THE MURDERS AT BILL'S O' JACK'S

For Francesca

THE MURDERS AT

BILL'S O' JACK'S

THE MYSTERY THAT STUNNED GEORGIAN BRITAIN

GILES WILCOCK

PEN & SWORD
HISTORY
AN IMPRINT OF PEN & SWORD BOOKS LTD
YORKSHIRE – PHILADELPHIA

First published in Great Britain in 2024 by
PEN AND SWORD HISTORY
An imprint of
Pen & Sword Books Ltd
Yorkshire – Philadelphia

ISBN 978 1 39903 586 6

A CIP catalogue record for this book is available from the British Library.

Typeset in Times New Roman 11.5/15.5 by
SJmagic DESIGN SERVICES, India.
Printed and bound in the UK by CPI Group (UK) Ltd.

Pen & Sword Books Limited incorporates the imprints of Atlas, Archaeology, Aviation, Discovery, Family History, Fiction, History, Maritime, Military, Military Classics, Politics, Select, Transport, True Crime, Air World, Frontline Publishing, Leo Cooper, Remember When, Seaforth Publishing, The Praetorian Press, Wharncliffe Local History, Wharncliffe Transport, Wharncliffe True Crime and White Owl.

For a complete list of Pen & Sword titles please contact
PEN & SWORD BOOKS LIMITED
George House, Beevor Street, Off Pontefract Road, Hoyle Mill, Barnsley, South Yorkshire, England, S71 1HN.
E-mail: enquiries@pen-and-sword.co.uk
Website: www.pen-and-sword.co.uk

or

PEN AND SWORD BOOKS
1950 Lawrence Rd, Havertown, PA 19083, USA
E-mail: uspen-and-sword@casematepublishers.com
Website: www.penandswordbooks.com

MIX
Paper | Supporting responsible forestry
FSC® C013604

Contents

Note: In pre-decimal British currency, there were 12 pence (d) in one shilling (s) and 20 shillings equalled £1.

Converting the value of money from 1832 into a modern equivalent is notoriously uncertain. Fairly precise values can be found on the website www.measuringworth.com, but a rough equivalent can be ascertained by multiplying by one hundred: £1 in 1832 would be worth just under £100 today; one shilling would be around £5 and one pence around 40p.

All quotations include original spellings and phrasing, but punctuation and capitalisation have been standardised where necessary.

Introduction

The parish church of St Chad serves the village of Uppermill in Saddleworth, a region historically part of the West Riding of Yorkshire but today within the administrative area of Greater Manchester. The building is not particularly close to the village centre; to reach it, the visitor must walk up a steep hill and down a quiet road which, after narrowing sharply as it passes the church, continues to wind through the countryside. When the Church Inn –the only nearby building –is closed, the area is almost eerily quiet.

St Chad's is an imposing structure, the main part of which dates from 1830–33, although the tower was rebuilt a few years later. Across the road, behind a stone wall and down some steps, is the churchyard. During the summer of 2023, a renovation project began to uncover some of the neglected graves located near the entrance. But to reach the most interesting section of the churchyard, the visitor must walk down the hill to the lowest parts. This western end is wildly overgrown at the time of writing, protected by trees and containing areas that are almost inaccessible. Only the south-western corner is easy to reach; and there, tucked up almost against the wall, is a grave so unusual that it has appeared in local guidebooks and featured in studies of epigraphs.

The memorial begins:

> 'Lie interred the dreadfully bruised and lacerated bodies of William Bradbury and Thomas, his son, both of Greenfield, who were together savagely murdered in an unusually horrid manner, on Monday night, April 2nd, 1832, W^{m} being 84 and Thos 46 years old.'

This unnerving opening is followed by an equally unsettling three-verse poem which effectively conveys something of the shock and horror experienced so long ago. For now, one verse will suffice:

> Throughout the land wherever news is read
> Intelligence of their sad end has spread.
> Those now who talk of far-famed Greenfield hills
> Will think of Bill o'Jack's and Tom o'Bill's.

When the rather gothic nature of the grave's setting is taken into account, it is not hard to see why the events described on that slab have captured the imagination of so many people over the course of nearly two hundred years.

William and Thomas Bradbury were brutally attacked in their home, a popular but vaguely disreputable public house on the edge of Saddleworth Moor, known as Bill's o'Jack's, sometime between 7 pm on the evening of 2 April 1832 and 11 am the following morning. Thomas died that Tuesday afternoon, his father in the early hours of Wednesday. News spread rapidly; to the nearby village of Greenfield, to the surrounding district of Saddleworth, and far beyond. No-one was ever charged with the murders and, contrary to the confident claims of later writers, no clear suspect emerged.

From the moment it was discovered, the crime intrigued people, not least because of the remote location and bloody nature of the deaths. Gossip and rumour drove the story; suspects were named and discarded with bewildering frequency. The one man to be arrested – who almost certainly had nothing to do with the case – was threatened by an angry mob. News travelled the length of the country; even several London newspapers followed the story closely.

Nor did the story fade after the two victims had been interred in St Chad's nearly a week after their deaths; the continuing macabre fascination marked by the famous inscription extended well into the next century. The prominence in the community of the Bill's o'Jack's public house – which continued to operate until 1937 – meant that the deaths of the Bradburys retained a grip on public imagination and cast a long shadow over the region. Even today, although surpassed in notoriety by the Moors Murders of the 1960s, the killings are remembered locally. Saddleworth Museum has a section on the story which features a set of items (including one of the probable murder weapons) dating from the time of the murders, and the Bradbury grave continues to draw visitors.

This ongoing, almost unbroken, interest in the Bill's o'Jack's case has given the story an odd sort of currency, as if it had only recently taken place. But the murders happened so long ago that they were closer in time to the English Civil War than they are to our own day; the Bradburys died only seventeen years after the Battle of Waterloo and five years after the death of Ludwig van Beethoven. Princess Alexandrine Victoria – the future Queen Victoria – was a 12-year-old girl, almost the same age as the niece of Thomas Bradbury who found him dying on the floor of his home.

These events took place at the tail-end of the Georgian period, which for a modern audience is comfortingly familiar in some ways, but in others utterly alien. Many differences to twenty-first century society are not immediately obvious but play a crucial role in understanding the story. To further confuse matters, the Georgian period is generally extremely well documented, but the Bill's o'Jack's murders fall into a historical black hole. Sources which would yield useful information about individuals do not exist for 1832 – the requirement to register births, marriages and deaths began in 1837; the census began to record details of households only from 1841. As Saddleworth had no police force, the only 'official' record is a scanty Home Office file stored in the National Archives.

Almost everything known about the case derives from a series of problematic newspaper reports from the days and weeks after the murders. There is a little more evidence, but not much. For example, two surviving eyewitness accounts of the hours after the discovery of the crime were largely based on hearsay and while they provide some interesting background, contain little useful information. Only the inquest generated solid evidence; while no official documents survive, the extensive newspaper coverage provides a moderate degree of confidence about what was said. These sources tell only a partial story in which some aspects are covered in the minutest detail but key questions are ignored entirely.

For these reasons, and many others, 'solving' the murders is impossible now. The identity of the killer or killers of the Bradburys remains as unknown today as it was on that April morning in 1832. There has been no shortage of theories over the last 200 years. But not even a 'confession' would offer a solution; there were several in the aftermath of the killings, none of which stand up to scrutiny.

Nor is there any underlying thread to draw the tale together. Not even the two victims are fully formed; by the time the sources pay any attention to them, they are already dead. There was no central figure around whom everything revolved. Instead, characters flit across the stage for a moment before disappearing forever.

With no 'main character', it is a difficult story to understand. Therefore, it is easier to explain events from the viewpoint of some of those ephemeral characters who drift in and out: the witnesses, the journalists, the suspects, the coroner. From their perspective, it is possible to perceive what was happening a little more clearly. And there are some factors which linger in the background: broader political events; trends in literacy; changes to the system of criminal justice; the growth of journalism; the unique nature of the Saddleworth area.

There are also two constants throughout the story. One is the scene of crime itself, the public house known as Bill's o'Jack's. The building is so prominent in the tale that it almost becomes a character in its own right. It was there before the murders and might have had a connection with what happened. It also survived long after its first proprietors and achieved notoriety through the manner of their death. But it no longer exists as it was demolished in 1937. Even though the path which led from the Greenfield-Holmfirth Road (the modern A635) down to 'far-famed

Bill's o'Jack's' survives, nothing remains of the building apart from a few stones and the old cellar (which post-dates the murders). The site is not accessible to the public and currently belongs to United Utilities, the water company which operates the Yeoman Hey Reservoir – completed fifty years after the murders and ultimately responsible for the closure of the famous pub.

The other constant is the story itself. From the moment a terrified girl stumbled upon that crime scene, it seemed to take on a life of its own. Within a few hours, a rudimentary narrative had been imposed on the confusing events by crowds which grew around Bill's o'Jack's. Even as time passed and solving the murders became effectively impossible, the story continued to be told, altered and 'improved'. Examining the route it took, and how its telling changed in the long years afterwards – how it was interpreted; the theories proffered; the portrayal of the victims and suspects – is almost as complicated as trying to untangle the events of 3 and 4 April 1832. The main character in the murders might actually be the story itself. In this sense, the grave of the Bradburys does not simply mark their resting place; it represented the birth of the legend.

Although the house in which William and Thomas Bradbury died is long gone, the surrounding area is in many ways unchanged today, apart from several reservoirs which now occupy the sites of what were once rivers and fields. The valley's spectacular scenery – often described as 'desolate', which is not necessarily pejorative – continues to attract tens of thousands of visitors. The sights which greet today's cyclists and hikers would have greeted the girl who walked from Greenfield up the same hill, one mild spring day in 1832.

The Morning After

On the morning of Tuesday, 3 April 1832, a young girl aged around 12 made her way out of the village of Greenfield and up the steep hill towards her grandfather's house. For now, even if it is probably inaccurate, it is better to use her name as reported at the time: Amelia Winterbottom. She had been despatched from her home in the area known as Fernlee by her mother, Nancy, to collect some yeast from her grandfather, who lived around three miles away. The route to his house was along the relatively new turnpike road which snaked up the valley and after passing his house, crossed Saddleworth Moor to reach Holmfirth, around ten miles from Greenfield.

Her grandfather – Nancy's father – was the 85-year-old* widower William Bradbury, more commonly known in the area as 'Bill o'Jack's'. This was his 'warty-name', a local practice whereby people were identified through their father: William, son of Jack, became 'Bill o'Jack's'. Bradbury lived in an old farmhouse which had been converted to a licensed inn. It occupied an isolated position, at least half a mile from the nearest building and just under two miles from Greenfield. The establishment had a chequered history but was well-known locally. Its official name was The Cherry Tree, but it was more commonly known, after its proprietor, as Bill's o'Jack's.†

The other resident of Bill's o'Jack's was the 47-year-old Thomas Bradbury (or 'Tom o'Bill's'), William's son and Amelia's uncle.

* William Bradbury's actual age is uncertain. Newspapers said that he was 85; his grave states that he was 84. But he was probably at least 88.

† Most writing about the murders uses 'The Moorcock' as the official name for Bill's o'Jack's, but this name was not adopted until later.

Although married with children of his own, Thomas lived with his father to assist in running the establishment; on her way up the hill, Amelia would have passed the home of Thomas's family, a place known as Sidebank, around a mile before Bill's o'Jack's.

The area in which the Bradbury family lived had undergone remarkable changes within William's lifetime. *Pigot's Directory* for 1828 noted: 'From a barren and almost uninhabited spot [Saddleworth] has become well inhabited, highly cultivated, and abounding with woollen and cotton manufacturers, and has gained considerable celebrity from the excellent quality of the articles produced in the district, as being equal to any made in the county'. The village of Uppermill, around two miles from Greenfield, was described as 'a thriving little hamlet'. Greenfield had its own section: 'The natural curiosities that may be contemplated in this romantic district are very interesting, especially those at Greenfield, where are immense caverns under the various hills, stupendous rocks, and several druidical remains, and the valley of Greenfield presents scenery picturesque and beautiful beyond description. In a sequestered situation at the extremity of this interesting vale, is a house of entertainment, well known by the name "Bill's o'Jack's", to which parties resort in the summer months, when upon an excursion to explore the natural wonders and romantic beauties of Greenfield'.

The spectacular scenery made quite an impression on the newspaper reporters drawn to Bill's o'Jack's and Greenfield in the days that followed. One wrote of the 'beauty and grandeur' of the area. Another noted: 'The traveller finds himself amid scenery of the most wild and desolate description. On his left is the summit of the hill called Oaderman [*sic*]*, along the side of which the road is carried. On his right is a deep and narrow glen, bounded by rocks and extensive moors, in a state of irreclaimable sterility'. A third journalist, not to be outdone in the descriptive stakes, wrote that the area possessed 'the

* The reporter had probably misunderstood the local accent and rendered the well-known Alderman's Hill (named after a legendary giant) as 'Oaderman'.

wildest, most barren, rugged' character. He noted the 'chasm' between the hills and described 'huge extending masses of stone and amongst, in some cases, perpendicular rocks, which while their look only adds to the dreariness of the prospect, they strike every gazing eye with awe and horror at their adamant and front'. The 'striking rocks', 'frightful precipices' and 'bleak moors' seem to have left this author, a young man called Edwin Butterworth who would play a key role in the story, rather unnerved.

For Amelia Winterbottom, these sights must have been familiar and perhaps she gave them no thought as she finally arrived at her grandfather's house between 10 am and 11 am. Bill's o'Jack's was perched on the hillside around a hundred yards down a path that looped to the right off the main road and re-joined it further up the hill. When she reached the house, the door was closed. She called out for her grandfather; perhaps she knocked. In any case, when she tried the door, it was unlocked.

As she entered, the bar area for customers was to her left; ahead, a flight of stairs led to the single room on the upper floor. There were no windows in the entrance passageway, so she might not have noticed the set of bloody footprints on the steps, nor the handprints on the wall. To her right was the main room of the house, which measured around three-square metres and had a paved stone floor, where her grandfather and uncle would usually have been found.

The former often sat on a wooden bench near the doorway. Perhaps she saw the blood spattered in this area. But her attention would have been entirely focussed on the scene before her.

Directly opposite her as she stepped into the room was a window, to the right of which stood a chair in its usual position next to the fireplace. But on the floor by this chair, in front of the stove, was a pool of blood. And in the middle of the pool, a man lay face down. More blood poured from a wound in the side of his head. Beside him was a dog (the girl did not recognise the dog, but he belonged to her grandfather). Not knowing who this man was, and thinking it could be her grandfather, she reached to touch him. At this point, the dog barked and sprang at her; this was the final straw. Terrified by all that she had seen, the girl fled. Hurtling back down the hill in a blind panic, she reached Binn Green Cottage, the home of a 52-year-old woollen weaver called James Whitehead who lived with his wife and four children, around half-a-mile from Bill's o'Jack's.

When Amelia Winterbottom arrived, Whitehead later recounted, she 'alarmed his family' by her account of 'a man bleeding to death on her grandfather's floor'. Having told the horrified occupants what had happened, she continued on her way home, carrying the news with her. Meanwhile Whitehead set out for Bill's o'Jack's, accompanied by his wife and another man (not identified at the inquest; *Wheeler's Manchester Chronicle* called him a 'neighbouring man'). When they entered, the dog came out barking at them. Whitehead recognised him as belonging to William Bradbury and calmed him down by calling his name: 'Laddie'. They found the man sprawled face down on the floor as Amelia Winterbottom had described. Whitehead did not recognise him; he was covered in blood and had severe head injuries which made him hard to identify. Whitehead and his companion initially thought the man to be dead, but he began to groan, although he never spoke any recognisable words.

More moaning from upstairs alerted them to the presence of someone else in the house. Whitehead went to investigate alone. He found William Bradbury, severely injured and half-dressed, lying in his bed. Whitehead, who presumably knew the elder Bradbury through living relatively close, asked him what had happened. According to Whitehead's evidence at the inquest, William's speech was unclear, and it took several attempts before he made himself understood. He eventually muttered what Whitehead heard as 'Pats, Pats' (the *Manchester Times* recorded this as 'the Pats, the Pats'). Whitehead assumed this to mean that Irishmen had caused the injuries. When asked if his son had been there, William probably – but not definitely – replied 'Aye'.*

Returning downstairs, Whitehead and his unidentified friend re-examined the first man. They turned him onto his back, but the only responses they received were further meaningless groans. They thought he was one of the assailants and attributed his injuries to the actions of Thomas Bradbury. The room was covered in blood and they noticed part of a pistol – the lock mechanism – and a bloody poker on the floor. Determining that help was needed, Whitehead went to find a surgeon while the other man fetched a constable. Whitehead's wife probably remained at the house as others began to arrive.

Earlier that morning, Whitehead had summoned Samuel Hegginbottom, the local surgeon, to his house because his daughter (probably Esther, who was 7 at the time) had been ill. Hurrying home to Binn Green, Whitehead discovered that Hegginbottom was still there and told him what had happened. According to the doctor's recollection in *Wheeler's Manchester Chronicle* (7 April), Whitehead informed him that an Irishman was bleeding to death. The two men returned to Bill's o'Jack's, arriving around 11:20 am.

When Hegginbottom entered the building, the wounded man still lay on the floor of the main room, although Whitehead noticed that he had rolled back onto his stomach. Those who were at the scene – as well as

* What William Bradbury might have said illustrates the uncertainty of the evidence in this case. The only witness to these words was James Whitehead, who described what happened at the inquest. Yet the different newspaper accounts of the inquest – supposedly recording the same events – had irreconcilable differences. The *Manchester Guardian* report (and notes made by the journalist Edwin Butterworth) said that, according to Whitehead's evidence, Bradbury replied 'Aye' to this question. The *Manchester Times* (which recorded Bradbury's culprits as '*The* Pats') said that Whitehead got no reply and 'the old man never spoke more'. The *Manchester Courier* omitted this question completely from its report. *Wheeler's Manchester Chronicle* said that Bradbury had taken 'several attempts to speak' before muttering 'Pats', and that 'The old man had said, in answer to a question, that his son Thomas had witnessed the "job"'.

Mrs Whitehead, it is possible that more people had arrived by this point – had left him on the floor, too terrified to do more. Hegginbottom quickly realised that he was not an Irishman; from his clothes, the surgeon recognised the dying man as Thomas Bradbury. Examining him, Hegginbottom identified numerous wounds to his scalp, several of which penetrated to the bone. His head and face were extremely swollen and he was incapable of speech. Although practically unconscious, Thomas unsuccessfully tried several times to get up. Hegginbottom could not find a pulse at the man's wrist and so ordered that he should be washed, have his head shaved and be put to bed.

The doctor, after briefly examining the room, followed a set of bloody footprints – evidently from someone wearing stockings who had stepped in a pool of blood – upstairs to find William Bradbury still in bed, but now having undressed himself fully. The old man was bleeding heavily from a wound to the left side of his head. Hegginbottom attempted to question him but the replies were unintelligible. The surgeon noted that William had several injuries, including one to his upper left arm where the muscle was cut through to the bone.

Hegginbottom left the house around noon to return home for his instruments, and noted when he went downstairs that Thomas was now fainting and almost dead. William, meanwhile, was ill throughout the afternoon and did not eat (which perhaps implies that food was offered and refused). By the time Hegginbottom returned, both men were in the same bed and he dressed their wounds. Around 3 pm, Thomas Bradbury died while Hegginbottom was still there. At some point – it is unclear if this took place before or after Thomas's death – Hegginbottom used his surgical knife to examine his injuries, identifying two fatal skull fractures. The doctor believed that William could have survived his wounds but for his extreme age; instead, he lingered for the rest of the day before dying at 1 am on Wednesday morning (4 April).

This account is the closest we can get to the 'truth' of what happened in the Bill's o'Jack's murders. It is largely derived from the testimony of the witnesses at the inquest – Amelia Winterbottom, James Whitehead and Samuel Hegginbottom – who described what they found on that Tuesday morning. Fortunately, apart from some minor differences in wording, all the newspaper reports agree on the essence of what was said. Although there is no guarantee that the witnesses told the truth, they were under oath and subject to cross-examination. Consequently, their testimony provides the most reliable evidence. If this was a modern criminal case, these would perhaps be 'agreed facts'.

Unfortunately, almost nothing else is certain. Only one witness – a man called Reuben Platt – had been with Thomas Bradbury the night before, but he had departed several hours before the attack must have taken place; no-one had seen what happened. Platt – who later became the unconvincing prime suspect for armchair detectives – had identified some potential culprits, but the only result was a desperate and ultimately fruitless search. Other than Platt's testimony, none of the evidence from the inquest provided even the slightest indication of who might have been responsible, nor what their motive might have been. Little else survives that would help, except a series of unreliable and contradictory newspaper accounts, laced with rumour or hearsay, some eyewitness descriptions of the chaotic scenes around Bill's o'Jack's on Tuesday afternoon and plenty of unsubstantiated gossip.

Complicating matters further, the murders became a familiar story in later years, a legend stripped of context. They came to be interpreted in isolation, not viewed as events from 1832. The unusually detailed intimacy of that morning after – the granddaughter's quest; the dying men struggling to speak; the muttered accusation against 'the Pats' – disguises the fact that it happened long ago, in a very different world. The obvious danger is that the modern 'investigator' might view the story through a modern lens.

To understand what led to the murders, and to explain the reaction to them, the events need to be returned to late-Georgian Britain to illustrate the circumstances of Saddleworth in 1832 and to provide that much-needed context. To comprehend what happened to the Bradburys, the world in which they lived must first be understood.

A Tumultuous Time

The Georgian era, which lasted from 1714 to 1837, does not quite have the same grip on modern imagination as the Victorian period that followed it. Nevertheless, it remains associated with the enduringly popular works of Jane Austen and, more recently, *Bridgerton*. Perhaps for some, it still conjures up images of *Blackadder*; for others it might be associated with the Industrial Revolution and vague recollections from their schooldays of being forced to memorise the names of inventions and inventors.

It was a time of frequent warfare – the Seven Years' War; the American War of Independence; the Napoleonic Wars – which established Britain as a world power. Domestically, it was a period of great social and technological change, driven by the growth of the textile and iron industries. The demand for power to feed the new technology caused an increase in coal mines, while a network of roads, canals and, eventually, railways developed to serve these industries.

William Bradbury would have directly felt the impact of these changes. When he was born in the middle of the eighteenth century, Saddleworth was isolated from the rest of Britain; until the mid-nineteenth century, it had no easy access to the wider world. Travel was difficult, not least because of Saddleworth's location in the Pennines. To reach the villages of Delph, Uppermill or Greenfield the visitor had to cross steep hills using roads which, until the late-eighteenth century, were little more than paths or narrow tracks.

This all changed with the surge in textile manufacturing. Weaving had been the mainstay of the northern economy for many years. But the nature of this industry changed dramatically during Bradbury's lifetime.

Enterprising manufacturers, hoping for a combination of enrichment and social advancement, began moving production into factories, away from the traditional system whereby weavers worked in their own homes. The process was accelerated by technological advancements which allowed these factories to become mechanised. Historians have debated the economic impact of these changes; the picture was not uniform and even in Lancashire, there were few large mills by the end of the Georgian period. Nevertheless, new mills sprung up, powered by steam engines and able to produce far more cotton than was possible through handweaving. The subsequent abuses by factory owners resulted in the Cotton Mills and Factories Act of 1819, which attempted to regulate this new world and prohibited the employment of children under the age of 9.

As employment shifted to factories, there was a relatively rapid movement of people from the countryside into towns and cities. Concurrently, although the explanation is disputed between historians, the population of Britain more than doubled between 1781 and 1841. By the time the Bradburys were murdered, around 13.3 million people lived in England. The effects were particularly pronounced in areas around Saddleworth. Between 1801 and 1851, the population of Manchester grew from 75,000 to 303,000; that of Huddersfield increased from 7000 to 31,000 in the same period.

Unsurprisingly, these changes had a knock-on effect. To feed the growing population, the amount of land used for agriculture increased. In many places, including Saddleworth, previously undeveloped land on hillsides began to be used for farming. Landlords exploited this by increasing rents, often dramatically. External factors also had an impact. The numerous wars with France between 1793 and 1815 drove up food prices and caused general inflation. And the end of these wars caused a collapse in the farming boom, bringing financial hardship.

In such uncertain times, people viewed the future with a combination of fear and optimism; suspicions that the country was in decline battled expectations of progress and betterment. But there was a febrile political atmosphere. Throughout the country, riots and public disorder, provoked by a variety of grievances, were common occurrences. The associated violence, looting and harsh reprisals from the authorities became a feature of everyday life.

A significant source of unrest was dissatisfaction with parliamentary elections. Rotten boroughs – unpopulated areas with a handful of voters – held disproportionate electoral power, having one or two members of Parliament while cities such as Manchester had no representation at all. A small group of men therefore wielded excessive influence, which was a recipe for bribery and corruption.

Attempts to reform the system in the mid-eighteenth century were halted after the French Revolution, owing to fears of opening the doors to similar turmoil. However, growing political pressure, driven by the Radical Movement, and widespread public unrest, such as the Bristol Riots of 1831, led to the passing of the Reform Act – not without a struggle – in 1832.

When the Bradburys were killed, the House of Commons had just passed the third Reform Bill. It faced further opposition in the House of Lords before it finally received Royal Assent on 7 June. However, even if it produced a fairer distribution of MPs, the act did not lead to anything approaching universal suffrage; it only enfranchised middle class male landowners who added political influence to their economic and financial power.

The broad trends of the Georgian Period had a considerable impact on Saddleworth. Because the hills and moorland that dominated the region were generally unsuited to profitable farming, the woollen industry had become crucial. One estimate suggests that by the end of the eighteenth century, almost 90 per cent of jobs in Saddleworth were associated with that industry. Part of the growth was driven by the switch to finer quality cloth made possible by technological inventions; an account from the end of the eighteenth century noted the increase since 1740 in the amount and quality of cloth produced in Saddleworth. Many mills were built; by 1800, there were twenty-one fulling mills (necessary for the creation of fine cloth) and forty-one scribbling mills (used to process and combine wool) in the region. Almost all had been constructed in the last quarter of the eighteenth century.

One important result of these changes was that Saddleworth became increasingly connected to the rest of Britain. The Huddersfield Narrow Canal – crossing the Pennines to link Huddersfield to Ashton-under-Lyne – was completed in 1811, but this was not enough. Saddleworth mill owners needed a better network of roads, and several turnpikes were constructed. One of these, begun around 1820, connected the village of Greenfield to Holmfirth over Saddleworth Moor. These projects required an influx of labour and many of the itinerant workers were Irish, a factor which had a huge bearing on the aftermath of the Bill's o'Jack's murders.

During William Bradbury's lifetime, Saddleworth experienced a huge growth in population, most likely driven by recruitment to the textile industry. Although we have no precise figures, probably between 1200 and 1400 people lived in Saddleworth in the mid-seventeenth century. By the 1740s, when William Bradbury was born, this had increased to around 4000. When we finally have accurate statistics, provided by the 1801 census, there were 10,665 people in Saddleworth. This figure increased steadily: 12,579 in 1811; 13,902 in 1821; 15,986 in 1831 and 16,829 in 1841. To accommodate the growing number of workers, weavers' cottages were built and new areas of habitation opened on the higher ground that was unsuitable for farming.

This growth was not necessarily seen as a good thing. A depression in the textile trade in the early 1800s, during the war with France, resulted in wages for workers dropping catastrophically throughout Britain, from between forty and sixty shillings per week in the 1770s to eighteen shillings in 1800 and five shillings by 1818. This disproportionately affected the areas around Saddleworth, where there were an estimated 4000 handloom weavers. As a result, almost a quarter of Saddleworth's population were receiving Parish Relief by 1817.

The people of Saddleworth refused to accept this modern world meekly. A particular grievance was the replacement of the old 'domestic system', whereby weavers worked from their own homes, with the new 'factory system'. And, as happened throughout Britain, there was anger at the reduction in wages that resulted from the use of new machinery in the factories. This even spilled into violence; on several occasions, 'Luddites' operated in Saddleworth and there were threats against mill owners. The combination of poverty, hardship, rising prices and falling wages caused increasing unrest. Harvest failures in 1795 and 1799 led to riots in which food was seized and sold at a reduced price before the diminished proceeds were returned to the vendor. Crowds from Saddleworth were also involved in food riots in Oldham and raided a shop in 1812.

But anger in Saddleworth was not limited to worries about food or wages. There was also a strong political element. For example, in 1807 only around one in 400 of Saddleworth's population had the right to vote. As a result, the area became increasingly involved in the reform movement. A government report from 1801 described the region as a 'centre of dissatisfaction' and several men from Saddleworth were imprisoned around this time. A military drill was held on Saddleworth Moor by 500 protesters in the mid-1810s, a reaction to a government crackdown that had resulted in the imprisonment – and even execution for treason – of reformers. And Saddleworth was among the hotspots to which the government sent spies to watch for potential troublemakers.

A sizable contingent from the region (mainly men from the areas close to the political hotbeds of Oldham and Lees) were present at one of the most controversial incidents of the Georgian period. In 1819, a crowd of around 60,000 men, women and children attended a meeting at St Peter's Field in Manchester to demand parliamentary reform as a response to growing unemployment and poverty. Local magistrates dispatched the Manchester and Salford Yeomanry Cavalry to arrest the organisers. This ended disastrously when a cavalry charge into the crowd killed seventeen people and injured hundreds. A contemporary Radical newspaper dubbed it the 'Peterloo Massacre' (after the Battle of Waterloo, which had taken place in 1815). Ten of the Peterloo fatalities came from Saddleworth. At the trial of one of the organisers, the prosecution produced the 'Black Flag of Saddleworth' as evidence that violent motives lay behind the protest.

Saddleworth, although far removed from the fictitious drawing rooms of Jane Austen, was therefore not some rural backwater completely cut off from the rest of the country; the changes of the Georgian period were keenly felt and not especially appreciated. The world in which William Bradbury died was almost unrecognisable from the one in which he grew up.

It is hard to believe that this did not impact on the lives of the two murdered men. Perhaps they were affected by the growth of factories; maybe the drop in wages pushed them to the brink of poverty. Were they involved in the military drill on the moors just a short distance from their home?

We don't know the answers to these questions, but we can take a closer look at what their lives would have been like.

Bill o'Jack's and Tom o'Bill's

In any tale of murder, the role played by the victims is always a short one, but their lives must be understood in order to explain why they died. Unfortunately, William and Thomas Bradbury – who should really be the central characters in the story – remain a mystery. Almost everything we know about them was written after their deaths, which coloured any interpretation of who they were and what they were like. Later evidence becomes unreliable because depending on the intentions of the author, they could have been portrayed as tragic victims or wicked individuals who got what they deserved.

It would be easy to focus on the information we don't have – to lament the lack of census returns or birth certificates – but there are some surprising amounts of detail to be found. The starting point should be the Bradbury family Bible. This was supposedly present in the room when William and Thomas were attacked, and spattered with blood. As a result, it became one of several 'relics' associated with the murders; its current home is Saddleworth Museum. But more interesting than the supposed bloodstains are the names in the front. In the fashion of the time, the Bible was handed down through the generations, and each new owner signed their name. And there, written neatly in ink, is the name William Bradbury. More prominent still is the name John Bradbury, almost certainly William's father; this would account for 'Bill o'Jack's' (Jack being a derivation of John).

With this information, the likely record of William Bradbury's baptism can be located in the records of St Chad's. He was christened on 8 March 1744 as the son of John and Helen Bradbury of Cover Hill; his father was a clothier. Assuming that this is indeed Bill o'Jack's, he was at least three years older than reported at the time of his murder. His age was variously listed as 84 (on his gravestone) or 85 (in newspapers and in his burial record for St Chad's); in fact, he would have been at least 88.

The family Bible provides a little more evidence. Both William and his father were able to write their names, an ability generally – although there are a few qualifications – taken as a sign of literacy, which was far from universal in this period. Statistics are hard to track down, but around 33 per cent of men in England and 38 per cent of men in the West Riding of Yorkshire (which included Saddleworth) could not write their name on marriage certificates in 1838–39. Broad trends also indicate that these figures would not have been hugely different in the previous century, but that rural communities were less likely to have been literate than urban ones and market towns perhaps had a higher rate of literacy than industrial ones. Quite where Saddleworth might fit into that pattern of trends is unclear, but if the ability of William to write his name does not mark him out as particularly unusual, it places him in the approximately 70 per cent of men in the area who were literate and implies that he had received some degree of education.

William can also be traced through his marriage. The announcement in the newspapers of the death of the 'wife of William Bradbury, innkeeper, Saddleworth' at the age of 80 on 14 March 1827 revealed that her name was Mary. From there, the records of St Chad's show that William married Mary Parry on 8 June 1772. William's signature is on the marriage register, but his wife could only make her mark; female literacy rates were much lower in this period than those for men. But most importantly for constructing any biography of William, the register reveals that he was a clothier like his father.*

William's life can be partially traced through the births of his four children because the baptismal register for St Chad's included the

* The record, repeated in the Bishop's Transcript for the marriage, says 'Clo^{r}'; adjacent records in the register which record the same occupation spell out the word in full.

occupations of fathers. For the thirteen years encompassed by the births, he lived at Fairbanks, an area in the hills between Diggle and Uppermill comprising an eighteenth-century farmhouse and a few other buildings. When his first child (also named William) was christened in 1772, he was working as a clothier. But when Mary was baptised in 1776, Bradbury was listed as a 'husbandman'; this usually meant a tenant farmer. And by the time of Nancy's (1783) and Thomas's (1785) births, he was once more listed as a clothier.

Therefore, William must have earned a living at Fairbanks from the weaving industry, perhaps cultivating some of the surrounding land to bring in more money. But most of his income must have come from small-scale weaving or selling what had been made by the family.

There might be another trace. A man called William Bradbury 'late of Dolefield in Saddleworth' was declared bankrupt in 1808. He was a woollen clothier and at the time of his bankruptcy had moved to Smallbridge, near Rochdale. This was not necessarily Bill o'Jack's; there were several men called William Bradbury living in Saddleworth, and Dolefield was not especially close to Fairbanks (although it is nearer to the site of the 1832 murders than Fairbanks). And yet the occupation fits.

But there is little doubt that even if he was never made bankrupt, Bill o'Jack's would have been a victim of the growth in textile factories and the collapse in wages for weavers. It is not a stretch that desperation, as factories absorbed the entire Saddleworth textile industry, forced him to enter a new trade, which in turn led to the opening of the inn which would forever be remembered as Bill's o'Jack's.

The history of the house which became Bill's o'Jack's is less clear. But its story is linked with developments in the area and the growing need for transportation routes across the Pennines. As part of a scheme to connect Manchester to Barnsley, where there was plentiful coal to keep factories working, a turnpike road was constructed between Greenfield and Shepley, via Holmfirth. Planning began around 1810 and work began in the 1820s, when additional links were also made to Huddersfield via the Wessenden Head Turnpike. Certainly the road was in existence by 1822 when it is marked on a map of the area.

The same map shows the public house known as Bill's o'Jack's, but it is uncertain how long the building had been there. It was probably a farmhouse originally, and possibly used for weaving before it acquired an alehouse licence around 1810. No doubt the intention was to take advantage of the construction of the turnpike. This would align with William Bradbury being discharged from bankruptcy around 1808. The new inn was initially called the Shooter's Arms and is named as such (with William Bradbury as landlord) in Baines's directory for 1822. It was later renamed the Cherry Tree, but as was common in the area, it soon became known by the name of its owner and was thereafter Bill's o'Jack's from 1828 at the latest.

From the beginning, the establishment was tied to the landscape around it. The attractions of the spectacular scenery, the rock formations (which local legend attributed to the work of giants or druids) and the opportunity for hunting or fishing meant that many people visited Greenfield from the late eighteenth century onwards. In 1828 James Butterworth, a local writer and the father of a man who had a crucial role in reporting the story of the murders, noted that the establishment was 'much frequented by numerous parties' during the summer months. But given that there were more easily accessible public houses in Greenfield, it is likely that its clientele largely came from these proto-tourists. *Wheeler's Manchester Chronicle* observed after the murders that 'the place has been the resort of the surrounding population on the Sabbath day, and has also derived considerable custom from the visits of such strangers as have been attracted by the beauty and grandeur of the surrounding country'.

As it happens, one of Bradbury's licences survives. Presumably displayed somewhere in the house at the time of the murders, it can currently be found in Saddleworth Museum and states that under the Alehouse Act of 1826, William Bradbury was entitled to run a brewery/inn at Greenfield. Signed by the Collector of Excise and the Supervisor of Excise, it was dated 27 October 1828 (although Bradbury had applied in February) and had cost £1. It permitted the brewing of between twenty and fifty barrels. This was presumably just one of several such licences as it required annual renewal; quite why this one has survived is unclear. But public houses were monitored by magistrates, who had power over renewals. Although we don't know when Bradbury learned to brew, he certainly did so because *Wheeler's Manchester Chronicle* described Amelia Winterbottom seeing 'liquor' left outside the house to cool on the morning of her gruesome discovery.

The apparently well-informed reporter for *Wheeler's Manchester Chronicle* provided more background about William and his alehouse. Although this was never corroborated elsewhere, there is no particular reason to doubt it. The article suggested that William and Thomas had supplemented their income from Bill's o'Jack's by working as stonecutters. But more importantly, William Bradbury had previously run a 'hush shop' – an unlicensed beer house – from Bill's o'Jack's, although no further details were provided in the *Chronicle*. In a separate incident, around 1830, he had been involved in a serious dispute with his landlord. He had attempted to 'set himself up as owner of the house, his title being founded upon long exemption from rent. He persevered pertinaciously in his determination to remain master of the building, until legal proceedings were adopted by the owner of the property'. Bradbury was removed from the house but, declaring that 'if he must leave Greenfield he would be carried away, heels foremost', he and his son Thomas 'immediately set about the erection of a hut close to the house, and in it they lived for some time'. The then-unoccupied hut was still in evidence in 1832. Around a year before the murder, some kind of understanding was reached and the Bradburys moved back in as tenants. But according to *Wheeler's Manchester Chronicle*, 'the publican's licence had been forfeited, and he was only enabled to practise as a retailer of beer' under the Beerhouse Act of 1830.

This Act was the culmination of years of debate. Alcohol was a frequent source of trouble in Georgian England. At a time when ordinary drinking water was frequently unhealthy, often dangerous, and occasionally deadly, alcoholic drinks were regarded as a viable alternative. But gin and whisky, the favoured choice for many, were seen as causes of drunkenness and debauchery; beer was considered less problematic. Therefore the Beerhouse Act of 1830 was Parliament's attempt to make beer and cider cheaper, reduce dependence on gin, and encourage people to establish alehouses without having to get the permission of magistrates. More than 24,000 beer shops sprang into existence in the first six months after the Act was passed.

The Beerhouse Act removed all duties on beer and cider and, by some estimates, would have cut the price of a beer by around twenty per cent. A licence, costing two guineas, permitted its holder (if they were a ratepayer) to brew and sell from their own house. It also freed beer houses from the influence of magistrates and placed them under the authority of excise officers. As there were suspicions that magistrates were paid by brewers only to award licences to those who would stock their beer, this change was quite popular. The only negative side to the Act was that beer houses could not sell gin or spirits and had to close at 10 pm. The latter provision was a competitive disadvantage because public houses could remain open as long as they liked (apart from during Sunday church services). The Act was popular, especially among the poor (who benefitted the most), but there was a moral backlash over the drunkenness which was supposedly evident in the aftermath. Therefore, despite what was reported in *Wheeler's Manchester Chronicle*, it is possible William Bradbury *preferred* to have the licence under the Beerhouse Act; he could have chosen to take that route independently of any other considerations.

The chequered history of Bill's o'Jack's indicates that William Bradbury was prepared to break rules – running a 'hush shop', fighting his landlord and occupying a makeshift hut after being (probably forcibly) evicted. If such niceties as licences did not unduly concern him, what else did he permit under his roof?

These events also raise the question of who William's landlord was, and that is not a straightforward story.

One of the factors lurking in the background of the murders was the practice known as enclosure. Through this process, common land – such as fields, moors or woodland, which traditionally belonged to the lord of the manor but was used by the whole community for grazing animals or growing crops – was divided into units, fenced or walled off and became private property. The main objective was to improve agricultural production to feed the growing population. Enclosure had been taking place for centuries, but from the mid-eighteenth century the process accelerated rapidly. Between 1750 and 1850, there were more than 4000 Enclosure Acts passed by Parliament, part of a wider trend in which over 5200 bills between 1604 and 1914 enclosed just under seven million acres – or around a fifth of England.

Unsurprisingly, this was enormously controversial and yet another cause of social unrest across Britain, not least because it was the wealthy who benefited. Ordinary people were deprived of their access to grazing for their animals, or land on which to grow crops and collect wood for fuel. Their only compensation might have been the granting of a small strip parcelled out from the old common land. As a result, many people left newly enclosed communities, accelerating the growth of towns and cities and ironically increasing the demand for agricultural produce and providing more reasons to pursue enclosure.

Enclosure was usually driven locally and Saddleworth was no exception. The catalyst was the death in 1791 of Saddleworth's last lord of the manor, a man called James Farrer. His will left instructions for his land to be sold off, so various merchants and manufacturers bought plots from which they hoped eventually to make a profit, either through selling it or cultivating woodland. Some of the land near Bill's o'Jack's was developed as part of this process; a plantation had been grown lower down the hill descending to Greenfield Brook which became known (and remains so to this day) as the Bill's o'Jack's Plantation.

However, the manorial rights to the moorland around Saddleworth were not included in this sell-off. Attempts to enclose the moors were strongly opposed by people who wished to retain their common rights. So the new landowners, who wished to enlarge their holdings, applied to Parliament for an Act of Enclosure in 1810, their argument being that more land was needed for agricultural purposes. This began a long and painful process, which took more than twenty years to complete, whereby a commissioner was appointed to examine in minute detail the claims of all interested parties. The final stages were taking place just as the Bradburys were murdered.

The final enclosure map – and accompanying complicated legal paperwork – published in 1834 shows the former common land split into a patchwork of plots given to numerous owners. In theory, these should have been demarcated by stone walls, which were pre-emptively marked on the map; in practice, this never happened because the cost proved prohibitive, especially with the reduced demand for farmland in peacetime. And over the subsequent thirty years the number of owners reduced as two men bought up the land; the intention to create land for grouse shooting would have made walls positively unattractive. However, these later events have no bearing on the story.

How might enclosure have affected the Bradburys? In one sense, not at all. The land surrounding Bill's o'Jack's was already in private ownership at the time of the Enclosure Act. The map of the area produced in 1822 shows the building located on land which had been enclosed for some time, quite possibly as part of the 1791 sell-off. At first, William Bradbury's landlord was almost certainly a man called James Whitehead (presumably unconnected to the occupant of Binn Green), but by 1832 the owner was probably a man called James Buckley, who through the enclosure process acquired several plots of land nearby. Although it is uncertain when or why the ownership changed hands, there was another connection to the murders. One of the Saddleworth magistrates who attempted unsuccessfully to make sense of events surrounding the murders was a man called James Buckley. This could have been a different man – the name was common in Saddleworth – but magistrates were almost always wealthy landowners and so it is likely that the magistrate James Buckley was investigating events on his own property.

Another mild curiosity is that the final enclosure maps – on which the land enclosing Bill's o'Jack's, unlike everything around it, was not given a lot number as it was already enclosed – feature a building labelled with the name of its occupier: William Bradbury, who was dead by the time the final document was produced.

If enclosure did not affect the Bradburys directly, it would have made a big difference to their lives. Suddenly, the landscape surrounding Bill's o'Jack's was placed, at least theoretically, off limits. Perhaps the eviction in 1830 was connected to the desire for Buckley to exploit the land; he certainly seems to have been set on owning large parts of the area. Perhaps it was connected to the loss of William's licence (especially if his landlord was also a local magistrate). Another factor might have been William's own claims as part of the enclosure; the final settlement showed that land was granted to a William Bradbury near Broadstone Hill, not far from Bill's o'Jack's (the hill can be reached from the Holmfirth Road before it bears east). This was around a mile from Fairbanks, where William Bradbury was once a husbandman. Even if this was not the innkeeper, it might have had some connection with him; his oldest son was also called William.

There is another interesting detail. The Enclosure Commissioner for Saddleworth was Ralph Fletcher from Bolton-le-Moors, a man with considerable experience of such a role. Fletcher died in early 1832, necessitating the appointment of another Commissioner. A meeting for anyone 'entitled to or interested in' the enclosure of the commons was advertised and duly held at the Swan Inn, Dobcross, to discuss the matter. On the list of attendees who signed the resulting document were some names which will become very familiar: Reuben Platt, who spent time with Thomas Bradbury on the night of 2 April; Ammon Platt, a witness to some of the events of the Tuesday morning; and most importantly, three men called Thomas Bradbury. Two of these differentiated themselves by adding that they were from Fairbanks and Runninghill respectively. At the end of the document, there are two signatures saying 'Thomas

Bradbury', although there is nothing to indicate which of the three men had signed.

However, we know that the Thomas Bradbury who was the son of William Bradbury (or as he was known locally, 'Tom o'Bill's') was literate and capable of signing his own name because, like his father, he had signed a marriage register after his wedding. And of the two signatures by Thomas Bradbury on the enclosure document, one bears a strong resemblance to Tom o'Bill's signature on the marriage register. While we cannot be completely certain, it appears very likely that our Thomas Bradbury was present at The Swan.

This might not seem especially important, and Thomas could well have attended numerous meetings about enclosure. But what makes the meeting to discuss Fletcher's successor slightly intriguing is that it took place on 19 March – less than a month before Thomas and William Bradbury were beaten to death. Although there was not necessarily any direct connection between the two events, it looks as if Thomas was involved in the issue of enclosure right up until his death and was taking an active interest in local affairs.

What else is known about Thomas Bradbury? As in the case of his father, there is information about Tom o'Bill's life in the parish records. Born in 1785, he was the youngest of William's four children, and in 1811 he married a woman called Ann Whitehead (whose baptismal record reveals her to have been the daughter of a clothier). At the time, he was 26 and she was 20, but that is not the most interesting part. The marriage took place at St Chad's on 10 January; *very* soon afterwards, Ann gave birth to the first of their five children. Augustus Bradbury was baptised on 30 April. At the time, the family lived at Knowl Top and Thomas was listed as a labourer. When their second child was born in 1814, they had moved to Sidebank, where Thomas's wife and five children continued to live until his death.

At some point between the birth of his sons Francis (1823) and William (1826), Thomas stopped being a labourer and became a clothier, according to the records of their baptisms. The article in *Wheeler's Manchester Chronicle* related that Thomas had been a stonecutter, like his father, but had recently 'worked for Mr James Bottomley of Greenfield Mills, in the vicinity'. Perhaps he or his father had financial worries? Perhaps he needed to join the great influx into the mills and factories to pay his bills? By 1832 Thomas did not live with his wife. Since at least the time of the 1830 'eviction', and quite possibly since his mother had died in 1828, Thomas lived with his father. The reasons are opaque but he certainly assisted his father in running Bill's o'Jack's.

Little else is certain about Thomas Bradbury – there is too much legend and not enough fact. But there are a couple of hints, dating from before the murders, that might fill out what is otherwise a vague outline. As well as his probable interest in enclosure, Tom o'Bill's might have been involved in political reform. The records of the various enquiries following the Peterloo Massacre in 1819 include a description of a minor incident witnessed by a captain in the 10th Foot Regiment called C. J. Tench, who had attended St Peter's Field out of curiosity on the day of the protest.

Following the cavalry charge, the crowd retaliated against the Yeomanry. In one of the incidents, a trooper called Hulme fell from his horse after being struck by a stone and was attacked by men and women armed with stones and sticks; Hulme had to be rescued by fellow soldiers. One of the civilians involved made a petition to the House of Commons that he had been wounded in the shoulder by a bayonet. Tench had seen the incident and wrote to inform the Treasury Solicitor that bayonets had not been used, but his statement included one tangential detail. Someone had told him the name of the man who had thrown the stone at Hulme; and Tench's source was a gamekeeper from Saddleworth called Thomas Bradbury.

Was Tom o'Bill's one of the Peterloo protesters? Bearing in mind the unrest permeating through Saddleworth, it is not far-fetched that a relatively young man like Thomas, who would have been 34 at the time, was politically active. But immediately, there are several notes of caution. An impressive number of men called Thomas Bradbury lived in

Saddleworth; there can be no certainty that this Saddleworth gamekeeper was Tom o'Bill's. Similarly problematic is the notion that Saddleworth even *had* gamekeepers as the moors had not yet been enclosed. For whom could he have been gamekeeper?

And yet there is one final piece of the somewhat sparse puzzle that is Thomas Bradbury's life before his murder. There are fragments of evidence that link him very closely to the moors. The first certainly predates his death.

A diary entry for 12 August 1829 (the opening of the hunting season), kept by a local man called George Shaw, revealed that four or five dogs had been poisoned with 'small pieces of muffin' in which leather buttons had been concealed. These 'had been evidently scattered about on purpose for mischief' near Bill's o'Jack's. According to Shaw: 'It is supposed that Thom o'Bill's has been the author of this diabolical action in revenge for being fined for shooting last year'. In other words, he was a poacher.

A week later Shaw recorded that Thomas had appeared before magistrates at Dobcross to answer questions about the poisoning, but as there was no evidence against him, he went free. The story was corroborated in newspapers, although no culprit was publicly identified. For example, the *Manchester Courier* reported how 'some miscreant on the night of the 11th ... placed a number of muffins strongly impregnated with poison in various parts of Saddleworth Moors' and that 'eight valuable dogs fell victims to this wicked stratagem'.

Shaw later wrote about the aftermath of the murders. He was absent at the time and only returned to Uppermill on 9 April, having read the previous day what had happened. On 21 April, he visited Bill's o'Jack's and observed in his diary: 'There was a great number of people at Old Bill's today. The struggle which deprived these poor unfortunate people of their lives must have been most terrific as Tom stood 6 feet ½ inch in height and was an extremely powerful man'. Perhaps many people had experienced just how powerful he was over the years.

The second fragment linking Thomas Bradbury to the moors is more problematic because it was written many years later, sometime between

1892 and 1894, when the murder had long since entered the realm of legend. He was mentioned in a hand-written document called 'The Annals of Saddleworth'. The identity of the author is uncertain, but it was most likely a Delph watchmaker and local historian called Joseph Brierley. Possibly the work was written with a view towards eventual publication. It was a collection from various sources of events from the region, dating back into prehistory but also including nineteenth-century controversies. However, the project was never completed and instead the notebook in which the 'Annals' were written is a chaotic, disorganised document without any clear structure and in which various items were started and apparently abandoned. Nor were they written sequentially in the book. Someone – possibly the author – added page numbers and made a note on which page a story was continued, but then the pagination was altered at a later time.

In short, it is a difficult document to decipher. But what does this have to do with Thomas Bradbury? One of the sections contains information about him, but it is uncertain where it came from. Much is written in the author's own words and references a book published in 1871. However, part of the text is claimed to be an account written by a man called Matthew Marsh who knew both William and Thomas Bradbury. It is not directly transcribed and it is impossible to be sure which are Brierley's words and which are those of Marsh. Nor is it clear when or where Marsh's original text – if it was indeed a text – was written. To further complicate the picture, part of the text is incomplete as a page of the notebook is apparently missing.

Therefore, it is hard to say whether the 'Annals' are another document based on the legend of the murders, or if they contain material which possibly predated the murders. Although we consequently cannot set too much store in what the 'Annals' say, there is just enough unique material – which matches what is known from elsewhere – to indicate that Marsh possibly knew more about Bradbury's background than anyone else who wrote about the murders.

The 'Annals' state that Thomas Bradbury – 'a wild sort of man' – lived separately from his wife because 'for years they could not agree'.

While interesting, that does not reveal anything particularly useful; more important is what the 'Annals' had to say about Thomas's habits. He was often to be found 'rambling' on the moors, where he 'made a living out of the game that he killed' – again, the link with poaching – and would 'boss and dictate to almost everybody who went there'.

Once again there is a link to the moors, but the 'Annals' go further and mention that there were a few areas on Saddleworth Moor that were private property even prior to enclosure (which was certainly true). The owners used watchmen/gamekeepers to keep people away and – according to the 'Annals' – Thomas Bradbury was employed to look after a plantation near Bill's o'Jack's (and possibly another area as well). It is a plausible scenario. If it is correct, it would be a strong indication that the Peterloo witness really was Tom o'Bill's.

Putting all this together, there is plenty of evidence to support the idea that Thomas Bradbury was heavily associated with the moors and with game, both in a semi-official capacity as a watchman/gamekeeper and, less respectably, as a poacher.

Little is known about poaching in Saddleworth at this time, although it clearly took place. For example, a newspaper story in August 1838 grumbled that poachers had captured a large amount of game from Saddleworth Moor overnight, and 'the consequence is that the birds are very scarce'. Game laws, dating back centuries, meant that landowners had the exclusive right to hunt game on their land. Legislation to protect these rights meant that punishment for poaching could be severe; for example, the 'Black Act' of 1723 made it a capital crime. That poaching remained a national concern around the time of the murders is clear from two further pieces of legislation: the Night Poaching Act of 1828 (which enacted punishments – including transportation – for poaching at night) and the Game Act of 1831 (which required the possession of a game licence to hunt and empowered the use of force by gamekeepers).

But the game laws were not aimed at individuals like Thomas Bradbury, who might have poached occasionally. Their target was the growing gangs of organised, violent poachers who worked at a much larger scale, often poaching considerable distances from their homes;

the kind of men who would all but empty Saddleworth Moor of birds in 1838. Poachers were often criminals for whom game was but one way of making money. If Thomas was not one of these career poachers, why was he spending so much time on the moors? Perhaps he was using his substantial physical presence to restrict access to the land or to extort from those who were using it; certainly, this idea circulated after the murders. In helping himself to the occasional bit of game, maybe Thomas was taking what he thought was rightfully his.

For all that enclosure was still ongoing, the moors remained common land for the time being, making the question of poaching a complicated one. This might explain Bradbury's interest in enclosure: his activities on the moors would have been jeopardised if the land was distributed to people who would place more of it under guard.

Or perhaps there was more to it after all. There was a long association between beer houses and poaching; often these establishments were a means of distributing the poached game. Bill's o'Jack's was even known as a place frequented by game hunters. William Bradbury was happy to run an illegal 'hush shop'; did he also allow poachers to use Bill's o'Jack's? Was William himself a poacher in his younger days?

There are many other unanswerable questions, the answers to which might shed light on the murders. When, where and why did the two Bradburys work as stonecutters? How wealthy were they? Were they among the many inhabitants of Saddleworth reduced to poverty by falling wages or the growth of factories? Were Thomas's actions on the moors driven by greed or hardship? Did William resent having to give up his work as a weaver? Were either of the men 'Luddites'? Or involved with the food riots? Does any of this have any connection with the murders? The answers will never be known – and lamenting the fact serves no useful purpose – but perhaps the questions need to be remembered in considering what we *do* know.

In some ways, these questions do not matter because it was the deaths, not the lives, of the two Bradburys which came to define them. The newspapers did not dig especially deeply into their backgrounds because the real identities of the two men – except as tragic figures – were irrelevant in telling a gruesome story.

The only exception came in the pages of *Wheeler's Manchester Chronicle*, which left a description of the pair at the time of their deaths. William 'was eighty-five years old, and though in his earlier days he was remarkably stout, his age had of course rendered him feeble. His son Thomas was a man in the prime of life: he was upwards of six feet high, a fine, stout, healthy fellow. It is the general opinion that he would have been able to overpower at least two ordinary men, unless taken without any weapon and off his guard. He has left a wife and a large family. The elder man was known through all the surrounding country. He was designated "Bill o'Jack's", and from the repute of his house and certain personal peculiarities his violent death has excited more general sympathy than any similar occurrence for a series of years'.

If 'personal peculiarities' seems a strangely oblique comment about one of the murder victims, that was as far as any newspaper went in describing them. But the killings very quickly moved on from being a matter for 'the surrounding country'; the story soon reached a much wider audience.

'Men of obscure birth and imperfect education'

At the time of the Bill's o'Jack's murders, the 19-year-old Edwin Butterworth was already an established author and news reporter. His first book, *Biography of Eminent Natives, Residents and Benefactors of the Town of Manchester* had been published in 1829, when he was 16. Employed as a researcher by Edward Baines – who was writing a history of Lancashire – Butterworth travelled widely throughout the county from his Oldham home. To supplement his income, he had begun to sell stories to newspapers. In a sense, Butterworth was following a family tradition. His father, James, was an author, local historian, and schoolteacher who had published a book on Saddleworth history in 1828. When ill-health prevented James from working as a reporter at local courts, Edwin took over the role and before long was writing about stories from across the region.

In 1831 Butterworth signed agreements with several regional newspapers, which at the time desperately needed coverage of the ongoing Reform Crisis, and he was soon responsible for a very high proportion of the Oldham news stories that appeared across Lancashire and Yorkshire. At the time of the murders, he received a guaranteed salary from the *Manchester Advertiser, Manchester Courier* and *Manchester Times*, totalling ten shillings per week. Other publications, including the *Manchester Guardian, Wheeler's Manchester Chronicle, Liverpool Mercury* and *Leeds Mercury*, paid him by the number of lines printed. Butterworth meticulously recorded each amount in a notebook.

Therefore it is unsurprising that as news reached Oldham that William and Thomas Bradbury had been murdered, a story of potentially enormous interest that would appeal to every newspaper, Butterworth made the five-mile journey to Saddleworth. In doing so, he unwittingly became one of the leading characters in the tale. His reports came to dominate the retelling and eventually to shape the legend.

Butterworth was not the only newspaperman to write about the murders, but because he achieved a degree of local fame through his writing, we know far more about him than his rivals, who remain faceless, anonymous figures. Yet in some ways, this was a good time to enter the profession that came to be known as journalism.

The late Georgian period was one in which newspapers thrived. Literacy rates had improved considerably in the late eighteenth and early nineteenth century. As a result, reading became more popular than ever, generating an enormous growth in the number of books and newspapers on sale. It has been estimated that newspaper circulation increased nationally from 2.4 million copies sold in 1713 to 16 million in 1801. The impact on daily life was considerable; the transmission of information became relatively straightforward and newspapers suddenly had enormous influence. 'Reading the news' became a communal act, bringing people together through print.

By the time of the Bill's o'Jack's murders, content had expanded from straightforward 'news' to encompass reviews, letters and comment. Nevertheless, newspapers in this period were very different from their modern counterparts. Many had an overtly political purpose, for example to push the Radical cause, to press for reform, to support the status quo or to represent a particular section of society. Furthermore, publishers were required to pay stamp duty – which was 4d per copy in 1832 and was not repealed until 1855 – and several other taxes (gradually repealed between 1836 and 1861) which pushed newspaper prices up to 7d, beyond the reach of most ordinary people. Publication was less frequent than it later became; although *The Times* appeared daily by 1832, most regional newspapers were only printed once or twice each week.

Despite the growth and popularity of newspapers, the journalist (a word that entered the English language in 1833) was not respected. In 1829, Sir Walter Scott described the profession as 'a disgrace and degradation' to his son-in-law: 'I would rather sell gin to poor people and poison them in that way'. The few famous names who contributed to newspapers, such as Samuel Johnson, mainly wrote essays; a few were crusading Radicals. The bulk of writing was done by anonymous men like Butterworth, who had been clerks or craftsmen, paid a pittance to find local news stories from their towns and villages. The *London Review* in 1835 classed them as 'men of obscure birth, imperfect education, blunt feelings and coarse manners, who are accustomed to a low position in society, and are contented to be excluded from a circle in which they have never been used to move'.

However, when he was not writing about reform, Butterworth had an eye for an interesting story, exactly what editors were increasingly seeking. Mainstream newspapers had gradually switched from overtly partisan reporting (often backed by political parties) to the pursuit of readership for commercial reasons. If eighteenth-century newspapers were focussed on parliamentary speeches, politics and foreign news, those of the nineteenth century were more concerned with stories that would appeal to the public and therefore increase sales.

It is therefore unsurprising that murder came to fascinate editors, writers and their audiences. There had been several famous cases prior to 1832. For example, the murder of Timothy Marr and his family in London in 1811 and that of John Williamson a few days later, attracted crowds of people to the scene of the crime. Numerous 'broadsides' – large-format, single-purpose sheets aimed at a popular audience – were published specifically to cover the story. Newspapers also featured exhaustive coverage. Although a gang was initially thought to have carried out the killings, the suicide in custody of an arrested suspect,

John Williams, satisfied the press and public that he was the perpetrator, even if the facts were not clear-cut.

The killing of William Weare by John Thurtell in Radlett, Hertfordshire in 1823 – a case which became known as the 'Radlett Murder' – was even more sensational. Newspapers reported every aspect of the story in depth, but the coverage went far beyond the factual; the press printed rumour and invented details. To feed the resulting public frenzy, souvenirs of the murder were sold, paid tours were offered of the relevant locations and the story was turned into several plays which were performed even before the trial was concluded. When Thurtell was found guilty, coverage of his execution (attended by approximately 40,000 people) was equally lurid.

In 1827, another notorious murder, that of Maria Marten by William Corder (known as the 'Red Barn Murder'), attracted similarly extensive coverage and public reaction. And the Burke and Hare murders of 1828, in which two men in Edinburgh killed sixteen people so that they could sell their bodies to anatomists, received enormous press attention. These cases remained well-known for much of the nineteenth century.

What made a particular story appealing for newspapers? Often it was the murderer rather than the victim who became the focus. Sometimes the attraction arose from particular circumstances. The Radlett Murder involved the glamorous sport of boxing and the world of gambling. The Red Barn Murder had an apparently sweet and innocent victim whose body was found in dramatic circumstances in the eponymous barn. And it was the shocking brutality of the Burke and Hare Murders that attracted attention. Occasionally a macabre detail became the focus. When the headless body of Hannah Brown was discovered in London in 1836, newspapers related with ghoulish relish how the murderer – her fiancé – had wrapped her head in a silk handkerchief and transported it, and various dismembered body parts, on an omnibus.

This fascination was the target of satire, in particular the essay 'On Murder Considered as one of the Fine Arts' by Thomas De Quincey, published in *Blackwood's Magazine* in 1827, which mocked sensationalist newspaper coverage of murder.

But murder was relatively rare in the 1830s. The number of executions for the offence had been falling since the mid-1820s and stood at an average of twelve per year (although this doesn't exclude the possibility that murderers were not being caught). And most cases were prosaic. For example, Thomas Patrick, the landlord of a public house in Colchester called the Yorkshire Grey, was murdered in 1827. He had sent for a constable after one of his customers, James Winter (also known as Reuben Martin), had tried to rob another man. Winter struck Patrick with a wooden board and killed him. Winter was executed that December, but while the story generated plenty of newspaper coverage, it never acquired the infamy of the Radlett Murder or the Red Barn Murder.

Even so, the public had acquired a taste for sensational crime. The people of Saddleworth were no different but it is unclear how aware they would have been of such national news. Wealthier people – merchants and manufacturers – could have subscribed to newspapers; some public houses might also have provided copies. And sometimes groups formed to pay a joint subscription. Such recycling was the pattern throughout the country and Saddleworth would have been no different. Regional newspapers certainly reported on events in the area, suggesting the existence of an interested audience.

However, before the events at Bill's o'Jack's, there had been little newsworthy crime locally. In early 1829, after a young man went missing from Saddleworth, a prisoner in Wakefield confessed to having murdered him because he planned to turn King's Evidence regarding a burglary in which he had been involved. And in October 1831 Hannah Watts, a 25-year-old woman from Dobcross, was charged with the attempted murder (by poisoning with arsenic) of Hannah Bowden, the wife of a man with whom Watts was co-habiting. Watts allegedly bought poison, stating it was for rats, and mixed it into cakes sent to Bowden. Those who ate them, including Bowden and her son, became unwell but ultimately recovered. However, Watts was found not guilty the following March as it could not be proven that she was the person who delivered the cakes. Otherwise, enterprising journalists had previously found little joy in Saddleworth. That was about to change dramatically.

The events of the morning of 3 April were certain to generate enormous interest. Even putting aside the public taste for sensationalism, brutality and gore, the unusual circumstances surrounding the murders – the remote location, the relative local celebrity of the victims and what proved to be the insoluble nature of the crime – proved an irresistible attraction for newspapers.

Butterworth was one of the first reporters to arrive, possibly around mid-afternoon on Tuesday. Unusually, a lot of information survives about how Butterworth worked owing to the vast number of his surviving notebooks, which were donated to the town of Oldham after his death. As was his usual practice, the notebook in which he wrote about the murders had been assembled from any paper to hand – in this case, fliers advertising his father's 1828 history of Saddleworth. He wrote in spaces around the print and on the back of the pages in tiny but legible handwriting. The notebooks were used to draft stories before he sent them to newspapers. He must have recorded facts elsewhere while he was investigating and subsequently assembled them into a coherent narrative ready for publication.

In the notebook in question, Butterworth's story about Bill's o'Jack's falls between a story dated Monday, 2 April 1832 and a report about a robbery at Lees Hill on Tuesday night. As it was written after William Bradbury had died,* it must have been completed by Wednesday at the earliest.

* Butterworth inaccurately recorded William's time of death as 10am, suggesting that he was relying at this stage on second-hand information. He was certainly in Oldham on Wednesday, reporting on a meeting.

However, Butterworth was not quite the first person to leave an account of what happened. Around noon on the Tuesday, an accounting clerk called Thomas Smith, who lived in Manchester, was travelling from Stalybridge to Holmfirth when he noticed a large crowd gathered outside Bill's o'Jack's. Curious, he wandered down to the public house and asked what was going on. Not only was he told what had been discovered that morning, he was able to look around the house; he even saw the dying men in their bed.

The only reason we know this is because Smith wrote a letter to Stephen Lavender, the deputy constable of Manchester, warning that the culprits were believed to have headed towards 'Oldham or Manchester'. Lavender passed the letter to the mayor of Liverpool in case they had travelled there with a view to escaping to Ireland, and apparently sent copies to newspapers, which published edited versions. The original no longer exists and the newspaper copies are all that survive. And this presents a few problems because there are two versions of Smith's letter.

The first appeared in the *Liverpool Mercury* on 6 April and was reprinted in several newspapers; the brief accompanying article noted that it had been modified slightly ('with a few verbal amendments'). The second version was printed in the *Manchester Courier* on 7 April alongside a more detailed account of the murders. This copy is simpler, suggesting that the *Liverpool Mercury* added details to the letter to provide context and background; the accompanying article in the *Manchester Courier* negated any such need. Other differences between the two versions indicate that the editor of the *Liverpool Mercury* made alterations for dramatic effect; for example, the *Manchester Courier* described 'bruises' on the two men but the *Liverpool Mercury* called them 'horrid bruises'. Also, the Liverpool version was addressed to that city's mayor and the name of the letter's author had been omitted; the *Courier* version was addressed to Lavender, signed 'Thomas Smith' and gave an address: 'My house is No. 16, Maskill-street, Chorlton Row, and warehouse, No. 17, Back George-street'.

If the *Manchester Courier* probably printed something closer to Smith's original letter, the two versions largely tell the same tale. Both were dated 3 April and sent from Huddersfield. Smith described his journey from Stalybridge to Holmfirth, via Greenfield, on the morning of 3 April (the modified version in the *Liverpool Mercury* gave the time as noon). He noticed a crowd of people around a 'lonely house' and, asking what had happened, was informed that a murder had taken place. He went in and saw 'a room about ten feet square, with a flagged floor' (i.e. covered in paving stones). Blood covered almost every surface, and a set of mahogany drawers had been smashed open. Following a trail of bloody footprints up the stairs, Smith found more people gathered around two severely injured men who were lying in bed. He was told they had been found around ten that morning and that a surgeon had seen them but could do nothing for them. Although the *Liverpool Mercury* letter opened with 'a most horrid murder was committed last night', this was an editorial addition as both versions of the letter otherwise made plain that by the time Smith departed, both men were still alive.

Smith stated that the younger Bradbury had not spoken, but he claimed that William Bradbury had identified his attackers as Irishmen; Smith also claimed that he had spoken directly to the older man. The two versions of the letter differ slightly on this point. The *Liverpool Mercury* had Smith reporting a direct conversation: 'He said that…' and 'On my asking him… he said'. The *Manchester Courier* was a little vaguer: 'The old man was almost incapable of speaking. I understand that he had said ...' This suggested Smith was merely relating what others had said. But this version also implied that Bradbury personally gave Smith a description of the men: he 'was unable to tell me the colour' of one man's coat. It seems certain that the original letter said – or at least heavily implied – that its author had a conversation with William Bradbury.

However, it is highly improbable that William spoke to Smith; everyone else agreed that he was incapable of being understood by this stage. It would be an incredible coincidence if the only person to whom William spoke, other than James Whitehead, was a random passer-by who recorded the information in a letter published in the press. Far more likely is that Smith wished to exaggerate his own role.

Smith also identified potential culprits. The *Manchester Courier* version stated: 'I understand that he had said that six Irishmen had come upon them in the early part of the evening, and had committed the deed and robbed the house'. The *Liverpool Mercury* version said: 'It is said that there were four or six of them, apparently Irishmen, engaged in the deed'. Perhaps the editor of the *Courier* thought that changing the number to an unambiguous 'six' was clearer for his readers.

If Smith never actually spoke to the victims, from where did his story originate? He could not have read anything in the press because his letter was written before any articles about the murder had been published. The most likely explanation is that he reported the garbled rumours in circulation as the men lay dying; he simply had spoken to the people crowded around or inside the house. He then wrote to Lavender as if he had first-hand information rather than simple gossip.

If Smith's 'evidence' about the crime itself cannot be trusted, being at best second-hand (although he described the inside of the house accurately enough), his letter tells us what everyone was saying during those first hours when Thomas was still alive: that the attackers were Irishmen and numbered around five and that robbery was the object. He wrote that one attacker was wearing 'fustian' (a type of material); as we shall see, this partially matches the description of a potential suspect seen the night before.* Smith's letter also revealed that onlookers had already gathered outside Bill's o'Jack's early on the Tuesday afternoon (before Thomas died), and that literally anyone could walk in to look at the bloodstained room or go upstairs to see the dying victims.

After his short diversion to Bill's o'Jack's, Smith presumably continued his journey to Holmfirth and played no further part in the tale.

* Smith wrote that they wore 'dirty fustian trousers and a ragged coat'; later accounts specified that it was a jacket made of fustian. Perhaps either the description or Smith's telling of it had become muddled.

When Butterworth arrived later that afternoon, the story had developed considerably and had begun to resemble that which emerged at the inquest. Unfortunately, it is impossible to know exactly what he did next. Did he interview witnesses? Or did he, like Smith, simply report what everyone was saying? It is hard to be certain, but the latter is more likely as the account he wrote in his notebook differed in several important respects from the evidence given by the witnesses at the inquest.

The notebook draft began:

> 'One of the most diabolical murders ever perpetrated occurred on Monday evening betwixt nine and ten o'clock at the well-known public house called "Bill's o'Jack's", situated at the upper end of the valley of Greenfield, in a remote, wild and dreary position of Saddleworth. The loneliness of the dwelling and the arid appearance of the surrounding hills seemed suited as a place of horror for the execution of such a shocking deed…'

He quickly got to the heart of the story; how an unnamed 'little girl, granddaughter to the old man' had been sent by her mother to get 'some barm [yeast] she had ordered the evening before'. When she went in, according to Butterworth, she found *both* men 'weltering in their own gore'. This must have been the belief on that first afternoon; the *Liverpool Mercury* version of Smith's letter similarly stated that both men had been found downstairs and carried up to bed.

Butterworth continued by saying how she met Hegginbottom on her way to the 'next dwelling'. However, he later altered his text – after his original version had been submitted to several newspapers – to state that she 'accidentally met a person called James Whitehead who fetched her Samuel Hegginbottom, surgeon of Uppermill and two other persons'. The next part of the text was also altered by Butterworth at a later date. Originally, he wrote how William Bradbury stated that 'in the absence of his son' he had been attacked by 'five Irishmen', who attacked Thomas later. Butterworth crossed out these parts and changed it to read: 'He and his son were attacked by Irishmen who left them for dead'. Again, the number five might reflect an early version of what was being said; Smith too had identified a specific number of Irishmen (between four and six). Butterworth also recorded several items that the family of the two men discovered to be missing, including some money. He originally wrote that seven pounds had been taken, but he subsequently struck this through and added that the money was usually in the drawer.

Incidentally, Butterworth often crossed out while writing, but this usually marked an abandoned phrase; these were clearly later corrections.

After this, Butterworth related the evidence of three witnesses: Abraham Dawson, 'a person in the employ of the Huddersfield Canal Company'; Reuben Platt, who had spent some time with Thomas Bradbury the previous evening; and James Whitehead who, according to Butterworth, spoke to Platt and the younger Bradbury the previous evening at a place called Scout Hill. Although no other sources seem to call the area Scout Hill, a map later sketched by Butterworth labelled the area roughly adjacent to Binn Green as 'Scout Hill'. He also mentioned a man called John Pollard, who saw five Irishmen drinking in an Uppermill pub late the previous evening.

If we compare what Butterworth wrote to the facts that emerged at the inquest, there were some obvious errors: the discovery of both men together; how Amelia Winterbottom encountered Hegginbottom during her panicked flight (although he later corrected this to say that she met James Whitehead); the suggestion (repeated nowhere else) that James Whitehead saw Thomas Bradbury the night before. However, he recorded the injuries to Thomas – including 'fifteen frightful gashes' and a broken skull – and William – whose 'left hand had become a complete jelly' – accurately enough.

This begs the question: to whom did Butterworth speak? Possibly he spoke to Hegginbottom, who was hardly shy in telling his story. It is even possible that Hegginbottom was still on the scene when Butterworth arrived at Bill's o'Jack's. But Butterworth's confusion over the role of Whitehead – whom he omitted from his first version of Amelia Winterbottom's tale – and the apparent invention of his participation the previous evening, more likely suggests that Butterworth was simply recording whatever bystanders were telling him rather than investigating particularly thoroughly. Similarly, Butterworth's detailed account of what Reuben Platt saw (which we shall examine later) largely reflected a story apparently in general circulation that first afternoon and it is likely that he wrote this down rather than speak to Platt personally.

Overall, other than these 'witnesses' (to whom he probably never directly spoke) there was very little from Butterworth that was not mentioned in Thomas Smith's letter. The likeliest explanation is that Butterworth was simply reporting the rumours in circulation that morning, almost exactly as Smith had done. If that was the case, it would not have been an isolated event; Butterworth faced occasional complaints about the accuracy of his reporting. In fact, just two months later his salary from the *Manchester Times* was reduced from five to three shillings following criticism of his coverage of a robbery trial in which he had questioned the truthfulness of the plaintiff.

Whatever the limitations of Butterworth's original report, it rapidly became the main version of the tale because he sold it to several newspapers: the *Liverpool Mercury* (for which his account book listed a payment of four shillings for forty-eight lines at a penny each), *Manchester Times*, *Manchester Courier* and *Leeds Mercury* (for each of which he was paid his standard weekly fee). And indeed, the articles about the murders in those newspapers – published on 7 April, apart from the *Liverpool Mercury*, which appeared a day earlier – were almost entirely based on Butterworth's manuscript. The only substantial difference was the addition of Smith's letter, which formed the bulk of the *Liverpool Mercury* report and which was a supplement to that of the *Manchester Courier*.

Each newspaper featured the version written *before* Butterworth made his corrections, so the reports mention 'five Irishmen', 'seven pounds', and Amelia Winterbottom meeting Hegginbottom on her way down the hill. It is not clear why he made those alterations *after* submitting his story; perhaps he was trying to interest other newspapers? Or maybe he tried to update his article but missed the publication deadline?

Other changes were made to his manuscript text before it appeared in print. Some of these might have come from Butterworth himself.

Editors in the past had been irritated when they discovered that rival publications had received identical stories from Butterworth. Therefore, it is possible that he provided different versions of his text to forestall criticism or to tailor his stories for different publishers. However, some cuts to the text were probably made by the editors for reasons of space or brevity. The *Manchester Courier* version was closest to Butterworth's original account in structure and phrasing and included all his witnesses. The *Leeds Mercury*, with some minor variations in wording, followed Butterworth's manuscript closely but merged the various witness accounts into a generic paragraph consisting of 'information of the [unnamed] neighbours'. The biggest changes were made for the *Liverpool Mercury* and *Manchester Times* stories, although their content was unmistakeably derived from Butterworth and retained much of his original phrasing. The *Manchester Times* added one detail of its own: 'the house was completely ransacked, and everything of value carried away'. This appears to be based on the letter of Thomas Smith which stated (in the *Liverpool Mercury* version) that 'every portable article in the house was carried off'.

If Butterworth's voice was already dominating, appearing in four newspapers, the effect was amplified when his account was 'recycled' – generally without attribution – elsewhere, something that was common practice at the time. For example, the *Lancaster Gazette* and the *Lancaster Herald* featured a straight re-print of the *Liverpool Mercury* article the day after it appeared. Over the following week, many newspapers featured Butterworth's work, which gradually spread across the country.

When newspapers reported the inquest a week later, Butterworth was less heavily used. Two versions survive of his account of those proceedings. The first was an extensive, detailed account in the notebook he was using at the time; the second was heavily abridged and written on a separate piece of paper (which someone later pasted, out of chronological sequence, into another notebook). At some point he must have written a third version, featuring parts of the other two, which was printed in the *Liverpool Mercury* (which paid him just under seven shillings for eighty-one lines) and the *Manchester Courier*. *Wheeler's Manchester*

Chronicle also used some heavily edited parts of Butterworth's longer account of the inquest. Even though he received his usual salary from the *Manchester Times*, the article in that newspaper seems to have had another author.

If Butterworth had slightly fallen out of favour, that might have been because he was not the only journalist telling the story.

The identity of Butterworth's rivals is unknown, but they carried out a far more thorough investigation. Their initial accounts of the murders were printed in the *Manchester Guardian* and *Wheeler's Manchester Chronicle*, both of which regularly featured Butterworth's writing. It is likely Butterworth at least offered them the story, but in contrast to the weeks before and after, his account book records no payment (literally listed as zero shillings) for 7 April from either newspaper. Perhaps his modifications to the article were aimed at interesting these two publications? Or perhaps after he approached them, they decided to send their own people. But the two stories that appeared without his involvement were far more comprehensive than Butterworth's own work.

A detailed article was published in the *Manchester Guardian* on 7 April which featured a description of the 'crime scene' and a plan of Bill's o'Jack's.* The author of this piece most likely spoke directly to Samuel Hegginbottom and Reuben Platt, as it included much of the evidence that they gave to the inquest (which had not taken place when it was printed).

The *Manchester Guardian* report said that the granddaughter (unnamed in this account) went upstairs after finding Thomas on the

* In the back of Butterworth's notebook, several pages away from his stories about the murders, are two quickly sketched plans; the second looks to be an attempt to improve the first. They are not labelled and are not connected to anything else on the page and seem to have been drawn before the story he wrote there (which was unconnected to Bill's o'Jack's). However, they look very similar to the layout of Bill's o'Jack's and the smaller of the two diagrams greatly resembles that printed in the *Manchester Guardian*. But if he did provide the picture, he was not paid for it.

floor, where she found her grandfather. This contradicts her evidence given at the inquest, that she ran after seeing the man downstairs, and might be either a misunderstanding or a conflation of her account with that of James Whitehead. Although the *Manchester Guardian* journalist said that Winterbottom went to the house of James Whitehead, he did not dwell on his part in the affair, but merely stated that Whitehead and his family found 'the facts to be as the girl stated'. The report described in some detail what Hegginbottom found, which matched what he said at the inquest, apart from the subtly different observation that William Bradbury was 'talking incoherently' rather than 'muttering' as stated at the inquest. The accuracy of this first article prompted the *Manchester Guardian* to congratulate itself a week later when it observed that it had already published much of what was said before the coroner. Whoever wrote the story printed on 7 April had clearly gone to some lengths to get accurate information.

Like Butterworth's story, the *Manchester Guardian* report was reprinted over the following days, for example in the *Leeds Intelligencer* on 12 April and the *Leeds Patriot and Yorkshire Advertiser* on 14 April.

The most comprehensive account written before the inquest appeared in the pages of *Wheeler's Manchester Chronicle* on 7 April; it took up three entire columns over two pages, a remarkable length. Even though it was published on the same date as most articles about the murders, it seems to have been written a little later as it included some details common to Butterworth and the *Manchester Guardian* but incorporated the latest developments that had not made it into other the other two accounts.

This author was far more cautious than his fellow journalists. He began: 'As the judicial investigation of the affair has been unavoidably deferred to the termination of the week, we have not been able to condense such a narrative as may be totally free from question, but it is believed that the circumstanced detailed below are generally correct'. And the account that followed was closest to that given at the inquest and showed some development from the story told by Butterworth. It began by setting the scene but showed far more awareness of the locality in discussing some of the history of Bill's o'Jack's, and – as we have seen – some of the personal history of the two victims.

The narrative of the murder began with an account of the previous evening and continued with the events of Tuesday morning. Bradbury's granddaughter (again unnamed) arrived around 10 am on a 'trifling errand' and saw 'some person lying insensible on the floor. The outer door was shut when she got there, and the only peculiarity was that the liquor which the old man and his son had been brewing on the previous day, and had put out to cool, was still standing at the entrance'. This tallied almost exactly with Amelia Winterbottom's evidence at the inquest and was the only newspaper report printed before the inquest to note correctly that she saw Thomas but not William. The extra detail about the liquor is unique – perhaps the author spoke to the girl?

'Much alarmed' by what had happened, she ran to the next house and told them that a man was bleeding to death at her grandfather's. Whitehead is not named; it simply stated that 'a person went with the girl to the house' – this was the only account to suggest that she returned to the scene and contradicted the inquest – before returning to fetch Hegginbottom, whom he told that 'there was an Irishman bleeding to death in old William's'. Upon returning together the unnamed Whitehead and the surgeon 'immediately' identified Thomas Bradbury before searching the house for his father. They found him upstairs, so the surgeon went for his instruments and returned with them, 'accompanied by two or three gentlemen', and dressed the wounds.

The account went on to describe the interior of Bill's o'Jack's in some detail, but made a few mistakes, as if the author had been misinformed. For example, it identified the building as being 'upon the left hand from Dobcross'. Dobcross is to the north of Greenfield and there is no road that directly goes from Dobcross to the site of Bill's o'Jack's. Also, it confused two of the downstairs rooms, mixing up the bar area with a pantry accessed from the main living room. More accurate was the description of the men's injuries – which almost exactly matched the evidence from the inquest – and details about the potential murder weapons found at the scene. There was also a list of items presumed stolen and a description of the damage done to some drawers. Finally, *Wheeler's Manchester Chronicle* reported a faintly ridiculous rumour, reproduced nowhere else and which the writer acknowledged was impossible to verify, that 'some toasted cheese is stated to have been found on the oven-top and part of a loaf upon the table, and it is conjectured that after accomplishing their main object in plundering the house, the murderers regaled themselves in the room where their victims were lying'.

The anonymous reporter was also able to expand on details provided by other newspapers. He recorded that William Bradbury recovered to some extent on the afternoon that his son died and it was hoped that he could explain what had happened. He was 'repeatedly interrogated by the surgeon and others, but though he betrayed, by muttering, a consciousness of the questions, not a sound escaped his lips which was at all distinguishable'. Putting aside the unanswerable question of who else was asking him, this contradicted what Butterworth said but suggests that the author did not speak to James Whitehead, who *did* claim that Bradbury said recognisable words.

What about the 'five Irishmen' deemed responsible by Smith and Butterworth? The reporter for *Wheeler's Manchester Chronicle* shed some light on how this rumour had evolved: 'It was at first conjectured, from some cause with which we are not acquainted, that five persons had been engaged in the murder, but there is good reason now to believe that the party consisted only of three'. This latter number was derived from the evidence of Reuben Platt. So where had the number five initially come from? Perhaps it was just another rumour? Part of the issue may have been perceptions that Thomas Bradbury could not have been overpowered by just one or two people. He was 'in the prime of his life: he was upwards of six feet high, a fine, stout, healthy fellow. It is the general opinion that he would have been able to overpower at least two ordinary men, unless taken without any weapon and off his guard'.

The report concluded with the letter by Thomas Smith as published in the *Liverpool Mercury*.

Although by far the best account of the murders to appear in that first week, the article from *Wheeler's Manchester Chronicle* was barely reprinted elsewhere (except rather randomly, for example in *Baldwin's London Weekly Journal* on 14 April) and until the 1980s was completely neglected by those who subsequently discussed the murders in print. This might have been because the newspaper ceased publication in 1842 and was perhaps more obscure than the others.

Almost all subsequent newspaper reports were based on these – mainly the Butterworth and *Manchester Guardian* stories – and many were copied verbatim. A handful of independently written articles also appeared which contain brief details of the story.

One early account appeared in the *York Herald* on Saturday, 7 April, stating that the Bradburys had been attacked by five Irishmen after the older man had been forced to 'disclose where his money was concealed'. The son had 'fifteen frightful wounds about his head and his skull was fractured'; some of the wounds were inflicted with a spade. The father was 'desperately mangled on his face and legs, his left hand was beaten to a jelly, and one of his legs and arms broken'. The report concluded with the information that 'two Irishmen have been apprehended on suspicion'. The mixture of rumour and accurate information might indicate a local source. Another early version appeared in the *Macclesfield Courier and Herald* and the *Staffordshire Advertiser*. This had details about the state of the house, but exaggerated its distance from other dwellings and reported that Thomas had been 'shot through the breast, the ball or balls entering under the arm at one side, and coming out at the other'. But some accurate information had trickled through; the author knew of 'sixteen wounds' to Thomas's head, and that the granddaughter of William 'had gone for barm'. The *Sheffield Independent* carried a brief story but this was little more than a reprint of a reward poster in circulation.

News had also rapidly reached London. On 7 April, the *Globe* and the *Morning Herald* printed a slightly dramatic account of the granddaughter's discovery: she 'knocked at the door several times, but no-one answered … [she] gave an alarm to some of the neighbours'.

Although it got some details wrong – for example, the article stated that Thomas had been found dead and William 'had been reported to be worth some money' – Irishmen were identified as suspects.

These newspapers clearly had access to some kind of source – perhaps details from Butterworth – but cannot have had a reporter on the scene. There are, however, two more sources which have rarely been used in retelling the story.

Even before the inquest, local authorities had offered a reward of £100 and wanted the Home Office to increase the amount to £200. To this end, three local magistrates – James Buckley of Saddleworth (who might have been William Bradbury's landlord), Lewis Fenton (of Spring Grove, Huddersfield) and Joseph Walker – wrote to the Home Secretary from Pontefract, where they were sitting at the Spring Quarter Sessions, on 5 April. The letter began: 'A circumstance of most atrocious desperation has just been perpetrated in Greenfield in Saddleworth'. It set out how William and Thomas Bradbury, 'joint occupiers of a Beer House under the new act' had been found around 11 am on Tuesday. The magistrates specified that neither man had spoken; the younger died 'almost immediately' and the older 'expired the following morning, being both unable to relate anything which might give a clue to the discovery of the perpetrators of so desperate a deed'. The three men who sent the letter, 'being acting magistrates for the above district', had 'just received by express a statement of the above melancholy event'. They had also received a copy of the reward poster, sent from Saddleworth and dated 3 April, which they enclosed with their letter.

The magistrates also sent to the Home Office a statement sworn before James Buckley and John Armytage, 'two of his Majesty's Justices of the Peace' and also dated 5 April, the Thursday after the discovery. This was made by Ammon Platt, a merchant 'of Heathfields in the Township of Quick'. Ammon Platt, who had been an attendee at the meeting to discuss a new Enclosure Commissioner alongside Thomas

Bradbury, does not appear in any of the accounts written at the time, nor in any subsequent retellings. But he provided some useful information. Although it is not entirely clear who he was (there were a surprising number of men sharing his name in the region) he was most likely born around 1785 and married to Esther Buckley. A later census return simply gives his occupation as 'landed proprietor'.

Ammon Platt told the magistrates how, around noon on 3 April, he had called on Samuel Hegginbottom, who informed him that William and Thomas Bradbury had been 'so dreadfully injured at their house in Upperwood, Greenfield … that he expected that they would both die very soon'. He showed Platt the pistol that he had brought from the scene, still bearing traces of blood and hair. Platt accompanied Hegginbottom back to Bill's o'Jack's as he went to treat the injured men; the pair arrived shortly after 1 pm. There, Platt said, he saw the bodies of the two Bradburys 'lying upon a bed in the chamber'. Also, 'in the first room in entering the house and where [Platt] supposes the murder was committed, the walls, windows and fireplace were sprinkled with blood and there was a large pool of blood on the floor. That in such room there was a spade covered with blood and it had a considerable quantity of hair upon it. That after minutely examining such first room (in which the drawers had been forced open) [Platt] went again upstairs and saw Dr Hegginbottom dress the wounds of Thomas Bradbury who had from twelve to fourteen severe wounds on his head. That [Thomas's] eyes were swollen up'. Platt detailed how Hegginbottom examined the wounds and skull of Thomas, determining that it was fractured, and then examined William. Thomas was 'in a complete state of insensibility' and died while Platt was still in the house. Platt reported that William 'was speechless', and he had heard that William died early the following morning.

Ammon Platt said that the two men had lived alone in the house they kept 'under the new Beer Act'. However, while he was there, Nancy Winterbottom – the daughter of William Bradbury and the mother of Amelia – and Thomas's wife Ann ('who did not live with him') were taking care of the two injured men. When Platt inquired into what had happened, he was told of the discovery that morning: the two men had been found by 'a granddaughter of William Bradbury going to the house for yeast as [Platt] has been informed'. Thomas Bradbury 'was found weltering in his blood on the ground floor of the first room on entering the house, and the father was found with his clothes on (except his shoes) laid up on the bed upstairs'. He described how 'there were foot marks of blood on every step going up the stairs and it is believed old Bradbury scrambled upstairs with difficulty after he was bruised and wounded never having come down again'.

This statement of Ammon Platt given on the Thursday is our only direct eyewitness account of events from the morning after the discovery and has the advantage of being sworn in front of magistrates. It does not add a huge amount to what we already know but reinforces some of the facts. This was Ammon Platt's only contribution to the story; he died in 1851.

In total then, we have six sources written within a few days of the murders as well as the inquest evidence. They provide a basic chronology of the events of 3 April. Between 10 am and 11 am Amelia Winterbottom arrived at the house. She found her uncle and fled in terror, by no later than 11 am, and got help from Binn Green. James Whitehead went to see what was happening with his wife and another man, found the two dying men and returned to his house to summon Dr Hegginbottom, who reached the scene by 11:20 am. He left for his instruments by around noon and returned with Ammon Platt at 1 pm. Nancy Winterbottom and Ann Bradbury were present among the crowd that had gathered, before Thomas Bradbury died around 3 pm.

Already, rumour and gossip had begun to create an explanatory narrative – the supposed theft, the five Irishmen – which was later reported by Thomas Smith and Edwin Butterworth. As more details emerged, the story was revised during the week and was more thoughtfully examined by the *Manchester Guardian* and *Wheeler's Manchester Chronicle*.

But there is one further interesting detail, recorded by Ammon Platt, that must already have been doing the rounds as he arrived. When he asked what had happened, he was told that (the unrelated) Reuben Platt had been with Thomas Bradbury the night before and had identified some suspects. There is no suggestion that Ammon spoke to Reuben himself, which indicates that by the early afternoon, everyone was already aware of what Reuben Platt had seen.

Reuben Platt was the only eyewitness whose evidence went further than a description of the bloody state of the victims and their house. His story instead promised the possibility of finding whoever was responsible because he had been with the two Bradburys on Monday evening and had encountered some suspicious men very close to Bill's o'Jack's.

The events that unfolded over the following days largely revolved around Platt's account of the night before.

The Night Before

Very little is known about Reuben Platt, although he seems to have been an unremarkable man. Yet he was a crucial character in the story and remained so when it was told and retold over the years, until he was gradually transformed into one of the key villains. He was born around 1791 and at the time of the murders was a woollen weaver* who lived at Primrose, a cluster of old buildings near St Chad's church, some of which dated back to the early eighteenth century.† Using modern roads, Primrose is three miles from Bill's o'Jack's, but there was a direct route across the hills of no more than a mile.

Platt had married Alice Hirst at St Chad's in 1813 and had two sons: James, who was 18 in 1832, and Henry, who was 11. His daughter Ann had died at the age of 6 in 1822. According to his own comments after the murders (in newspapers and at the inquest) he was a friend of Thomas Bradbury and had occasionally assisted at Bill's o'Jack's during busy periods. Although Platt was nominally a weaver, there is no indication of whether he worked from home or in one of Saddleworth's mills. Perhaps, like so many others, he had been affected by falling prices.

That is the sum of our knowledge about Platt and even in later years when grim suspicions posthumously circulated about his role in the murders, he remained something of a cipher in the various retellings.

* The *Manchester Times* inaccurately reported at the inquest that he was a carter.

† The Platt family had lived at Primrose since the 1700s. Within Reuben's lifetime, a man called Joseph Platt of Primrose had been awarded six acres of adjoining land when the Manor of Saddleworth was broken up in 1794. The Poll List of 1832 identifies Reuben and three other Platts living there.

But there are a couple of tantalising points that might fill in some background for this shadowy figure. The first is that he attended the meeting about appointing a new Enclosure Commissioner; perhaps he accompanied Thomas Bradbury, a fellow attendee. The second is the faintest suggestion that, like Thomas Bradbury, he was a poacher. To understand this, it is better to let Platt's story emerge as he told it.

The short version is remarkably straightforward. Platt called into Bill's o'Jack's late on Monday afternoon and, after having a drink or two, walked to Road End – a crossroads in the village of Greenfield – with Thomas Bradbury before the two men went their separate ways. But what made these unremarkable events the focus of everyone's attention was that, on their way down the hill, they encountered three men who aroused the suspicions of Thomas. And when the dying Bradburys were discovered the following morning, these three men quickly became the leading suspects.

Several variants of Platt's story appeared in print; each was fundamentally consistent but differed in minor details, as if being told afresh. Out of all the witnesses, only Platt's evidence appeared in every newspaper report published before the inquest. That does not necessarily mean that journalists interviewed him because there is evidence that, even before Thomas Bradbury died, Platt's story was in wide circulation around Bill's o'Jack's. Ammon Platt knew some of the words alleged to have been spoken by Thomas on Monday night, and Thomas Smith knew that one of the supposed attackers had been wearing 'fustian'. These details can only have come from Reuben Platt. Either he was present telling his story to the crowd that first afternoon, or it had already circulated widely.

Therefore, many people could have shared Platt's narrative with the three journalists. But it is also possible they spoke to him personally. Butterworth – whose original report was usually the least precise – wrote an account of Platt's evidence that closely matched what he said at the inquest. *Wheeler's Manchester Chronicle* was even more detailed, while the *Manchester Guardian* seemingly quoted Platt directly. Each journalist either had a very accurate source – most likely Platt himself – or the story was so well-known that its details were unvarying whoever told it.

This suggests Platt enjoyed the limelight and was eager to tell anyone who would listen. What was it that he said?

Around 4 pm* on Monday, 2 April, Platt walked across the hills from Primrose in the direction of Greenfield. The *Manchester Guardian* (7 April) recorded that he planned to watch two men exercising their dogs but missed them and spent some time at a quarry† watching men loading stone onto a wagon. He then followed the wagon down to the main road, where he met Thomas Bradbury outside Bill's o'Jack's. According to the *Manchester Guardian* (7 April):

> 'When near Bill's o'Jack's [Platt] saw the younger Bradbury, who was standing by the roadside. They were old friends, Platt being "a bit of a sportsman himself", [was the author quoting him directly?] and having occasionally assisted the Bradburys in waiting on company when they were crowded. Tom said to him, "How far art 'o for this way, lad, to neet? [How far are you going tonight?]" Platt said, "I think I shall go down by th'Road End, an' by th'Upper Mill". Tom said he was going down to th'shop, and would be company for him to Daniel Whitehead's [shop]. Platt and Tom then went down to the house and Platt had a pint of

* The *Manchester Times* report of the inquest recorded this as 7 pm.

† This might have been the Greenfield Hall Quarry, marked on an Ordnance Survey map twenty years later.

> beer which he drank and paid for, whilst Tom was preparing for his errands. When they came off, Tom said to the old man, "Father, I'll leave you sixpence in silver and some copper, lest anyone should want change whilst I am away".'

No other newspaper account was quite as detailed nor included direct quotations, let alone used dialect which might have been impenetrable to some readers. However, the same article recorded Alderman's Hill as 'Oaderman's', so it is surprising the author could render such speech accurately. But there was another curiosity: Platt's story appeared twice in the same article. The section which directly quoted Platt's conversation came after the bulk of the story had been told, as if it had been added afterwards. Perhaps there were two writers, one of whom mis-transcribed Alderman's, and the other of whom recorded Platt's speech, perhaps having interviewed him.

If we can rely on the *Manchester Guardian* – which was accurate in details that can be corroborated – there are two interesting points about Platt's evidence. Firstly, he must have been quite close to the Bradburys if he sometimes worked in Bill's o'Jack's 'when they were crowded'. In which case, the brutal death of a friend must have been quite traumatic for Platt, possibly explaining one or two minor inconsistencies in his evidence. Secondly, Platt seems to have indicated that one of the reasons that he knew Thomas Bradbury was that he too was 'a bit of a sportsman'. To a modern audience, this might have suggested that they took part in games together, but in 1832 the word 'sportsman' almost always meant someone who hunted animals. Was Platt, like Thomas, an occasional poacher? That might explain his attendance at the meeting to discuss a new Enclosure Commissioner. And were Thomas's activities on the moors so well-known that Platt's audience – not necessarily the readers of the *Manchester Guardian*, but whoever was listening as he held court – would have realised how the two became friends?

Each version of Platt's story, including the one he gave at the inquest, agreed that he spent some time in Bill's o'Jack's waiting for Thomas to be ready and that Thomas left money for his father. Butterworth reported that Thomas needed candles, although it is not clear if this was what Platt said or if it was inferred because candles were found in Thomas's pockets. The two men left for Road End between 6 pm and 7 pm, just as dusk was falling. According to Butterworth's original report on the murder, they were seen by James Whitehead at Scout Hill, but that was probably an error.

Not far along the road into Greenfield, they encountered three men resting at the side of the road – according to the *Manchester Guardian* (7 April), 'at a considerable pile of stones, cut and squared for building'. According to *Wheeler's Manchester Chronicle* (14 April), Platt told the inquest that Thomas, seeing them, remarked: 'There are three Irishmen there. I don't like them, and am afeard of leaving my father by hisself'.

As Thomas and Platt approached, one of the three men asked how far it was to Holmfirth (the distance from there, as the pair informed them, is around eight miles). The *Manchester Guardian* (7 April) added: 'They seemed to be men on travel and out of work, spade men or navigators, and Tom mentioned a person who had a job of cutting stone near Holmfirth and said they might perhaps get work with him. They then went away slowly, as if tired and foot sore, and Tom said he did not like them'. Every version of Platt's story is clear that only one of the three men spoke; the others were notably silent. At the inquest, Platt said that the conversation lasted five minutes, which seems a long time for what was reported. Most versions agree that Platt and Thomas watched the three men make their way up the hill, which Butterworth recorded as 'appeared to skulk away their time considerably by stopping and sitting down on the walls and stones lining the road'. This was also the impression given in the *Manchester Guardian*'s description of them as 'tired and foot sore'. The latter article also recorded that Thomas, while they were waiting for the men to move on, 'began to measure the stones by his step, as if he were employed in making a calculation'. It is not quite clear what this meant, or why the reporter included it, but it reinforces the impression that Platt spoke to that reporter and maybe even showed him these stones as he told the story.

Thomas told Platt that he believed one of the three men had stolen a pair of stockings from his father's house. Most versions of Platt's evidence from the inquest say that the stockings belonged to Thomas; the initial reports in the *Manchester Guardian* and *Wheeler's Manchester Chronicle* said that his father owned them. According to the latter, Thomas also said the man had stolen a shilling from his father, but this was not repeated elsewhere. Platt's evidence clearly suggested that Thomas knew the men, and that they had spent time in Bill's o'Jack's.

However, one aspect of the story Platt told the newspapers had subtly changed by the time of the inquest. Initially, as Butterworth recorded, 'Platt positively asserts that the men were Irish', even though only one of them spoke. The only original version that went any further appeared in the *Manchester Guardian*, which reported Thomas's observation to Platt that the suspected thief 'could not face me'. By the time of the inquest, Platt did not think that the man who spoke had an Irish accent but was convinced that one of the others was Irish. Furthermore, Platt now said that the suspected thief kept his back turned the whole time so that neither he nor Thomas saw his face. Although Platt's earlier certainty that they were Irish had either vanished, or been mis-reported in the first place, he seemed convinced of the nationality of at least one of the men. Did he know them too? He also stated (according to the *Manchester Guardian*'s 14 April report on the inquest) that Thomas 'had a dread of them'.

One explanation for how Thomas or Platt supposedly knew that the men were Irish is that Thomas (and probably Platt) knew them already. It is also possible that they identified the men's nationality through their accent (although Platt later asserted that the only man who spoke did *not* sound Irish). But it is equally possible that Thomas or Platt made an assumption based on how the three men dressed. Working class Irish men in England would almost all have been labourers of some kind and therefore dressed accordingly. And a particular style of 'simple' dress was associated with Irish workers in the minds of the English public, although it is hard to be certain if this reflected reality or was a prejudiced assumption. Thomas and Platt might have categorised the men as Irish – accurately or otherwise – based on little more than their dress and general appearance.

Furthermore, a key feature of every description of the three men (including Smith's) was that they wore fustian. This was a thick, heavy cloth associated so closely with working men that it was adopted as a symbol of identity by the Irish Chartist leader Feargus O'Connor in the 1840s. Whoever else these men might have been, they were clearly manual workers employed nearby.

Platt described their clothing – the main hope for identifying and arresting them – several times. As recorded by Butterworth: 'One wore a blue linen slop [outer garment], another a black coat and a third drab trousers and a fustian jacket'. A further description, which can only have come from Platt, was included in a reward poster offering £100 for information: 'One man had on a drab and decayed olive velveteen shooting jacket, stout made, full red face, and stood about five feet, nine inches high. Another man had on a blue slop, slouch shabby hat; and another, a tall thin man, shabby black coat, short light coloured trowsers [*sic*] and had on a pair of quarter boots. One of the men had a large aquiline nose, on which was a scar'.

At the inquest, Platt went a little further: 'I noticed them more particularly through Thomas's observations. One wore a torn shabby hat, blue slop and darkish coloured cotton trousers. One was a tall man and *they looked like Irishmen* [emphasis added]. One wore light coloured trousers and half boots, an old shabby black coat and had a piece rent out of his hat. The third would not be seen and turned his back on us, because Thomas said to me, "I believe he is the man that once stole a pair of stockings of mine". The third had an olive fustian, velveteen jacket with large laps. The buttons of the jacket had a rim round their shanks'. He may have added (not all the inquest reports mention this) that the tall man had a dark complexion.

After the three men had passed Bill's o'Jack's, Platt and Thomas continued their journey. Only the *Manchester Guardian* (7 April) reported their subsequent movements in any detail: '[They] met a man with some hats in a sack, who was going to Holmfirth. Tom told him there were three men before [i.e. where Thomas and Platt had just been]; and "they were three bad ones, Irishmen"; but if they had kept on the road, they were two miles before and he might not see them'. Thomas and Platt parted company at Daniel Whitehead's shop at Road End, where the former went to make his purchases. The same article said that Thomas bought some coffee, tea and half-a-pound of candles. These candles were found in his pocket after he died, 'crushed and sodden in blood', but the coffee and tea 'are missing with the rest of the plunder'. If Platt had already left Thomas by then, how did the author know what he had bought? Did someone speak to Daniel Whitehead?

Meanwhile, Platt went past Road End to Uppermill, 'where he called at a beer shop kept by one James Bowker, and from thence he went home to his residence at Primrose, near Saddleworth church'.

Wheeler's Manchester Chronicle (7 April) had a little more on Thomas Bradbury's subsequent actions, albeit with a different list of items purchased: 'He then called at a shop and bought some flour, candles, etc. He has a wife and six or eight children [actually five], who, strange to say, have been in the habit of living not with him, but in a separate house at a place called Sidebank, about three-quarters-of-a-mile from his father's. He called to see them after he had been at the provision shop, and left there for his father's house about half-past eight o'clock'. The source for these movements (and the different 'shopping list' to that in the *Manchester Guardian*) is unclear.

None of this was mentioned at the inquest.

Although it might be tempting to dismiss these mysterious Irishmen as a figment of Platt's imagination – and some later writers would attempt to do so – other people also noticed them. A throwaway comment in the *Manchester Courier* report, which unlike the rest of the article did not come from Butterworth and is of uncertain provenance, stated: 'Two other persons saw the same three men on whom suspicion has fallen, lurking in the neighbourhood'. The most authoritative corroboration came in *Wheeler's Manchester Chronicle*, which reported: 'They [the three men] were seen, however, at Road End about six o'clock and previously also at different points, before [Thomas Bradbury] and Platt met them. At each period they were loitering and their bearing was so remarkable as to attract the particular observation of everyone who encountered them'. The same account stated that a constable asked people who claimed to have seen the trio on Monday night if they recognised a potential suspect a few days later. The witnesses were Thomas Placow, a wagoner, who saw them around 6 pm; another man called Thomas Bradbury (not a known relation of Tom o'Bill's, but one of several local men who shared his name); and 'several other persons'. Finally, Smith's letter stated, regarding what he believed were the four-to-six Irishmen involved: 'I have also learnt that persons of a similar description were seen a few miles further on the road earlier in the afternoon; one of them wore a white straw hat'.

Unfortunately, there were no definite later sightings on Monday night. According to *Wheeler's Manchester Chronicle* (7 April): 'Although Thomas Bradbury watched the three men beyond his father's dwelling, neither the persons in [the next house along from Bill's o'Jack's] nor some people who were working upon the road [in the dark?] and must have observed them had they gone forward, remember to have seen any such men pass'. And the *Manchester Times* inquest report said that someone – the wording is unclear who, but it might have been Platt – had later made enquiries further along the Holmfirth road but the three men had not passed by.

In any case Holmfirth – if that was their actual destination – was eight miles away and crossing Saddleworth Moor at night can hardly have been an attractive proposition. They might have followed the reverse route of Reuben Platt and headed towards Primrose over the hills. And although no-one saw them further along the road that night, they might easily have passed on unseen to Holmfirth or Huddersfield (via the Meltham and Wessenden Head Turnpike) given that the alarm was not raised until the following morning. Even if there really *were* people working on the road that night, they would not have been looking out for anyone; the alarm was only raised the next morning.

Given all these uncertainties, we do not really know what became of the three men. But one of them might have left something behind. *Wheeler's Manchester Chronicle* mentioned in the article published on 7 April: 'The murderers left nothing at or about the house that can afford any assistance in their detection except … an old slouched hat which was found in the house and appears to correspond with that described to have been worn by one of the men whom Bradbury and Platt met'. This mysterious hat might have been discussed at the inquest, but only the *Manchester Times* and the *Manchester Guardian* reported it. According to the latter, the hat was physically produced at the inquest: 'It was a shabby, old, crumpled one, with part of the brim torn off; the witness [Platt] said, "This is the hat the Irishman had on".'

If this was such a vital piece of evidence, why did no rival newspapers mention it? Why was it part of the description issued of the three suspects if it had been left behind? And why did that poster not make more of the hat being torn as that might have helped to identify its owner? Butterworth, in his exhaustive article about the inquest, corroborated the presence of a hat, yet he stated that the item belonged to a man who had been arrested on suspicion of involvement (i.e. it had *not* been found at the scene); and according to Butterworth, Platt could not be certain that this was the hat worn by any of the three Irishmen. Did the journalists get a little too excited and misunderstand to whom the hat belonged? Did the other newspapers ignore the issue as it had been established that the hat was unconnected to the three Irishmen?

As we cannot entirely trust the sources here, assessment of the hat is tricky. Even if a hat really was left behind in the Bradburys' house, does that place the Irishmen at the scene? The number of visitors to the scene in the days afterwards meant that anyone could have left a hat there; it is unclear exactly *when* it was found. Nor do we know that it was the same hat; it may have been a common design. And it is even possible, if Platt had inflated his own role or was enjoying the attention, that he saw the hat in the house later on and decided to add it to his description. The hat cannot definitively prove that the three men had anything to do with the murders.

Although most of what we know about the night before comes from Reuben Platt's evidence, there was another witness, albeit one not called to the inquest: a man called Abraham Dawson who lived in a hut at Upperwood which was the next house along from Bill's o'Jack's. Most mentions of him can be traced to Butterworth's first article, which identified him as a worker for the Huddersfield Canal Company. He was walking up the road (i.e. towards Holmfirth) between 9:30 and 9:45 pm on Monday, 2 April when he came across William Bradbury's dog (with the implication the dog was heading down the hill). Continuing onwards, Dawson 'heard as if company tippling in the house, and thinking it was the case he proceeded onwards, to a house a quarter of a mile further where he lodged'. It is unclear whether Butterworth spoke to him, or whether Dawson's tale was also being widely retold on Tuesday afternoon. As this is followed in his notes by the account of James Whitehead supposedly seeing Bradbury on Monday evening, it is likely that Butterworth was reporting hearsay.

Wheeler's Manchester Chronicle published a very similar version of events, although Dawson is nameless and simply 'a man … passing along the high-road'. While near the Bradburys' house, he 'fancied there must be some boisterous company within' because of the 'great noise'. Not giving it much thought, he carried on up the road, where a 'large dog which Bradbury kept came running from the house, apparently much frightened. When it had got some distance it lay down on the opposite side of the way'. This version of the encounter with the dog takes place *after* he passed Bill's o'Jack's; it is sufficiently different to Butterworth's to suggest that the author could have spoken to Dawson himself but might simply be an alternative version of what Butterworth had heard.

However, Dawson appears to have gone out of his way to discuss the murders in the aftermath of the inquest. Although the *Manchester Guardian* did not mention him in its first report, he appeared in that newspaper's postscript to the inquest published on 14 April. The writer said that Dawson was either visiting or staying with a man, Joseph Matthews, who lived in at the top of the hill: 'Abraham Dawson, a stone-cutter in the employ of Mr Patteson*, of Manchester, went up the road at about half-past nine o'clock that night, and heard a noise in Bill's o'Jack's. On arriving at the hut of … Matthews, he remarked that "he thought old Bradbury had some rough company".'

If the three accounts cannot quite decide upon Dawson's occupation, they agree on the main details: he heard a commotion at Bill's o'Jack's between 9:30 and 9:45 on Monday night, when he was returning home. But it was not unusual or concerning enough to raise the alarm or investigate further. We don't know if William Bradbury had more than one dog, but if Dawson saw Laddie, that raises a question: the door to Bill's o'Jack's was closed when Amelia Winterbottom arrived next morning, so how did the dog get back inside the house if he was in the road when the 'commotion' took place?

For whatever reason, Dawson was not called to the inquest – possibly because the coroner was not too concerned with establishing *when* the murders took place as much as getting an idea of what happened. Yet Dawson's claims, which there seems little reason to doubt, gave a potential time for the attacks. It is unfortunate that Dawson was never questioned further; a more concrete description of what he heard might have yielded valuable evidence.

Platt's narrative of what happened the night before became crucial in the days that followed as it provided the only indication of who might have been responsible for the brutal murders. His description of the suspects circulated widely and drove a frantic search over the following days and weeks, during which time almost every stranger in the area was viewed with frightened misgivings. The result bordered on chaos.

* Patteson's was a Manchester firm of masons which also dabbled in statuary.

The Hunt for Suspects

As news of the murders spread, and strangers were closely scrutinised for any resemblance to the descriptions provided by Reuben Platt, a man passed through Saddleworth, unaware that he was about to become a major character in the story of Bill's o'Jack's. He had no association with the Bradburys, nor was he anywhere near Greenfield at the time the two men were attacked. But he had the misfortune to be in the area when the simple fact of his nationality made him an object of fear and suspicion.

Charles Mullen, born in Ireland around 1802, had moved to England to look for work, although we don't know exactly when. Eventually, he settled in Maryport, Cumberland, where probably no more than a couple of years before the murders, he married a woman called Elizabeth. Not long after she gave birth to their first child, he left his family in Brampton (near Carlisle) to find further employment. None of this was particularly remarkable because at this time, a huge number of Irish-born men sought work in England.

According to the 1841 census (the nearest one for which Irish births were recorded) out of England's total population of just under 15 million, 284,000 people had been born in Ireland – just under 2 per cent – of which a slightly higher proportion were men. In the West Riding of Yorkshire, which included Saddleworth, around 1.3 per cent of the population (15,000 people out of 1.1 million) were Irish-born. But in nearby Lancashire, that figure rose to 6.3 per cent (106,000 out of 1.7 million), and around a quarter of these people lived in Manchester, where the Irish-born accounted for 13 per cent of the population. Figures for Saddleworth were lower, around 1 per cent, but statistical variations mattered less than popular perception, and the Irish faced enormous prejudice.

Contemporary writers viewed the Irish as a 'social evil', concentrated in overcrowded ghettos riven with crime, squalor and disease. There was no understanding – economic or sympathetic – of the forces which led to the creation of slums populated by Irish immigrants; the only proffered explanation was one of 'moral degeneracy'. This was especially marked in 1832 when a cholera epidemic ravaged Manchester around the time of the murders; at least one writer associated the disease with the 'Little Ireland' area of the city.

The prejudice was driven by several factors, including religion and politics, but at its heart was the irrational fear which has been directed at immigrants throughout history. The Irish were explicitly viewed as a distinct – and inferior – race, and identified as a social problem, for example through the belief that the number of Irish paupers was affecting the poor rates. Working men feared that Irish labourers would take their jobs, as they were willing to work for less money in harsher conditions. In short, the Irish were seen as a threat and treated accordingly. In a case as brutal as that of Bill's o'Jack's, even discounting Reuben Platt's evidence, the engrained prejudice meant that no-one questioned the idea that the murderers *had to be* Irish; it was a natural (albeit unjust) assumption.

Mullen had worked in many places over the years. At some point, probably before his marriage, he had been in Greenfield, working on the turnpike road. By April 1832, he was working as a navigator* on a canal near Methley in Wakefield, employed by a man he knew only as 'Irish Jemmy'.

* A navigator – often abbreviated to 'navvy' – was a labourer employed in the construction of canals, roads and railways.

The weekend before the murder, Mullen had spent time drinking in Leeds. During the daytime on Monday, 2 April, Mullen and his colleague (a man called John Coombe) fell into a drunken brawl in Leeds – *Wheeler's Manchester Chronicle*, inadvertently but perfectly demonstrating anti-Irish sentiment, said that 'having got drunk, [they] like all other Irishmen fell to fighting' – and were dismissed from their jobs either on the Monday or early on Tuesday. Mullen had continued drinking in Leeds on Monday and found himself at a place known as 'Nancy Piper's' before returning to his lodgings late that night. After another day of heavy drinking in Methley, Mullen sobered up on Wednesday and set off towards Manchester, intending either to find more work or to journey home to his family in Cumberland. He spent Wednesday night in Huddersfield before continuing the following morning.

Unfortunately for Mullen, he continued to bear the signs of his fight while heading towards an area where, fuelled by Reuben Platt, everyone was on the lookout for such things, particularly if those exhibiting injuries were Irish. On the road to Delph, Mullen passed a wagon driver who warned him that the marks on his face would probably result in his arrest, but Mullen pressed on regardless.

Later that Thursday, Mullen was seen near Marsden and was an immediate target for suspicion. A local man began to question him, but dissatisfied by his answers ran to nearby Dobcross for help and returned with a group of men determined to detain Mullen. As they arrived, Mullen sat down by the road in despair and simply said: 'I'm not the man you want'. Nevertheless, he was taken to Dobcross and examined at the King's Head public house where blood was found on his shirt.

At this point, a modern reader might expect that the police had become involved, or that a detective had taken charge, questioning suspects or gathering evidence. But when Mullen was arrested, Saddleworth had no police force and the first English detectives would not be recruited for another ten years. So who led the investigation into the murders of the Bradburys? The short answer: no one. In effect, there was no investigation to lead. So what did criminal justice look like in 1832?

As areas became increasingly urbanised in late Georgian Britain, law and order was a growing concern. Between 1810 and 1830, the number of criminal trials in England and Wales more than trebled but few places outside of London had their own professional police force. Saddleworth, for example, had nothing until the West Riding force was instituted in 1858. Therefore, in cases like Bill's o'Jack's, no central authority existed to lead the investigation. That does not mean that crime was ignored. Public disorder was handled by the Yeomanry or by soldiers, but day-to-day justice was solely in the hands of magistrates – known also as Justices of the Peace – who were usually wealthy landowners with good social standing but little legal expertise. Although the role brought considerable authority and local power, the heavy workload and vast responsibilities discouraged potential candidates from coming forwards. Nor did magistrates have a uniformly good reputation; many were suspected of corruption.

Day-to-day issues in an area like Saddleworth were the concern of the parish constable, an unpaid position awarded by magistrates and given to (frequently reluctant) local men – often farmers or tradesmen – for a year at a time. However, a constable only fulfilled his limited duties in his spare time. He could arrest anyone who broke the law, his presence might deter potential wrongdoers and he might be called out if there was trouble or violence. But he was not an investigator. So what happened after a crime was committed?

In the eighteenth and early-nineteenth centuries it was the responsibility of a victim (or someone with an interest in the case) to identify the culprits who had broken the law and to organise their own prosecution in the courts. Therefore, in the case of Bill's o'Jack's, it was the angry local people, on the lookout for suspicious Irishmen, who led the 'investigation'. A constable might be persuaded to assist, but he would expect to be paid for his time. It was a different matter if a suspect had been apprehended; at that point a constable was more likely to become involved.

That is what happened in the case of Mullen. After he had been detained in the King's Head, a constable was summoned. He searched Mullen but did not find anything incriminating (such as stolen money). But the limitations of the role of constable quickly became apparent; the crowd that had brought Mullen to Dobcross refused to disperse. Several people who had got into the room before the constable arrived refused to leave and began to cause trouble. This crowd had predetermined Mullen's guilt. *Wheeler's Manchester Chronicle* recorded: 'Several individuals thought proper to pronounce their opinions upon the man in language which did little credit either to their feelings or their understandings'. One man wanted to take Mullen outside and hang him; another wished to take him to the next room and 'pugilistically prove that he … was one of the murderers'; a third threatened to stab him. Other onlookers shouted questions at Mullen. When he (understandably in the circumstances) replied with 'uncivil answers', they seem to have been somewhat shocked. Eventually, and with some difficulty, the onlookers were removed from the room.

In an attempt to prove that Mullen was one of the strangers seen on Monday night, Reuben Platt was called. However, Platt was unable to identify him for certain. He said that Mullen might possibly have been the man wearing a 'blue slop' who kept his face hidden but he was far from sure. Others who had seen the three men in the area on Monday night were also called. Two witnesses believed that Mullen might have been the man in blue, but others did not recognise him.

Mullen explained to the constable how he had been injured, and how he came to be in Saddleworth. He stated that he was familiar with the area through his work on the Greenfield road but was unfamiliar with both Dobcross and the area around Bill's o'Jack's. Some locals wondered if the hat he was wearing might have belonged to William Bradbury, but Mullen said he had picked it up after his fight having lost his own; two neighbours of William confirmed the hat was not his. Meanwhile, attempts were made to corroborate Mullen's tale. By a coincidence, a 'respectable merchant' from Methley named Dennison was in Dobcross and after questioning Mullen was satisfied that he had been working where he said. And a Saddleworth constable called Waterhouse went to Methley on Friday to investigate further.

None of this looked especially promising in terms of having found one of the murderers; even *Wheeler's Manchester Chronicle* judged that the charges against Mullen were 'vague'.* But there was just enough suspicion to warrant the involvement of someone in authority, which meant finding a magistrate.

When there was a case against a suspect, deciding what to do next was the responsibility of the local magistrates, beginning a process that varied with the seriousness of the charge. Relatively minor offences could be dealt with solely by the magistrates at what were known as 'petty sessions'; these were sometimes held in the homes of magistrates or at a local building such as a public house. The magistrates also ascertained whether a case should be heard at a higher court. More serious crimes were tried before a jury at quarter sessions, courts which met four times each year, under the jurisdiction of magistrates from across a county. Capital offences, including murder, were tried before juries in the major towns of a county at the twice-yearly assizes, presided over by judges recruited from the ranks of experienced barristers.

But the process of prosecution before a court – which had to be done by the individuals affected – was expensive and time-consuming. As a result the poor were often unwilling to pursue cases. The breach was partially filled in many areas (including Saddleworth) by prosecution

* The article in *Wheeler's Manchester Chronicle* gave so much detail about Mullen and his story that it is likely the journalist was present when he was arrested and questioned, or had spoken to someone who was there.

associations: members paid a subscription in return for which they would have financial support if ever they needed to prosecute an offence. By 1832, expenses were often paid for individuals who were pursuing a case but there was still no system of public prosecution.

However, there was never even remotely enough evidence against Charles Mullen to warrant a trial. And because no-one was ever charged with the Bill's o'Jack's murders, the case was never prosecuted before a court.

Once Mullen was safely held in the King's Head, the constable sought a magistrate, but that was not straightforward. Two of the Saddleworth magistrates were away at the Pontefract Quarter Sessions; a third, the Reverend Evans of Grasscroft (around four miles from Dobcross) was 'seriously indisposed'. Eventually, Evans agreed to question Mullen, and around 4 pm the prisoner was conveyed to the magistrate's house. On the way, he was 'followed by a great concourse of people. All the inhabitants of the surrounding country flocked to the roadside, and influenced by his [Mullen's] ungainly exterior, pronounced condemnation as he passed'. *Wheeler's Manchester Chronicle* stated: 'The women were, as usual, the least measured in their epithets. Several elderly dames expressed their readiness to undertake the task of execution, and to spare the labour of the gallows-building by appropriating the next tree to the unholy office'. Evans remanded him in custody until the inquest. Mullen grumbled about the threats he had received and Evans told the constable to make sure there were no recurrences. Mullen was taken to be held at the William the Fourth public house at Road End. On the way, he was once more jeered by the crowd, 'notwithstanding the strenuous interference of the constable', although not as severely as before.

He spent Thursday and Friday night in custody at the William the Fourth. But the frenzied search for Irish suspects had not ceased with his arrest, and the chaotic pseudo-investigation continued. In a state of heightened tension, any stranger was going to be a suspect, particularly if they were (or appeared to be) Irish. Although a few men were held by constables, there was insufficient evidence to detain anyone for long, and no-one other than Mullen seems to have appeared before magistrates that week. Nevertheless, the various lists of alternative suspects – published in newspapers on 7 April – was long.

Edwin Butterworth, in the draft of his article, said that John Pollard, 'a young man living at Lees but working in the neighbourhood' saw 'five Irishmen in a public house at Upper Mill before dusk on Monday evening'. They had been drinking there until they had 'spent up'. Butterworth recorded: 'In consequence of what had been adduced, suspicions have fallen on either the three or five Irishmen seen as the perpetrators of the deed and the disappearance of the two Emeralders [presumably Irishmen] who were working on the new road to Huddersfield, which passed through Greenfield, has excited still stronger suspicions'. Butterworth reported that an 'active search after the villains has ensued' and he seemed confident that there would be bloody marks on the clothing of anyone involved, or that there would be some sign on them of the violent struggle. Failing that, he hoped they could be identified through having items or money stolen from Bill's o'Jack's.

The newspapers that printed Butterworth's article supplemented it with more up-to-date information. The *Manchester Courier* said that a man matching the description of one of Platt's Irishmen was being held at Delph (this probably referred to Mullen) and the *Leeds Mercury* recorded: 'Suspicion attaches to two Irishmen, who have been apprehended'. *Wheeler's Manchester Chronicle* reported that on Monday, 2 April, a man called Garside, the constable of Stalybridge, had seen three men – who 'had most villainous looks' and whom he deduced were Irish – talking to two Irishmen with whom he had dealt previously. Although the newcomers were unfamiliar to him, he had suspected they were up to no good and so observed them carefully. Garside did not see them again but remembered them when he heard of the murders on Wednesday. According to *Wheeler's Manchester Chronicle*, he believed they were the three men seen by Platt based on the descriptions circulated.

Wheeler's Manchester Chronicle also revealed that a man was being held in Huddersfield on the Friday, although the writer did not think anything would come of this; similarly a man in Manchester was expected to be released from custody imminently. Another man called Francis Barker from Yorkshire was being detained at Shudehill on the grounds that he had tried to change a £10 note at the Lower Ship public house and had left a slop (the item of outer clothing) there early on Tuesday morning. The alarm was raised later that day, but when Barker was located on Thursday, he denied having so much money. Although the constables who questioned him suspected he had indeed possessed £10, they discovered that he had not left a slop on Tuesday. Instead, he had left a different item of clothing two weeks earlier. Even though he refused to account for his movements on Monday, the constables quickly lost interest.

Even as innocent men continued to be arrested based on little more than their appearance or accent, the story of the murders continued to excite people in the area. The *Manchester Guardian* described the double murder as causing a 'sensation' on the Tuesday and Wednesday: Bill's o'Jack's 'was visited by many hundreds of persons of both sexes, and of all ranks in society'. By Wednesday, the bodies had been washed and laid out in an 'antechamber' ready for the inquest.

Interest continued to grow. *Wheeler's Manchester Chronicle* also reported on the crowds in attendance: 'The house has been visited by several thousand persons, nearly all of whom contributed their mite in aid of the funeral and other expenses'. And yet this perhaps underplayed how many people came. The article related that the roads to Bill's o'Jack's had been 'actually crowded' all week. Given that even today the roads in that area are easily gummed up by tourists in the summer months, it is not hard to imagine queues stretching in all directions. There were hints that tempers frayed: 'So eager has been the desire to obtain admission to the house, that the greatest difficulty has been experienced in preserving anything like order. So late as yesterday (Friday) there was positive fighting for precedence'. The writer expected that the house would be an 'object of attraction' for some time to come.

By this stage, according to *Wheeler's Manchester Chronicle* (written towards the end of the week) most of the signs of the murder had been cleaned up; however the bloody clothes the two men had been wearing were on display in the main room, as were the presumed murder weapons. The bodies, cleaned up and with the wounds dressed, were in 'a still smaller room, of which the roof at one part is only about a yard high'. Only their faces were visible, so 'their appearance is not peculiarly striking'. Butterworth noted that 'hundreds of people have daily flocked to visit the scene of this barbarous tragedy'.

However, around the time of Mullen's arrest, the Saddleworth magistrates belatedly began to impose some order on proceedings, because even in a justice system which appears strange to modern eyes, they had certain responsibilities. As a breach of the 'King's Peace', murder required more direct intervention from them. Therefore, the Saddleworth magistrates should have taken an immediate interest in the murders. But matters were confused because, as the constable discovered when looking for someone to deal with Mullen, two of the Saddleworth magistrates were attending the Pontefract Quarter Sessions, which by an unfortunate coincidence, had begun on Monday, 2 April and continued until Wednesday. And because the Reverend Evans was too ill to act, no-one in authority was in a position to do anything on the Tuesday or Wednesday when there was the greatest chance of finding the culprits.

Therefore the aftermath of the murder was somewhat directionless. Only John Buckley, a Saddleworth constable – and most likely the man summoned to Bill's o'Jack's by James Whitehead on Tuesday morning – was proactive. The same Tuesday, he had a poster printed offering a reward of £100 for information about the murders, including the description given by Reuben Platt of the prime suspects. News about the murder and a description of the wanted men was also circulated to the surrounding areas.

It was not until the Thursday that some semblance of order entered proceedings when Buckley travelled to Pontefract to ask the magistrates what should be done before they returned to Saddleworth. Judging by the rapidity of their reaction, this must have been the first they had heard of the murders. Immediately, they sent a letter from Pontefract, dated 5 April, to the Home Secretary requesting money to increase the £100 reward that had already been offered for information. This was fairly common practice.

Given the difficulties of prosecuting crime and the vagaries of the court system, financial incentives were provided by the Home Office in capital cases to encourage individuals to prosecute or for witnesses (even accomplices of the culprit) to come forward. Generous rewards were offered for successful prosecutions. The prospect of monetary benefit for the capture of criminals encouraged professional thief-catchers such as the famous 'Bow Street Runners' but also led to cases of abuse such as the 'Macdaniel Affair' of 1754, in which a group of bounty hunters deliberately prosecuted innocent men on capital charges to secure the reward money.

The letter to the Home Secretary was signed at Pontefract by the Saddleworth magistrates, James Buckley and Joseph Mallalieu, and a Huddersfield magistrate called Lewis Fenton. Also enclosed was the sworn statement from Ammon Platt – an odd choice of witness in the circumstances as he was only able to report everything second-hand – to back up their claim. Perhaps Platt had travelled to Pontefract (from where the letter was sent to the Home Office) with Constable Buckley, or perhaps the two magistrates who took his statement on 5 April (James Buckley and John Armytage) had gone to meet him.

An announcement duly appeared in the *Gazette* on 10 April offering a total reward of £200 – half from Constable Buckley and half from His Majesty's Treasury – for information leading to a conviction, and a pardon to anyone (except the murderers) who came forward. This was another common incentive offered by the Home Office to encourage accomplices to turn King's Evidence. But by the time the announcement appeared, the inquest had been held and the trail was already growing cold.

The Inquest

The man responsible for the inquest was Michael Stocks junior, a 33-year-old solicitor and magistrate from Halifax. He came from a wealthy and influential family; his father, also named Michael Stocks, had preceded him as a magistrate and was an important local figure. An owner of coal mines, a well-known Radical and supporter of the reform movement, Stocks senior made the newspapers in 1831 when an attempt was made to remove him as magistrate, largely because of his political views, after a controversy which tangentially involved his son. Later in 1832, Stocks senior stood unsuccessfully as the member of Parliament for Halifax in the constituency newly created by the passing of the Reform Bill.

Michael Stocks junior had qualified as a solicitor in the 1820s and in 1826 had been elected unopposed* as the coroner for Halifax after the death of the incumbent. This was an important position at the time, far more than an administrative role. Coroners were elected – usually for life (although Stocks resigned in mysterious and controversial circumstances in 1837) – by freeholders of the county in which they held the position. They were required to investigate any sudden or unexplained death, for which purpose an inquest was called. These had no set venue but were held in any suitable building – often a public house – close to where the death had occurred. As coroners were responsible for a large area, they often had to travel considerable distances as part of their role.

* Although uncontested elections for the office were quite common, Stocks achieved this through a technicality. He and his opponent agreed to draw lots to decide who should be coroner.

To listen to the evidence at an inquest, local juries were selected by the parish constable. Depending on the wishes of the coroner, these ranged in size from twelve to twenty-three men, but there were no restrictions on who could serve; there was, for instance, no property qualification. The jury was required to view the bodies of those deceased and to inspect any relevant locations. They could question witnesses and sometimes called witnesses themselves. However, the primary purpose of the inquest was simply to identify a cause of death. Further questions were matters for higher courts. The coroner did not investigate more deeply because that was not his role. However, when the inquest verdict was murder or manslaughter, the jury named the perpetrator if possible; such cases automatically went to trial at the assizes. And the document recording the proceedings and verdict, signed by the jury and coroner, became the indictment for any charge at the trial.

Usually an inquest took place within a day or two of a death, but as so often in the Bill's o'Jack's case, the Quarter Sessions caused a delay. Stocks was in Pontefract, most likely in his capacity as a magistrate, so was unavailable for most of the week. The Bradburys' inquest was finally held on Saturday, 7 April, at the William the Fourth public house – where Charles Mullen remained in custody – very close to the place Reuben Platt had parted company from Thomas Bradbury a few days earlier. Although no-one could have been sure at the time, it proved to be the only formal investigation into the murders.

It began at 9 am with the swearing-in of the jury, who then went to Bill's o'Jack's to see the two victims and to inspect where the murders had taken place. The *Manchester Times* was the only newspaper to record this part of proceedings: 'There a most melancholy scene presented itself. The bodies of father and son lay side by side on a bed in the back room, literally covered with plaisters [*sic*] laid over the wounds which they had received in this most sanguinary struggle ... the great quantity of blood that lay up and down [the house], formed a sight the most horrible that has ever been witnessed in that part of the country'.

Because the jury members had attended what today would be called the 'crime scene', the inquest did not dwell on any descriptions except where it was mentioned in the evidence of James Whitehead and Samuel Hegginbottom. Fortunately – or not, depending on your perspective – the newspaper reports written in the immediate aftermath of the discovery, combined with the evidence from the inquest and the other available sources, provide us with a remarkably detailed picture of the room on that Tuesday morning. In fact, as the poem on the Bradbury grave phrased it, the 'bloody scene of catastrophe' was one of the factors that generated much ghoulish fascination.

Quite possibly, the curious jury members inspected the whole house for themselves to understand its layout. What did they find? Although Bill's o'Jack's is long-gone, plenty of information survives, quite apart from the photographs taken of its exterior in later years.

Detailed descriptions appeared on 7 April in the *Manchester Guardian* and *Wheeler's Manchester Chronicle*. Additionally the *Manchester Guardian* printed a plan of the interior (suspiciously similar to an unpublished sketch in the back of Edwin Butterworth's notebook) which was reproduced in several newspapers. This diagram, however, was slightly misleading because it made the rooms look larger than they were. A better plan appeared ninety years later in A. J. Howcroft's *Tales of a Pennine People* (1923), which showed the inn at the time of the murder (and how it had been altered in the intervening period).

The main entrance to Bill's o'Jack's opened out onto a small passage. On the left was the area where customers went to drink. No-one seems to have given this much thought, suggesting that there were no signs of violence there, but it means that we know nothing about that room. On the right was the main room, where the father and son would have spent most of their time; for example, William Bradbury was known to sit on a wooden bench by the room's entrance. Only around three square metres (Thomas Smith in his letter said it was ten feet square), the room was not large, which might explain how almost every surface came to be covered in blood following the attack on the inhabitants. A sense of its size can be gathered from the only known photographs taken inside Bill's o'Jack's, shortly before it closed in the 1930s. These show a couple being served at a table by a window, next to the large stone fireplace. In fact, the corner of the table nearest to the camera probably marked the spot where Thomas Bradbury was found a hundred years earlier.

By the time of that photograph, Bill's o'Jack's had been remodelled; the 'murder room' was something of an attraction, becoming the place where customers were served. But in 1832, it was the private living room. Apart from William's bench, it contained wooden drawers and an armchair; *Wheeler's Manchester Chronicle* mentioned a table and chairs too. Thomas Smith described the floor as being paved stone.

William and Thomas had been laid out for the jury to see in a small room – described by most sources as a pantry or buttery – that could only be reached via the main room and was at the opposite end of the house to the entrance. Howcroft's plan indicated that this had a small window and therefore would probably have been quite dark. *Wheeler's Manchester Chronicle* (7 April) suggested that the room had a ceiling which sloped downwards, being only a yard from the floor at one point. Howcroft's plan seems to indicate another door to the house next to the pantry, but this seems to have been a later feature not present in 1832; such a door was not mentioned elsewhere and did not feature in the *Manchester Guardian* drawing.

The only other room was upstairs, reached via the staircase from the entrance passage. Like the bar area, it attracted little attention from journalists or witnesses so, apart from the bed, we know nothing about its contents.

If the details about the other rooms are fuzzy, that was because everyone was understandably focussed on the bloody state of the main room. The *Manchester Times* report on the inquest indicated that it had not been cleared up even by Saturday when the jury visited. Was this for their benefit or to entice more visitors to the grisly scene? Earlier reports described the scene on Tuesday morning in gruesome detail.

Blood covered every surface – the walls, the fireplace, the mantlepiece, the stove, the window – and those first on the scene said that the floor was literally swimming with it. There were spots, splashes and finger-marks – as if someone had reached out to steady themselves – all around, but the heaviest concentrations were close to the chair by the window and around the stove. Additionally, bloody footprints led upstairs, left by someone wearing stockings, as well as equivalent traces along the wall where the same person – almost certainly William Bradbury – had supported himself. These led to the bed in which the older man had been found.

Places around the room told more of the story. At the door to the small pantry was what Hegginbottom described at the inquest as 'two pounds of coagulated blood'. Where Thomas was found lying, a large bloody pool stretched from the window to the fireplace. Inside the pantry, a mark in the wall opposite the doorway looked as if it had been created by a blow from a sharp object. Nearby was what the *Manchester Guardian* called 'a mark as if a bloody head had been dashed against the plastering; the walls all around are spotted with blood'.

The supposition was that Thomas had been attacked as soon as he entered the house, because his pockets contained crushed candles, bought the previous evening. *Wheeler's Manchester Chronicle* also reported that a bag of flour had been abandoned by the entrance. Although the flour was not mentioned anywhere else, Ammon Platt said that Thomas had purchased some, which might indicate he had seen it in the house.

Several probable weapons were found at the scene and had been laid out for the jury – or curious visitors – to see by the Saturday morning. The *Manchester Times* reporter saw: 'Three bludgeons, covered with blood, the largest about a yard long and between two or three inches thick'. Other items had been in the room when Thomas Bradbury was discovered on Tuesday morning. The *Manchester Guardian* (7 April) noted: an old spade which was already worn, broken from its handle and 'from its appearance might have been dipped in blood'; a 'bent and bloody poker'; and an angur (a type of drill, possibly like an auger, but not a misprint), the handle of which was 'covered in blood'. Ammon Platt said that when he entered the house with Hegginbottom, the spade was still there, 'covered with blood and it had a considerable quantity of hair upon it'. *Wheeler's Manchester Chronicle* also described an old spade shaft, covered in blood. Two other weapons had been removed; they would make an appearance at the inquest.

When the jury returned to the public house, more representatives of the press were in attendance, making Stocks uneasy. One of the journalists present was Edwin Butterworth; before the witnesses were called, Stocks questioned why he was there. Butterworth informed Stocks that he was 'professionally employed' but this did not satisfy the coroner, who pressed the matter further, drawing an admission from Butterworth that he was a reporter.

Although Stocks said that he did not object to the presence of journalists at the inquest, he requested that the names of the witnesses and the full details of their evidence not be reported in any newspaper. According to the *Manchester Guardian* (the only newspaper to record this exchange between Butterworth and Stocks), the coroner believed that giving too much information 'might be hurtful, and could not be attended with beneficial effects, and in his opinion, it would be sufficient if the public knew the narrative of the evidence, without going into particulars'.

This curious episode was in fact a re-enactment of a battle playing out across the entire court system of Britain over the concern that press coverage could – and often did – threaten the prospect of a fair trial. Every detail of a case was often reported, Bill's o'Jack's was no exception. By itself, this was potentially prejudicial to a defendant but some journalists went further and invented their own facts. For example, *The Times* coverage of the Radlett Murder in 1823 falsely stated that the suspect, John Thurtell, had a prior record as a murderer.

Sometimes newspapers – *The Times* being notorious – effectively found the accused guilty long before a jury heard their case; Thurtell was condemned by the press before he went to trial and something similar happened to the banker Henry Fauntleroy in 1824. Although prejudicial public comment about the accused was prohibited and could lead to a charge of contempt of court, newspapers in the early-nineteenth century had little regard for such laws. Even when there were explicit judicial bans on reporting, newspapers sometimes printed stories regardless, such as in the case of the Cato Street Conspiracy (a plot to murder the Cabinet) of 1820.

Therefore coroners often attempted to stop newspapers publishing details of inquests. But in the case of Bill's o'Jack's, it was already impossible to cork that bottle because the story – and a lot of the evidence that Stocks was about to hear – had been printed that very morning and was being read across Britain. Of the witnesses, only Amelia Winterbottom had previously been anonymous, listed simply as William Bradbury's granddaughter. Perhaps that was why the newspapers largely ignored the coroner's request; there was no point suppressing what was already known.

The writer for the *Manchester Guardian* compromised slightly, giving only a condensed version of the inquest evidence, and observing: 'We do not feel ourselves at all bound by the coroner's opinion, though in this case we readily comply with his request, because the witnesses detailed very little that was not known before'. He added that his newspaper had already published almost everything, but added a few new facts, including the name Amelia Winterbottom.

Despite the warning from Stocks, Butterworth made extensive notes about the inquest, far fuller than appeared in any single newspaper, which he might have intended to generate several articles. For example, the entry ended with a general comment about rumours in circulation, a description of the scenery around Bill's o'Jack's (which he might have intended to begin a different piece) and an annotated sketch map of the area. Some of this long version appeared, in a heavily edited form, in

*Wheeler's Manchester Chronicle.** He also wrote an abridged version on separate paper (later stuck into the front of a different notebook) but the reports on the inquest published in the *Manchester Courier* and *Liverpool Mercury* used a combination of both versions of his story. Butterworth was also paid that week by the *Manchester Times* – even though the inquest article seems to have been written by someone else.

Two inquests were held in the William the Fourth that day. The first, which investigated the death of a newborn child whose body had been found on Thursday, took up the rest of the morning. This death might have had a bearing on the story of the Bradburys, but for the moment it can be put to one side.

Finally, at around 2 pm, the inquest into the death of the Bradburys began. It lasted around three hours. First to give evidence was the granddaughter of William Bradbury; she related how she had found her uncle four days earlier. Most articles about the inquest included her name – Amelia Winterbottom – which had been omitted from earlier reports; only *Wheeler's Manchester Chronicle* obeyed Stocks's instruction to keep her anonymous. But there is some doubt whether her name really was Amelia.

Her mother must have been Nancy Winterbottom, the daughter of William Bradbury who attended Bill's o'Jack's on Tuesday afternoon. But there is no record of Nancy and her husband Benjamin having a

* According to his own account book, Butterworth was paid for 46 lines at a rate of one penny per line, which totalled 3s 10d, by *Wheeler's Manchester Chronicle*. However, this was more likely to have been for a separate article (of 43 lines) about the continued hunt for suspects that matches an entry in his notebook. Yet the main article on the inquest followed a similar structure to Butterworth and included some of his notes and asides, even if it was heavily re-written. It was close to 200 lines in total. It is unclear why he was not paid for this work on the longer article, unless he was given a nominal amount for the basic reporting but his notes were written up by someone else.

daughter called Amelia. This could simply reflect an omission from the parish registers; perhaps she was not baptised for some reason. However, Nancy *did* have a daughter called Mary, baptised in September 1820. This would make her the right age for the girl who entered Bill's o'Jack's on Tuesday morning; the newspaper accounts of the inquest agreed she was approximately 12 years old. And when the story of the murders was retold nearly forty years later, the girl's name was altered, without explanation, to 'Mary Winterbottom'.

If, as seems likely, the girl who raised the alarm *was* Mary Winterbottom, why was she called Amelia at the inquest? Perhaps it was an attempt at keeping the witness anonymous. Or perhaps she was known, for whatever reason, as Amelia although her real name was Mary. A further curiosity is that Thomas Bradbury and his wife had a daughter called Amelia, but she would have been 18 at the time of the murders – too old to be mistaken for a 12-year-old.

The next witness was James Whitehead, whose insistence that William Bradbury said 'Pats, Pats' played an enormous role in the growth of the legend in the following years. Butterworth noted that Whitehead – whom he described as an old man although he was only 52 years old – was hard to hear when he gave his evidence.

Amelia (or Mary) Winterbottom and James Whitehead could only describe how they came to find the two Bradburys, but neither could shed any light on how or why they died. The next witness, the surgeon Samuel Hegginbottom, finally provided a few answers. He had already played an unusually large role in the story, but his appearance at the inquest would not have been a certainty in this period.

By 1832, there was some tension around the role of science in determining the cause of death at an inquest. Advice to coroners in the eighteenth century specified that it should be jury members who examined wounds on bodies, to ascertain their severity and the likely weapon. Until the middle of that century, even the opinion of relatives or servants was accepted as sufficient to determine how someone died. But an increasing demand for expert testimony during criminal trials – particularly as the need for guilt to be proved 'beyond reasonable doubt' became more established – slowly changed expectations for inquests, as did a growing awareness that non-expert witnesses were not above perjuring themselves to earn the various financial inducements available for successful prosecutions. For this reason, medical evidence was often heard at an inquest, but some doctors were reluctant to testify, not least because payment for doing so was at the discretion of the local parish.*

As the demands grew for specialist evidence at inquests, there were parallel calls for coroners to have some kind of medical background; they had previously been recruited from the world of politics. The result was a gradual professionalisation of the office of coroner that had already begun by the time Michael Stocks arrived in Saddleworth. Even if he was firmly in the 'political' category of coroner, he seems to have demanded evidence from doctors. Both inquests held on 7 April heard medical testimony. In the case of the child death, two surgeons offered their opinions, but the Bradbury hearing relied on the evidence of the man who had examined the two victims.

Samuel Hegginbottom was around 38 years old at the time of the inquest and had been a surgeon in Uppermill for some time; he was one of nine advertising in Saddleworth in *Pigot's Directory* for 1828–29. Married since 1817, he had five children, the youngest having been born in 1818. Little else is known about him; he does not seem to have given evidence at any other inquest. But Hegginbottom had proven an extremely enthusiastic amateur detective when he visited Bill's o'Jack's. As well as examining the two Bradburys, he had made a careful survey of the house and helped himself to some items found at the scene.

Hegginbottom's evidence was thoroughly described – with a certain macabre delight – in newspapers. Similar details, which must have

* Laws were passed in 1836 that made it compulsory to pay doctors for testifying at an inquest.

originated from Hegginbottom, had also appeared beforehand in the press. Therefore, a great deal is known about the condition of the dying men.

William Bradbury had the lesser injuries. He was found in bed. From the footprints on the steps, he appeared to have been attacked before struggling upstairs and getting into bed. *Wheeler's Manchester Chronicle* (7 April) described 'bloody traces all along the wall; on the stairs the impression of feet, his stockings being saturated with blood, were distinctly visible. He had experienced great difficulty in mounting the stairs, and seemed only to have effected this by crawling on his hands and knees, step by step, and dragging one foot after the other'. Ammon Platt also hinted at this, describing 'footmarks of blood on every step' left when William 'scrambled upstairs with difficulty after he was bruised and wounded never having come down again'. William had partially undressed; Hegginbottom reported that he had removed his coat and waistcoat. Hegginbottom found him lying on his right side in bed. He had a 'severe cut' to the left side of his head that was bleeding heavily and 'opened to the temporal artery'; there was a lesser wound on his right side that Hegginbottom discovered when turning him over.

Pulling down the bed covers, Hegginbottom discovered more wounds: lacerations on his left arm, the muscles in his upper arm cut through to the bone; the fingers of his left hand also lacerated; his knee severely bruised.*

Some of the earlier newspaper reports were obviously based on first-hand observation. For example, the *Manchester Guardian* (whose reporter may have interviewed Hegginbottom) said that William's fingers

* According to the inquest report in *Wheeler's Manchester Chronicle*, Hegginbottom believed that the wounds (especially those to William's fingers) were caused by the pistol he found; he also believed that an indentation in the old man's head matched the lock of the pistol. However, it is likely the writer was mistaken because the *Manchester Times* mentioned only that the indentations in *Thomas's* head matched the pistol.

on his left hand 'were cut to pieces' and his left wrist and elbow were 'cut and mangled in a shocking manner, the muscles being cut through to the bone, which was broken to pieces'. He was covered 'from head to foot' in bruises. This report suggested that the spade, broken from its handle, was the most likely weapon used on the old man. *Wheeler's Manchester Chronicle* also contained a description in its first report: William's left arm was almost 'battered to a mummy' from the elbow to the wrist and he had been struck on the forehead above his eyes by 'a blow ... which must have immediately blinded him' and had also 'completely closed his eyes'. Ammon Platt also stated that William's eyes were severely swollen. Hegginbottom told the inquest that William had died through blood loss, but would likely have survived had he been a younger man.

One of the stranger aspects of the whole story is that William went to bed; if the men were attacked together, why would he go upstairs when his son lay injured on the floor? Perhaps such apparent callousness indicated that his injuries and blood loss had impaired his judgement. Or did the attack on Thomas occur after his father had left the room? Was William already injured when Thomas returned from his visit to Road End? Or was he lying on the floor like Thomas – perhaps one of the pools of blood belonged to him – and went upstairs after regaining consciousness when whoever was responsible had gone?

Thomas was much more severely injured. Hegginbottom told the inquest that his head had swollen so much that 'they could scarcely touch it with their finger end without putting it into a wound', which was why he was unrecognisable when he was discovered. James Whitehead also told the inquest that Thomas's face was 'marked with bruises and streaming with blood'. He had 'fifteen or sixteen holes' of varying sizes on his scalp which were cut down to the bone, the largest of which was four inches long and the others around half an inch. Hegginbottom stated that the 'holes' were around half an inch deep. All the wounds were bleeding heavily when Hegginbottom saw them. When discovered, Thomas was lying face down; James Whitehead turned him over but by the time Hegginbottom arrived, he had returned to his front.

Hegginbottom examined Thomas when he returned with his instruments, when his head had been shaved (by whom?). Using his surgeon's knife, he enlarged the openings in Thomas's scalp and discovered two fractures: one on the right side was four inches long and 'cut down to the parietal bone' (the side of the skull), the lower part of which was 'much depressed'. The second was on his forehead; his *os frontis* was shattered – perhaps accounting for the mark on the pantry wall. Both fractures, said Hegginbottom, would have been fatal – the second would have been particularly deadly. It is not entirely clear whether Thomas was still alive when this examination took place; if not, this might have been a rudimentary post-mortem. Hegginbottom also reported that Thomas was bleeding a great deal from the ears and nose. He also had a severely fractured finger on his left hand, and various marks on his other fingers. Hegginbottom believed that the pistol had been used to inflict the injuries. The *Manchester Courier*'s report on the inquest indicated which items might have been used: the pokers, a 'sword-stick' and the shovel.

The initial report in the *Manchester Guardian* added a little more about Thomas: 'His head and face appeared to be a mass of clotted gore' and 'though apparently unconscious, he made frequent attempts to rise from the floor, but each time sunk again into the pool of blood in which he had been lying'. The only additional detail was that he was 'cut and bruised all over the body' and died while his wounds were still being dressed. *Wheeler's Manchester Chronicle*'s first report added that he had cuts all over his legs, knees and feet, and one of his legs was particularly badly injured. He wore a bloodied white apron, in which he had been seen the previous evening. Unlike his father, Thomas made no attempt to speak but merely groaned.

While Hegginbottom was giving his evidence at the inquest, he produced two of the potential murder weapons that had been removed from the scene. One of these was the remains of what Hegginbottom called 'a sword-stick of beech'. The Saddleworth constable, Buckley, was able to tell the inquest that it was in fact an ornamental walking stick that Thomas Bradbury had received from a friend; it had been hollowed out and holes had been pierced into the sides to transform it into a large flute. It was broken, as if used to hit someone repeatedly.

The second weapon was a broken pistol. James Whitehead had seen part of it, the lock, or firing mechanism, 'lying on the floor, covered with blood' in the main room. The rest of the weapon had been found outside the house. The initial report in the *Manchester Guardian* on 7 April noted that it was found 'lying amongst a clump of heath, beside a footpath leading from the house to the high road'. But Butterworth's notes from the inquest reveal that it was not Hegginbottom who found the pistol; as he was leaving the scene to get his instruments, 'a little boy' (presumably one of the rapidly gathering crowd) picked it up around 200 yards from the house and gave it to him. Quite why Hegginbottom kept the pistol and walking stick and took them home (where he showed Ammon Platt the pistol) is unclear.

The best description of the pistol (variously called a cavalry or a horse pistol) was published in the *Manchester Guardian* on 7 April. The writer had clearly inspected it, which is further evidence that he spoke to Hegginbottom, and noted that its hammer, trigger guard and butt end had broken off but the trigger and pan was still intact. According to the *Manchester Guardian*, this pistol was loaded with powder and ball, but had evidently been used to strike someone; however, other sources indicate that the ball had fallen out. The 'lock, stock, and barrel were covered with blood, and betwixt the stock and the head of one of the screws was a portion of hair, known by its light sandy colour to have belonged to Thomas Bradbury'. The pistol was described as 'old and clumsy'; it had brass mounting and the guard was marked with the number 21. On the plate of the lock was a crown and the letters G. R. (for George Rex; i.e. King George) as well as the marking 'D'EGG'. This revealed that the pistol had been made by Durs Egg (1748–1831), a Swiss gun-maker who opened a shop in London in 1772; his clients included George IV when he was the Prince of Wales.

The markings suggest that it was a Light Cavalry Volunteers pistol, manufactured between 1810 and 1820. It would have been used by a trooper in the Yeomanry Cavalry; such pistols were still in active use until the mid-1830s. However, as the pistol was described as old; it might not have been in official use anymore. The Yeomanry was generally, but not exclusively, recruited from more respectable members of society. In rural areas, it comprised mainly tenant farmers or tradesmen. It is probable that the pistol dated back to the expansion of the Yeomanry during the numerous wars at the beginning of the nineteenth century.

The ownership of the pistol was not clarified at the inquest, nor was it discussed to any extent except how it had been used as a bludgeon. The *Manchester Guardian* report on 7 April, however, explicitly stated: 'It is known not to have belonged to the Bradburys'. It must have remained in Hegginbottom's possession at least until the inquest; had it belonged to the Bradbury family, perhaps he would have been less likely to keep it. Gun ownership was not widespread in Britain and in theory it was largely forbidden. For example, the Vagrancy Act of 1824 had provisions for the arrest of 'any person with any gun, pistol, hanger, cutlass, bludgeon or other offensive weapon ... with intent to commit a felonious act'. But in practice, nothing prevented anyone holding onto an old firearm; for example there were occasional concerns about armed former soldiers, discharged after service in the wars against France, causing trouble.

Overall, there is insufficient information to identify a likely owner of the gun. As tempting as it might be to state that the killer had been a member of the Light Cavalry Volunteers, it is just as likely that the murderer or murderers (or someone connected to them) had acquired an old pistol for whatever purpose they had in mind. Whoever possessed the weapon also had access to bullets and powder, but the fact that it misfired might suggest that its owner did not take especially good care of it. Its abandonment also indicated a lack monetary or sentimental value.

Even if we could establish a connection between the pistol owner and the Yeomanry, membership was not exclusive enough to tell us anything useful: he might have been a landowner, a farmer or just a local tradesman. Nor do local membership lists exist for us to check.

After giving his medical evidence, Hegginbottom made way for Reuben Platt and the inquest moved on to determining if Charles Mullen had any involvement. But it is worth dwelling a little longer on what Hegginbottom said.

The severe injuries to the hands and arms of both men indicate that they were attempting to defend themselves from blows. Does that mean they were unarmed during the struggle? William's lesser injuries indicate that the intention was merely to disable him. He was hit once on the head (perhaps the injury on the opposite side of his head was caused by a fall after being struck) and was evidently conscious enough to move upstairs. The injuries to Thomas were far more vicious and were such that his attacker(s) must have continued to strike him long after he was incapable of offering resistance. The ferocity might be further gauged by the damage to the pistol. Perhaps the bent poker and shattered walking stick also give some clue as to how badly injured he must have been. However, no-one knows which weapons were used by the attackers and which might have been snatched by the victims to defend themselves. The wounds to his legs reported in *Wheeler's Manchester Chronicle* also suggest that Thomas was attacked while lying on the floor and kicking out in defence. Either this attack was driven by furious anger against Thomas, or he put up such a fierce resistance that he had to be repeatedly struck before he fell still.

Based on the state of the room, the author of the article in the *Manchester Guardian* (7 April) reconstructed what he thought had happened. He noted that William often 'reclined' on the wooden settle near the door, resting his head on the hob. The author conjectured – probably based on the concentration of blood in that area – that the attackers found him there and struck him with the spade until it broke, as William attempted to defend himself with his left arm. The author then speculated that the attackers were surprised while 'plundering' by the arrival of Thomas; they attacked him immediately but the pistol misfired and 'the stock was broken by a blow'. His version had Thomas retreating to the pantry, where his attackers followed and overpowered him. At this point, he fell and left the pool of blood found in that room. The author supposed that Thomas 'rallied' and 'rushed into the house, probably fighting in his own country way with his hands and his feet, or with some weapon snatched in the moment of desperation'. There were signs of a struggle on the wall of the pantry, and another near the 'two-armed chair' by the fireplace, where 'a bundle of feathers tied in paper, and depending [*sic*] from the ceiling, seem to have caught a descending blow, of such force that the paper is cut as if with scissors'. The author concluded that this is where Thomas was 'pent up and finally overcome'; the place where he was found the following morning.

The biggest problem with this version is the events in the pantry. If Thomas was attacked immediately upon entering (and the presence of flour at the door would suggest this to be the case), why would he 'retreat' forwards into the house? A surprise assault would have been more likely to make him head back outside to give himself more time and space. Did he rush to his father's defence? Or run into the house to confront whoever was inside? Was he confronted with a pistol – possibly even outside the house – and forced to go into the smaller room?

The pistol contained powder, but it had not been fired. According to *Wheeler's Manchester Chronicle*, the bullet was found in the pantry (Butterworth said there was a bullet in his first report but did not give its location; presumably this was among the gossip circulating that first day). However, no other source mentioned the bullet, and the matter did not arise at the inquest, so caution is necessary. But *if* the bullet was in the pantry, that might be where the pistol misfired; perhaps Thomas was forced in there at gunpoint. After the misfire, perhaps the attacker decided to use it as a bludgeon until it fell apart, accounting for the gouge mark in the wall. And judging by the further markings, Thomas's head was smashed into the wall, at which point he collapsed.

On the other hand, despite what was believed at the time and printed in the *Manchester Guardian*, the pistol *could* have belonged to the Bradburys; perhaps it was Thomas who brandished it. It would have made sense for them to have access to a weapon given the isolated nature of their house and the possibility of trouble from drunk or aggressive customers. They might not have broadcast the fact, not even to their families. And George Shaw recorded in his diary that Thomas had been fined for shooting game in 1828, although a cavalry pistol was hardly effective for hunting. Overall though, it seems unlikely that the gun belonged to the victims. There were no contemporary suggestions that it belonged to anyone but an attacker, and Thomas's various adventures on the moor would have been an opportunity for him to wave a pistol around had he owned one. Everything we know about him suggests this was not an opportunity he could have resisted, but there is no hint that he did so.

The evidence does not really establish how many people attacked the Bradburys. Contemporaries speculated that Thomas was so strong that it would have taken three people to subdue him, but that does not factor in the loaded pistol which would have given one assailant all the initial advantage. And if the weapon misfired, the panicked desperation of a single, unexpectedly disarmed attacker facing a much stronger opponent in a life-or-death struggle might account for the brutality of the attack. Or perhaps there were two people involved, one for each of the Bradburys. Or maybe three or more? Yet a key point is that Thomas Bradbury was not simply subdued; he was beaten to death. Why did the attacker(s) not flee before this point, especially if Thomas had been lying in the pantry long enough for a pool of blood to accumulate? Or did that not belong to him? Was he restrained and then attacked? What would that suggest about the attackers and their motive?

Clearly there are questions here that can never be answered. But there is one last point on which it is worth dwelling: the timing of the attack. Thomas Bradbury and Reuben Platt left Bill's o'Jack's around 7 pm. The initial report in *Wheeler's Manchester Chronicle* suggested that Bradbury visited his family at Sidebank and left there around 8:30 pm. Abraham Dawson heard noises from Bill's o'Jack's around 9:30 pm. Therefore it was assumed that the attack took place around 10 pm on Monday night. Based on the evidence of the candles in his pocket (and perhaps items left by the door), he had just returned from Daniel Whitehead's shop. Every subsequent retelling has taken this view; that Thomas was attacked that evening when he returned home, well before midnight. But he did not die until early afternoon on Tuesday. This means that he survived with a doubly fractured skull and severe blood loss for more than twelve hours. He was still conscious enough at noon the following day to make sounds and attempt to rise. Even at the time, this drew comment. *Wheeler's Manchester Chronicle* (7 April) noted: 'It is a matter of surprise to every individual who has seen the bodies of the murdered men that they lived so long after the perpetration of the attack upon them'.

Several doctors and medical practitioners to whom I have mentioned this scenario are dubious that Thomas could have survived so long. Both the blood coming from his nose and ears and the depressed fracture (which was different to the forehead injury that probably occurred in the pantry) suggest intercranial pressure. Several of them agreed that Thomas was unlikely to survive more than four hours and possibly as little as one hour after falling unconscious (with caveats about not knowing the full medical details, and the unpredictable nature of such injuries). However, a forensic pathologist suggested that, while survival of less (perhaps a lot less) than twelve hours was perhaps more likely than the notion he lived up to sixteen hours, it was not implausible given how little is known about his injuries, and how the nature (and survivability) of such injuries is unpredictable even in modern medicine.

But if Thomas had survived for a much shorter time than generally supposed, that opens the possibility that he was attacked not long before Amelia Winterbottom found him on the Tuesday morning. That would widen the number of possible suspects considerably and remove the three Irishmen from the picture (although it would not rule out a motive of theft). It would tidy up the (admittedly small) issue of how the dog 'Laddie' could have been in the house that morning when he was seen outside by Abraham Dawson the night before. But in that case, what did Dawson hear on the Monday night? Maybe it was a coincidence. Or maybe the Bradburys had a guest that night, and the confrontation – or whatever it was – took place over an extended period. Is it even possible that Thomas did not arrive home until that morning?

Having posed yet more unanswerable questions and taken speculation considerably beyond the confines safely allowed by the evidence, it is time to return to much firmer factual territory.

Consequences

After Hegginbottom had given his evidence, Reuben Platt was called and told his story to the jury. Finally, he was questioned about Charles Mullen, the man in custody. Platt confirmed that he had seen him the previous day and reaffirmed his doubts, saying that if indeed he was one of the three men, he was the one who kept his face hidden: 'The prisoner is about the same size, but the man was "hutch'd of a lump" and we never saw his face'. The remainder of the inquest was taken up by deciding what was to be done about Mullen (although the report in the *Manchester Times* omitted any mention of him, and the *Manchester Courier* only touched on him briefly).

Waterhouse, the Saddleworth constable, reported that Mullen's former overlooker confirmed most of the tale he had given earlier in the week. He had indeed been fighting in Leeds during the day on Monday, but more importantly Waterhouse had spoken to two men who had been with Mullen at his Methley lodgings on Monday night. He had also discovered that he had arrived for work at 6:30 on Tuesday morning (presumably being dismissed shortly after), so he could not realistically have travelled to Saddleworth and back in the interim; he could not have been responsible for the murders. Nevertheless, as his former employer did not know his whereabouts between Saturday and Tuesday, Mullen was brought into the room to be questioned. All the newspapers described him as a powerfully built man. Butterworth said he was 'a robust, muscular Irishman presenting some wounds and scars on his face, which first led to his apprehension'. The *Manchester Guardian* described him as 'a stout, powerfully built man, with all the characteristics of the genuine Irish physiognomy'.

Mullen accounted for his movements between Saturday and his apprehension on Thursday. Most of the period had been taken up with an extended drinking session, but his story tallied well enough with what Waterhouse had discovered and with a letter that had been sent by Dennison, the man from Methley who had been in Dobcross when Mullen was arrested. Mullen was also able to name various men with whom he had spent time in that period, although no-one seems to have followed this up. He also gave convincing explanations for the bruises on his face (from the fight) and even how he had acquired the hat that aroused such suspicion on Wednesday.* The coroner and jurors were therefore satisfied that he was innocent.

Mullen was set free and presumably returned to Cumberland. There are just a few traces of the rest of his life. A man called Charles Mullins of Maryport appeared at the Cumberland Sessions in January 1838 after being charged with assault against a constable. The trouble arose when Mullen had borrowed a coat from a man; suspecting that he was going to steal it, the latter spoke to a constable, who arrested Mullen. But Mullen's wife then accused the constable of requesting thirty shillings to release Mullen who, he had told her, would be otherwise transported. However, at the sessions, there was no bill against Mullen and he went free. Instead, he appeared as a witness against the constable, who had been charged with fraud for taking the money from his wife. The constable was found not guilty.

The censuses of 1841 and 1861 (there is no clear trace of him in 1851) reveal that Charles Mullen continued to work as a labourer. He died in Maryport in 1868.

After Mullen's release, the jury went away to consider and shortly returned with two verdicts of 'Wilful murder against some person or

* The discussion around Mullen's hat might be the reason there was some confusion over the item produced in court – whether it belonged to him or had been found in Bill's o'Jack's.

persons at present unknown'. By around 5 pm, it was all over. *Wheeler's Manchester Chronicle* reported that between three and four hundred people were present at the William the Fourth through the day to follow the inquest. However, a combination of morbid curiosity and the chance for a drink seems to have motivated this crowd more than any desire for justice. The *Manchester Guardian* noted with disapproval that the inn was 'crowded to excess' by locals, 'many of whom conducted themselves as if entirely unconscious that a tragedy so mournful had been enacted'.

According to the *Manchester Guardian*, Saturday, the day of the inquest, was very wet and so 'few persons, comparatively speaking, visited the scene of the murders'. But Sunday, 'a clear, though cold day' saw the valley 'thronged by an immense number of visitors' from the regions around Manchester and over the hills from Huddersfield and beyond. The journalist described people arriving by horse, in carriages and on foot; there were long queues outside Bill's o'Jack's and 'it is computed by those who were on the spot, that 30,000 persons visited it on Sunday alone. The crowd was so great, that it was found necessary to place constables at the door to the house, who admitted visitors by twelve or fourteen at a time. Fortunately no accident happened, and, with the approach of night, the multitude gradually disappeared, and the wilds resumed their wonted loneliness and silence'.

Finally, on Monday, the bodies of the two Bradburys were taken by hearse from Bill's o'Jack's, via Uppermill, to Saddleworth church, a distance of around four miles. The *Manchester Guardian* reported that 'as the procession passed along the road, the dwellings were all deserted, and the people flocked together to bid a last farewell to Old Bill o'Jack's and his son Tom. At Uppermill the crowd increased and became still more numerous in the churchyard'. At the church – which was still in the process of being built – a hymn was sung, 'and few eyes remained dry during the ceremony', before father and son were buried together in the bottom corner of the churchyard in the grave that is still there nearly two hundred years later. The curate who officiated at the burial made a note adjacent to the two entries in the parish register: 'Barbarously murdered on Monday night 2nd April'. Everyone returned home, and life went on.

But the spectre of the murdered father and son refused to go away.

The diary of George Shaw indicated that people continued to visit the house where the two men had died. He had been away from Saddleworth when the Bradburys were killed, and only returned to Uppermill the following day. On 21 April, he went to see the scene for himself and recorded: 'There was a great number of people at Old Bill's today'. So for at least two weeks after the murders, curious people were still arriving to look even if, as Shaw observed in his diary, it was no longer likely the culprits would be caught.

There was one additional detail recorded by the *Manchester Guardian*. Its report of the inquest and burial concluded with a final eyewitness account. The writer recorded that 'Joseph Matthews, a stone-cutter, residing in a small hut on the road towards Holmfirth, states that, hearing of the murders, he went down to Bradbury's, where he found Tom on the floor, and spoke to him but he did not answer. He asked the old man who had done it, and he said four or five "Irish Pats". He asked him what time, and he said "Soon at night"; he also said that one of his attackers wore "a dark, ragged, torn coat", and another "a blue frock [coat]"'.

Matthews' claim is compromised by coming so late, a week after the murders; the alleged utterance of 'Pats' was doubtless by then a well-known detail locally given that story had spread so rapidly. This is probably enough to dismiss his evidence. But the phrase 'soon at night' does not quite make sense in response to the question of when he was attacked, and if Matthews was making it up, why not just 'at night'? It may be what a confused, mortally injured old man might say. But perhaps Matthews only *thought* this was what he had said. Or maybe the whole thing was a fabrication.*

* Matthews lived in a hut at Upperwood, at the top of the hill on which Bill's o'Jack's was to be found. At the time of the murders, Abraham Dawson, the man who heard the disturbance on Monday night, was living with Matthews, to whom he observed that 'old Bradbury had some rough company'. The 1841 census records Joseph Matthews, a 38-year-old stone cutter, still living at Upperwood with his wife and three children.

Butterworth, possibly bruised by his dispute with Stocks, seems to have been left in a more melancholy mood by the inquest. Having completed his account in the notebook, he digressed into a description of the 'sombre hue and savage cast' of the 'wild romantic' mountains. He also observed how the growing number of rumours was making it difficult to be sure what had happened.

Meanwhile, during the chaos of that week, the Bradbury family had been left to pick up what pieces they could. The newspaper reporters had little interest in them; they were more concerned with gruesome details of blood stains, smashed pistols and suspicious Irishmen travelling the countryside. Ammon Platt's sworn statement revealed that Nancy Winterbottom (William's daughter) and Ann Bradbury (Thomas's wife) were at the house attempting to take care of the dying men on the Tuesday afternoon, but little else is known about what the family did.

The dynamics of the situation might have been complicated given that two branches of the family were involved. William had three other children: the 59-year-old William, the 56-year-old Mary, and the 48-year-old Nancy. Given the complete lack of evidence, it is tempting to suggest that Nancy was closest to her father, given that her own daughter Amelia/Mary was visiting him on the morning of the discovery and her own prompt arrival at the scene. However, William's other children might also have attended.

As for Thomas, he had five children: Augustus (aged 21 in 1832), Amelia (aged 18), John (aged 11), Francis (aged 9) and William (aged 7). But Thomas had not been living with his family, although he had supposedly visited them the evening before his death. Whatever the state of his marriage, it is understandable that his wife Ann would have been on the scene quickly, even if only because she was desperately wondering how she could support her children as a widow.

Clearly, her thoughts had immediately turned to the future. *Wheeler's Manchester Chronicle* implied that those who visited the murder scene were encouraged to pay their 'mite'. Butterworth (in notes written during the week commencing 16 April) recorded: 'The money collected on the spot by the relatives of the deceased from the multitudes who flocked every successive day to witness the brutal spectacle has been applied towards the expenses of the funeral and partly divided amongst the relatives'.

The obvious questions – such as who organised this, and which relatives were involved – cannot be answered. But the amount did not go as far as they hoped. *Wheeler's Manchester Chronicle* stated on 21 April: 'The furniture of the Bradburys is to be sold for the benefit of the widow of "Tom o'Bill's", and a rare harvest doubtless she will reap. It is stated that the proceeds of the exhibition at the house during the week succeeding the murder are by no means so great as those who were called upon to contribute have had reason to conjecture. Report says that the children of Thomas Bradbury [*sic*] insisted upon an equitable partition of the money, and that, consequently, the widow had for her share only about two pounds, fifteen shillings and fourpence'. Only Augustus out of Thomas's children was an adult and he would not have been challenging his own mother for a share, so the reporter clearly meant to say the children of *William* Bradbury. An almost identical story appeared in the *Manchester Guardian* on the same date, saying that 'we have been requested' on behalf of 'the widow and five children of Thomas Bradbury' to 'contradict a statement currently made, that they had derived great pecuniary advantage from the parties who went to view the bodies. The money given on that occasion was divided among all the sons and daughters of old Bradbury, and all that the widow received was £2 15s 4d'.

Something is not quite right here. What was the nature of this 'conjecture'? How did the writer (who might have provided both articles) hear of it? And how did both newspapers know the exact amount received by Ann Bradbury? This could represent the faintest echoes of tension among the surviving family. Perhaps William's three children disputed Ann Bradbury's claim to be the sole beneficiary of the collection taken at the house. Once more, the complicated family situation must have played a part; the house was rented by William but Thomas was also living there. In that case, who should have received the money taken? But the same problem would have applied to the auction; the contents of the house would presumably have belonged to William, not Thomas. Perhaps Ann's in-laws agreed that she could sell that if she gave them their share of the collection.

However, these events can be interpreted differently. The only modern writers who have studied the murder in depth – Neil Barrow and Terry Wyke, both of whom have written extensively for the Saddleworth Historical Society on the case – suggested in a 1987 article that the story of Ann making little money from the collection was a response to gossip in the locality that she had profited from her husband's death.

The auction of the Bradbury furniture was advertised in the *Manchester Guardian* on 21 April for the following Friday (27 April) at noon, 'for the benefit of the widow of Tom o'Bill's' and to be held at Bill's o'Jack's itself ('on the premises occupied by the two unfortunate individuals who were cruelly murdered on Monday evening the second instant'). Listed for sale was the 'whole of the furniture, consisting of drawers, tables, chairs, glasses, china, earthenware, brewing utensils, beds, bedding, and all the other goods, chattels, and effects, late the property of the above-named persons'. That long list contradicted the claim in the *Manchester Times* during the week of the murder that the house had been ransacked and 'everything of value carried away'. Unfortunately, the newspapers were silent on how much money was raised.

It is worth spending a little longer thinking about Ann Bradbury's 'equitable portion' of the takings from those who visited the crime scene. If the newspaper report was correct, her share amounted to £2 15s 4d. If that amount was split with William Bradbury's other three surviving children, that would have meant that over £11 had been shared between them.

Although the cost of the funeral, which must have come out of these takings, was not reported, there are some hints. Given that it involved a hearse and an ornate memorial, it cannot have been cheap. Funeral expenses varied during this period, including by location, but some figures survive from the region. For example, a funerary society established for teachers at Delph Independent Sunday School in 1821 guaranteed funeral costs of £2 in return for a quarterly penny fee. At a slightly later date, the Saddleworth Friendly Family Burial Society of Uppermill guaranteed £4. This was clearly a minimum amount and depending on the funeral, costs could have been considerably higher; for example, a relatively expensive burial in Austerlands in 1859 cost £5 3s 19d. Another indication – although it is of dubious origin – is that William Bradbury was supposed to have told his family that he had saved £7 for them to bury him (which was the origin of the idea that the murderers stole £7 from the house). Even if he never said these words, it was a realistic enough funeral cost for it to be reported as fact. If we estimate that between £5 and £10 went to the funeral, that would mean that between £15 and £20 was collected from those who came to view Bill's o'Jack's.

At the time, and in later years, the Bradbury family (and subsequent landlords of Bill's o'Jack's) exploited the legend quite effectively. Making money from visitors to the scene of a murder was not particularly unusual. For example, after the murder of William Ware, tours were offered of the relevant scenes of the crime, and the location of the Red Barn Murder became a scene of grisly pilgrimage. Similarly, William Probert – who was present at the Radlett Murder but escaped any charge by turning King's Evidence against John Thurtell – had fallen behind on his rent so his landlord auctioned off most of his property, which attracted ghoulish interest from people fascinated by the murder.

A difference between these earlier 'famous' murders and those at Bill's o'Jack's was the nature of the location. The Radlett Murder took place less than twenty miles from London; the Red Barn Murder was further away but attracted the interest of London publishers which distributed sensationalist penny broadsides to keep audiences updated. Those thrill-seekers who queued outside the Bradburys' house in order to see their bodies or to look at the blood-stained walls might have travelled a considerably further distance. And despite the relative isolation of Saddleworth, the story spread widely.

Accurate and detailed versions of the story began to be printed in places hundreds of miles from Saddleworth. On 9 April, *The Times* reprinted the article on the murders from the *Leeds Mercury* – one of those based on Butterworth – under the heading 'Barbarous Murders and Robbery'. The same article was reprinted in that day's *Morning Chronicle* in London and the *Brighton Guardian* two days later. And in fact, that article or the *Manchester Courier* version appeared the same week in newspapers published in locations as diverse as Edinburgh, Belfast, Antrim, Fife, Nottingham, York, Westmorland, Dublin and Cornwall. Therefore the report, even if it was quite out of date by this point, reached a very wide audience.

Although this was a time before such stories generated reaction from readers' letters (which, although they were printed in newspapers, generally had a political focus), and recycling of stories was common, there is just a hint that interest was more than usually widespread. For example, the *Morning Chronicle*, a week after printing Butterworth's *Leeds Mercury* article, published another, which it noted was 'a more circumstantial account of these murders than has yet been published', taken from the *Leeds Intelligencer* which was in turn an edited version of the first article in the *Manchester Guardian*. And the following day (17 April), the *Morning Chronicle* reprinted the *Manchester Guardian*'s report on the inquest, which took up a full column. The *Albion and Star*, one of the London newspapers to print the story on 9 April, gave an update (taken from several sources) on 24 April. Another London publication to cover the story in depth was the *True Sun* – a Radical newspaper among whose reporters was a young Charles Dickens – which featured three abridged reprints from other publications in April and a fourth in May. And *The Times* had a final article on the murders on 5 May. Publishers would not have kept the story alive for weeks had the interest not been there.

But somehow, the Bill's o'Jack's story never *quite* ignited in the same way as the Radlett, Red Barn or Burke and Hare Murders. That was because it was murderers, not victims, who fascinated the journalists and reading public; those famous cases featured extensive coverage of the trial and execution of the culprit. Even less engrossing stories, such as the 1827 murder of Thomas Patrick in Colchester, generated plenty of column inches for a longer period of time owing to the capture of the perpetrator. Bill's o'Jack's had no similarly neat conclusion. And so it burned brightly for a month before fading.

Instead, what set Bill's o'Jack's apart from the other murders was not just the mystery of who was responsible – something which might have appealed more during the growth of the cult of detectives in the middle of the nineteenth century or the advent of crime fiction – but the fact that its memory smouldered for a very, very long time.

The Red Bredburys and Other Unlikely Candidates

The fuel that kept the story alive and fed the legend for over a century emerged in the days following the funeral with the appearance of two apparently plausible suspects. As they were a father and son, they offered a villainous counterpoint to the victims, but the claims against them – which initially looked strong – proved to have little substance.

They were by no means the only men arrested after the inquest, but the parallel 'investigations' were marked more by a sense of futility than any expectation that the murderers had been caught. The *Leeds Intelligencer* recorded on 12 April that 'several other individuals have been taken into custody in various places, two in Manchester, under circumstances of some suspicion, but on subsequent inquiries, it was found that there was no ground whatever to detain them on this charge, and no one now remains in custody'. On 13 April, the *Liverpool Mercury* concluded its report on the inquest by saying: 'Two men answering the description of the persons near the cottage on the night of the murder were apprehended on Monday evening [9 April], at Rotherham, in Yorkshire, and are still in custody'.

Butterworth's report on the events in Rotherham – which appeared with minor variations in the *Manchester Courier* and *Wheeler's Manchester Chronicle* on 14 April – demonstrated the complete lack of method or co-ordination in the ongoing search and, as had been the case with Charles Mullen, how men were arrested on the basis of little more than prejudice and guesswork.

At Dobcross on Wednesday, 11 April, two constables (Hudson of Rotherham and Dalton of Huddersfield) told the Saddleworth magistrates

James Buckley and the Reverend Mills (who had presumably recovered from his illness) how they had apprehended two men – Samuel Jarvis and William Stevenson – who were 'applying for relief at the vagrant office in Rotherham', simply because their clothing looked similar to that worn by the three wanted Irishmen. Reuben Platt was consulted by the magistrates, but without having seen the men, he could provide no more than a cautious affirmation that their descriptions – that of Jarvis in particular – *might* indicate some likeness to his three suspects. The constables reported that 'they refuse to say where they were on the fatal night. One of them describes himself as a joiner, from Manchester. They spoke neither pure English nor Irish, though the taller looked like an Irishman'. However, neither man showed any signs of being in a recent fight, nor possessed any incriminating items. When they finally gave a satisfactory alibi, they were released.

Butterworth also recorded in his notebook (on two separate occasions) the story of some men seen at Hooley Hill near Ashton-under-Lyne on the night the Bradburys were believed to have been attacked, which seems to have reached him via two sources: Constable Heywood of Oldham and Constable Buckley of Saddleworth. Both officials had apparently received letters about three Irishmen who had arrived at a public house around midnight on Monday, 2 April, covered in blood as if they had been fighting. They had asked for a drink, which the landlord provided after they promised to finish quickly and leave. If these men existed – which is perhaps doubtful – they were never found.

Other, almost certainly innocent people continued to be caught up in the search. Butterworth also reported that 'the constables of Huddersfield are in active pursuit of three suspected persons living near that town'. After Butterworth's article, the editor of *Wheeler's Manchester Chronicle* (14 April) added an update: 'The man whose apprehension in this town was mentioned in the last *Chronicle* has been discharged. It was reported yesterday that three men were in custody in Liverpool, but such is not the fact'. A man was also arrested at Tadcaster the following week; the *Huddersfield and Halifax Express* said that he was an Irishman who had with him 'an instrument used in tobacco cutting, and said he was a cigar maker'. The man claimed to work in York, but this 'proved untrue', which along with his tobacco cutter and nationality may have been enough to arouse suspicion. But as with the other suspects, nothing further came of this. Two men were also arrested in Liverpool but released on 24 April.

Many of these arrests carried an air of desperation, particularly given the varied locations, miles from Saddleworth.

Just as the search for the murderers seemed doomed to failure there came an apparent breakthrough: a father and son were arrested at Holme near Huddersfield. They lived in Bradshaw, near Holmfirth. Unlike every other suspect, these men were believed to have an unquestionable motive. Their name, like the victims, was Bradbury. No-one could quite agree on whether they were related: the *Manchester Courier* claimed they were no relation to William and Thomas; the *Huddersfield and Halifax Express* identified them as 'distant relations'; *Wheeler's Manchester Chronicle* said they were 'half cousins'. A much later account, recorded in the problematic 'Annals of Saddleworth' – written in the early 1890s but possibly containing material from 1832 – also indicated that Thomas was their cousin.

The suspects were commonly known, according to the *Manchester Courier*, as the 'Red Tom Bredburys'. This was the only contemporary account to use that name, but we shall stick with it to distinguish these suspects from the victims.

Each of these newspaper accounts, all published on 21 April, was based on a report by Butterworth. But the piece that appeared in his notebook had some very important differences from the version in newspapers and provided the most thorough account of what happened. The older Red Bredbury and his 'associate' (as Butterworth phrased it) had been detained on Monday, 16 April, and their house was searched. They appeared before the magistrates on Wednesday and again on Saturday, being remanded in custody in the meantime. Butterworth was not entirely certain why. His explanation was preceded by the disclaimer: 'We believe the following to be the causes of their detention'. But newspapers were less hesitant. *Wheeler's Manchester Chronicle* and the *Huddersfield and Halifax Express* had a partial caution – 'it is said there are strong facts against them' – but the *Manchester Courier* reported everything as an unequivocal fact.

According to Butterworth's cautious account, the two men were locally notorious poachers who hunted on Saddleworth Moor. Shortly before the murders, according to the story, the elder of the Red Bredburys was charged with 'unlawfully chasing a hare on the Greenfield plantation'; this was most likely the trees near Bill's o'Jack's which later came to bear its name. The witness against him was Thomas Bradbury. Butterworth explained that the older Red Bredbury and Thomas Bradbury were to appear on the first day of the Pontefract Sessions. Butterworth's original notes said that these began 'a few days after' the murder; the *Huddersfield and Halifax Express* used this wording, but *Wheeler's Manchester Chronicle* and the *Manchester Courier* subtly altered this to the far more incriminating start date of the 'day after the murder' (which presumably meant Tuesday morning). In fact, the Sessions had begun on Monday, 3 April.

Butterworth's story reported that the Red Bredburys appeared at Pontefract, and the defendant 'claimed an acquittal on the ground that his accuser could not appear against him as he had been murdered'. The magistrates, unaware of any such murder, were suspicious that the accused knew of it so quickly. Butterworth did not attempt to explain why it would have taken two weeks to follow up on these suspicions, but if he was correct that they were arrested on Monday, 16 April, and held until the Saturday, there must have been enough evidence to justify keeping them in custody. However, all Butterworth had discovered was that they had been seen in Saddleworth at the New Inn* near to St Chad's church around 7 pm on Monday night, where they had a drink

* Later renamed as the Church Inn.

before saying they were on their way to Holmfirth – the road to which passed Bill's o'Jack's. He also revealed that the search of their house had concluded 'without the discovery of anything likely to implicate them in the crime'.

The newspapers were selective in what they published of Butterworth's article. None of them reported that the search of the house had produced no results. *Wheeler's Manchester Chronicle* pompously declared that it would not report the 'other suspicious circumstances', which would 'risk propagating false rumours about men who must be considered innocent until they are proved the contrary', but still printed everything that Butterworth had said except the unsuccessful search. Only the *Huddersfield and Halifax Express* showed any restraint, restricting its reporting to the fact of the arrest of the two men and that Thomas Bradbury 'was to have appeared against one of them at Pontefract Sessions, a few days after he was so brutally butchered; they were also seen at Saddleworth on the day of the murder'. The article noted that there were 'other suspicious circumstances' but the newspaper did not wish 'to propagate mere rumours'.

But not a single newspaper included an inconvenient detail recorded by Butterworth: that 'a publican at Holmfirth' claimed the two men were at his house before the murder had taken place and therefore, if that man was telling the truth, they could hardly be guilty.

The two Red Bredburys appeared a second time before Huddersfield magistrates on Saturday, 21 April, having been held in custody for almost a week. Despite the clamour surrounding the murders, no reporters were present. The only information that survives comes from brief articles – based on a report by Butterworth – which suggested that several witnesses were called and examined at length. Eventually the magistrates were satisfied that the Red Bredburys had a solid alibi and could explain 'the circumstances which caused them to be suspected'; they were therefore acquitted.

It is hard to know what to make of this episode. The decision by the magistrates to hold the Red Bredburys in custody for several days indicates that there was *something* to investigate. Although there were no reports into what form the enquiries might have taken, presumably it was a constable who searched the house of the two men. Perhaps someone travelled to Holmfirth to check the alibi reported by Butterworth. Maybe the records of the Pontefract Sessions were checked (although as the magistrates were probably present at those sessions, that might not have been necessary). The hearing before the magistrates on the Saturday would have been less formal than the inquest, but perhaps witnesses corroborated the Red Bredburys' story.

The most important detail, however, is what the magistrates did – or rather did not do – next. They could have remanded the two men for longer and sent the case to be heard at the next assizes, where capital crimes were tried. Had they discovered any incriminating evidence or suspicious circumstances, that would have been their inevitable course. Even if the case were not convincing, they could have passed it on, washing their hands of a story which had attracted national attention, to satisfy the public demand that someone be charged. But having taken the matter seriously enough to hold the Red Bredburys for almost a week and investigate in some depth, they chose to release them. The conclusion must be that there was very little evidence against either man; the magistrates believed them to be not guilty.

This is not altogether surprising because the story as uncovered by Butterworth does not stand up to scrutiny. No-one named Bradbury or Bredbury appeared at the Pontefract Sessions (for which records survive and for which detailed newspaper coverage exists). Nor would the case have been omitted from the record because there had been no prosecution; the newspapers list those acquitted and those for whom there was 'no bill'. If the Red Bredburys *were* in court, it was not at the Pontefract Sessions of April 1832. And the suggestion that the magistrates first heard of the murders from the mouth of the Red Bredburys does not fit the facts. It is fairly certain that the Saddleworth magistrates who were at Pontefract heard of the murders on Thursday when Constable Buckley asked them how they wanted to proceed and they immediately wrote to the Home Office. Had they learned what happened in such suspicious fashion, they would have mentioned it in that letter or taken immediate action against the suspects. That they did neither of those things suggests that the story was not true.

If the Huddersfield magistrates were satisfied the Red Bredburys were innocent, others were less convinced. Suspicion lingered around them. An article in the *Huddersfield Chronicle* in 1851 discussed the death of a 59-year-old man called James Bradbury from Whitewalls in Austonley. It observed that he 'had always been suspected of being concerned in a most dreadful murder which took place in Greenfield, Saddleworth, about nineteen or twenty years ago … The exact reason why suspicion clung to this man we are not prepared to give. Some individuals assign one [reason], some another, but the one we have most frequently heard is that at the time of the murder a lawsuit was pending between James Bradbury and someone else, and that Bill o'Jack's, his son, or both of them, were to appear in evidence against the said James Bradbury'. The newspaper repeated the tale first told by Butterworth of how James Bradbury informed the Pontefract Sessions that his accuser was dead – following the line taken by the *Manchester Courier* that this took place the morning after the attack on William and Thomas.

The *Huddersfield Chronicle* hinted at some rumours in circulation: 'Popular report further says that some time ago [James Bradbury's son] died, and that during his illness the father would not allow anybody to visit him. Another reason which we have heard … is that he has always, ever since the occurrence alluded to, had the appearance of being miserable, of having a weight on his mind, but this might be only a vulgar conjecture arising from the fact of his being suspected'. Similar stories in both Saddleworth and Holmfirth suggested that the father had admitted to the murders while under the influence of drink but although these 'confessions' were proven false, the stigma did not fade. Journalists for the *Huddersfield Chronicle* had investigated a few other rumours but could find no evidence of any confession. The reporter concluded that any purported admission of guilt by James Bradbury to his family was probably untrue, on the not unreasonable grounds that the family itself – the only possible source – would be unlikely to leak the story to the public.

It is impossible to be certain if this James Bradbury who died in 1851 was one of the Red Bredburys accused in 1832, because contemporary accounts were very vague about the identities of the two suspects. The only detail to emerge at the time was that they lived in Bradshaw. But there *might* be another potential hint in the 'Annals of Saddleworth' to link James Bradbury to the suspects. It must be emphasised once again that this document dates from the 1890s, which must cast doubt on anything it says. However, some of the relevant sections are based on older material, the origin of which is unclear and undatable. According to the 'Annals', the Red Bredbury involved in this episode was called Jamie Bradbury, Thomas's cousin, and he was known locally as 'Jammy o'Bradshaw's'.

There was certainly a family living in Bradshaw called Bradbury, and they had a definite link to Saddleworth. The most prominent member, Job Bradbury, lived in Austonley (a region which includes Bradshaw) and had six children. His wife Hannah had been born in Saddleworth around 1786. On tax records, Job is listed interchangeably as Bradbury and Bredbury. Also living in Austonley in the early 1800s was a man called Thomas Bradbury/Bredbury; perhaps this was 'Red Tom Bredbury' referred to by Butterworth, but there is no way to know.

Except for the record of his death, James Bradbury cannot be traced with certainty. One possible candidate can be found in the Quarter Session records for 1819, when a James Bradbury of Austonley was found guilty of assaulting a Joshua Schofield in Saddleworth to the point that 'his life was greatly despaired of'. Although Bradbury denied the charge, he was 'fined sixpence and discharged'. If the incident involved the same man whose death was recorded in the *Huddersfield Chronicle*, it is the only independent contemporary evidence that the family's negative reputation was in any way deserved. Another candidate – perhaps the same man – was a clothier and farmer called James Bradbury, born in Saddleworth, who lived in Fairbanks in 1841 and was imprisoned for debt in York Castle at the time of the 1851 census.

But even if the Red Bredburys *could* be definitively identified, they should be entirely ruled out as suspects. The case against them centred on their supposed involvement in the Pontefract Sessions. Without this, the entire story collapses. If they were not at Pontefract – which they almost certainly were not – they cannot have attracted the suspicion of the magistrates, nor demonstrated incriminating knowledge of the murder. And Butterworth, from whom all the evidence originated, had already established their alibi. Every subsequent report was subtly altered to strengthen the case. This careless – or perhaps deliberately sensationalist – reporting meant that the Red Bredburys have been strong suspects ever since. The evidence against them never warranted such prolonged attention.

Once the Red Bredburys had been freed by the Huddersfield magistrates, Irishmen again came under press scrutiny. The *Huddersfield and Halifax Express* concluded on 28 April 1832 that the murders must have been committed by the three men seen by Platt and the newspaper claimed that they were seen on the road to Ashton that night by a man returning home; this same man had supposedly heard noises from Bill's o'Jack's earlier in the evening. As this appears to be based on the claims of Abraham Dawson (who would not have been anywhere near the road to Ashton late at night), this was at best a distortion and at worst a fabrication. In either case, the man supposedly heard one of the trio, speaking in a conveniently loud Irish accent, say: 'If it had not been for that spade, I should have been done for'. A spade had, of course, been found at the scene covered in blood, as everyone would have known by then. Like much of the 'evidence' after the inquest, this can be safely discounted.

The article concluded that 'the wretches would have been secured' but for the absence of so many officials at the Pontefract Sessions. Given the number of suspects investigated, the obsession with finding Irishmen, and the lack of conclusive evidence against anyone, this seems unlikely.

Even four years later, the idea that Irishmen were responsible stubbornly lingered. When five Irishmen were arrested at Manchester for highway robbery in 1836, rumour connected them with the 1832 murder.

Following the release of the Red Bredburys, the press and apparently the authorities lost interest. The fascination did not go away – within a month, a play based on the murders was performed in Oldham – but all hope of solving the case apparently evaporated. However, in the years that followed, other 'confessions' briefly made waves before being forgotten.

The first came almost a year after the murder. On 18 March 1833, a navigator called Nathaniel Stannyer, from Bollington near Macclesfield, handed himself in to the constable of Compstall Bridge (near Stockport) and claimed that he had been one of those responsible for killing the Bradburys. But by the time the magistrates examined him, he had changed his story and said he had been drunk when he 'confessed'. He was remanded until the Saddleworth constable could be informed of the case, but as nothing further was reported he must have been released. The continuing interest in the Bill's o'Jack's case can be gauged from how widely this 'confession' was reported; an article which told the story was reprinted nationally, including in several London publications.

The next 'confession' occurred in 1845. A man called John Mitchell was working as a navigator when he went into a beer shop in Huddersfield on 15 April at 6 am and stayed until noon, drinking eight pints of beer. Towards the latter part of his visit, as he became progressively more drunk, he interrupted a man reading aloud a newspaper report of a murder trial and began singing a song. The landlady told him to stop as it reminded her of a song about the Bill's o'Jack's case. He began to claim intimate knowledge of the story, eventually saying – to much protest from his fellow patrons – that he was present at the murders and 'saw the first blow struck'. He went on to say that 'the old man used the spade manfully, and if we had not killed them they would us'.

Mitchell's version of events was that, on that night in 1832, Thomas Bradbury had gone for candles and when he returned 'we thought he was too strong for us, so we knocked him down at his entrance'. Mitchell claimed to have been arrested at Holmfirth the next day because his clothes were bloody, but subsequently released.

After Mitchell had gone on at length, a constable arrested him after getting a warrant from a magistrate. At this point Mitchell's story changed; he denied all knowledge and said that he had begun working on the Shepley Lane Head and Greenfield Turnpike Road shortly after the murders, during which time he had learned of the story. When James Buckley, still the Saddleworth magistrate, heard of Mitchell's tale, he wearily replied that the man had been before him on numerous occasions and was 'an idle, drunken, dissolute blackguard' and although Mitchell had 'ill-used his wife' Buckley did not think he was connected to the murders. He was 'discharged with a reprimand'. And Buckley was doubtless correct; everything Mitchell described would have been common knowledge or could have been read in newspapers.

Another 'confession' came from the opposite side of the world eight years later. On 5 March 1853, the *Huddersfield Chronicle* printed (with his permission) a letter from a man living in Australia to his brother who still lived in Huddersfield. The article stated: 'We do not give the name of the writer, yet we have every confidence in his veracity'. But even if he was as truthful as the newspaper hoped, his letter presented evidence that, at best, was several times removed from the original source.

The author was actually telling someone else's tale – he had been given a 'statement' (it is not clear whether this was in a conversation, through a letter, or if he had read the story elsewhere) in October 1852 from Robert Whitehead, a sheep farmer living in Australia at Springs Creek, 'about 160 miles' from Melbourne. By a remarkable coincidence, Robert Whitehead was almost certainly the son of Daniel Whitehead, the owner of the shop visited by Thomas Bradbury on the night he was attacked. The bulk of the letter was taken up with what appears to be a transcription of Whitehead's statement.

Whitehead in turn had been told the story in late 1851 or early 1852 by a wool carrier to whom he spoke in a public house at 'Port Fary' (presumably Port Fairy), a town in South-West Victoria, about 180 miles from Melbourne. The wool carrier entered and said to Whitehead: 'I know you and I knew your uncles'. After asking if the murder at

Saddleworth had ever been solved, the wool carrier told him that he had been working on the nearby canal at the time. He said the murderer was 'a young man hawking tape in a basket in Saddleworth', and related the hawker's story to Whitehead.*

Shortly after the murders, the hawker had been arrested for robbing a drover at Leicester and was therefore transported to Sydney in Australia. The hawker was later hanged for murder in Hobart, but not before confessing to the wool carrier. According to this confession, the hawker had only intended to rob the Bradbury's house and so sent William upstairs out of the way. However, the old man subsequently came back down. The hawker struck him on the head and Bradbury crawled upstairs. At this stage, the narrative became muddled – perhaps unsurprisingly given how many hands the story had passed through by the time it appeared in the newspaper – and described Thomas Bradbury entering the house on two separate occasions: as the hawker was searching the drawers *and* as he was about to leave. Whichever version was the one given by the hawker, the outcome was the same: 'Seeing Tom coming he turned back, and as Tom entered the door he knocked him down with the fire poker'.

As the basis for a confession, this is not a particularly robust source given the multiple levels of hearsay – the hawker told the wool carrier, who told Robert Whitehead, who told the anonymous author of the letter which was sent to the newspaper. Even if we believe that each person was telling what they believed to be the complete truth, the probability of garbled transmission would be high. While the basic tale seems plausible enough, it does not account for the violence of the attack on the Bradburys (an observation made by the *Huddersfield Chronicle* writer), nor does it mention all the implements used as weapons, particularly the pistol. And once again, nothing was described that was not common knowledge in 1832.

* A hawker was a person who travelled from place to place selling cheap goods. It was a precarious sort of occupation and hawkers were not respected.

The modern writers Neil Barrow and Terry Wyke have identified the most likely person to have made this confession as James Hill, the only man executed at Hobart in the 1830s and 1840s, from Leicestershire. According to their research, Hill was baptised at Church Gresley in Derbyshire in 1810 and worked in various occupations before twice being convicted of theft; on the second occasion in 1841, his sentence was transportation to Australia. There, he briefly became more respectable until he was charged with the murder of an elderly woman in 1846 – although it is not clear why he did so, it is possible he was disturbed during a robbery. He was found guilty and hanged. When the judge passed sentence and concluded with the usual remark 'May the Lord have mercy on your soul', Hill muttered that 'there was little chance of that'.

However, James Hill was a very common name – shared by many who were transported to Australia – and we can never be certain whether all these facts relate to the same man. And even if they do, we will never know if James Hill made the reported confession, nor – if he did – whether it was genuine. With such uncertainties, it is unlikely that the solution to the murder is to be found here.

There was one interesting passing comment at the end of the *Huddersfield Chronicle* article about the hawker: 'In any case there should appear any reasonable grounds for hope that … this singularly brutal and most mysterious murder may be cleared up; and "the thousand and one" dark insinuations which are aimed at certain families in the locality – as connected with this transaction – may thus be set at rest for ever'. Is this alluding to suspicions against the Red Bredbury family? Or against someone else?

This final 'confession' from Australia attracted only passing attention, although it did influence some later dramatisations of the murders. Like the earlier 'confessions', the story of the hawker offers little evidence, nor any plausible solution to the mystery. In fact, these confessions mark a turning point. Any hope of finding the guilty party was long-gone, and the Bill's o'Jack's murders had begun an irreversible transition into the realms of legend.

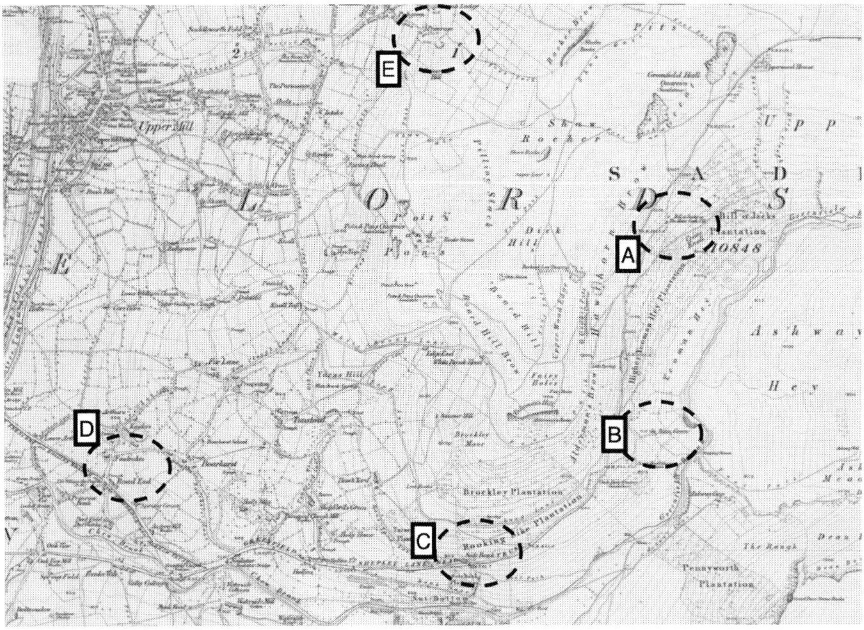

The Ordnance Survey map of Greenfield from 1854, the first such survey of the region. Relevant locations are marked: (A) Bill's o'Jack's; (B) Binn Green (the home of James Whitehead); (C) Sidebank (the home of Thomas Bradbury's wife and children); (D) Road End (to where Thomas Bradbury and Reuben Platt walked together on the night of 2 April 1832) and Foulrakes (where Esther Porritt worked); (E) Primrose (the home of Reuben Platt). (Reproduced with the permission of the National Library of Scotland/CC-BY (NLS))

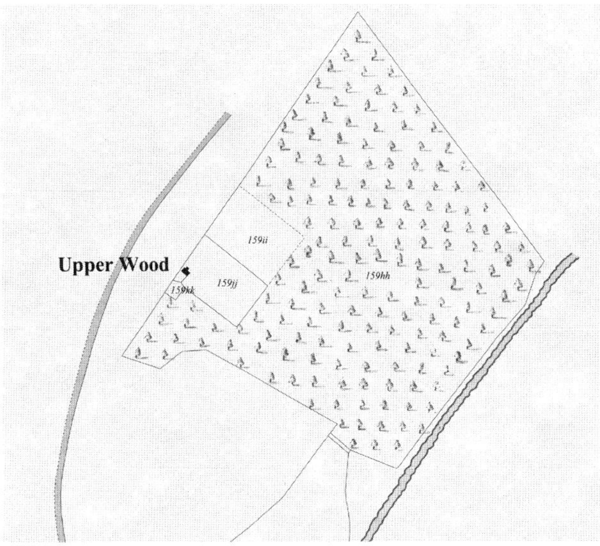

The location of Bill's o'Jack's in 1822 from a recreation of a contemporary map. (Reproduced, with permission of the Saddleworth Historical Society, from *Mapping Saddleworth Vol II*)

Visitors to Bill's o'Jack's, c.1902. (Courtesy of Saddleworth Museum)

A side view of Bill's o'Jack's photographed around 1910; the extension of the building can be seen at the back. (Courtesy of Saddleworth Museum)

A postcard of Bill's o'Jack's from c.1903. (Courtesy of Saddleworth Museum)

One of the only two known photographs of the interior of Bill's o'Jack's (the other is a similar one taken at the same time and printed in a newspaper). It was taken in the room where the attack happened and roughly where Thomas Bradbury was found lying a hundred years earlier. (Courtesy of Saddleworth Museum)

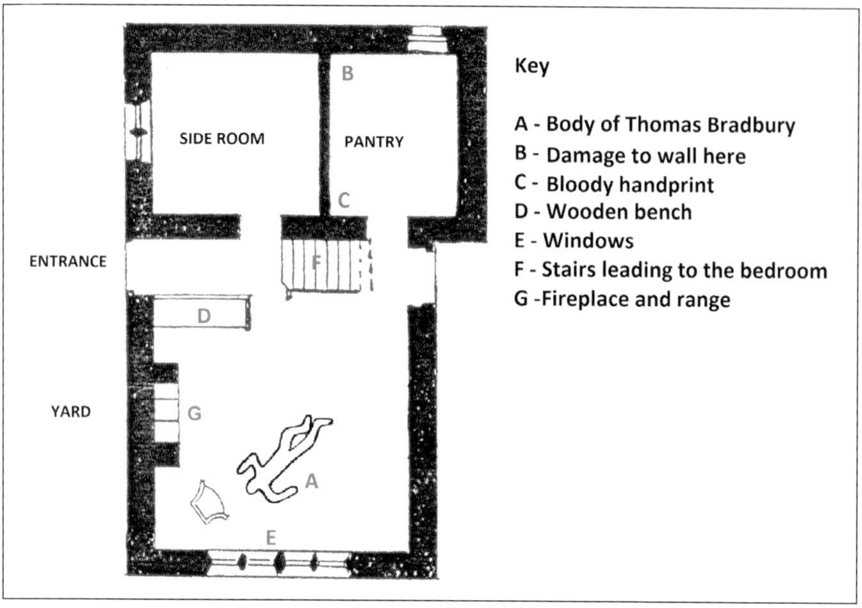

Above: A plan of Bill's o'Jack's in 1832, created by Saddleworth Museum, based on the plan produced by A. J. Howcroft. (Courtesy of Saddleworth Museum)

Below: Primrose, where Reuben Platt lived, photographed c.1955. (Courtesy of Saddleworth Museum)

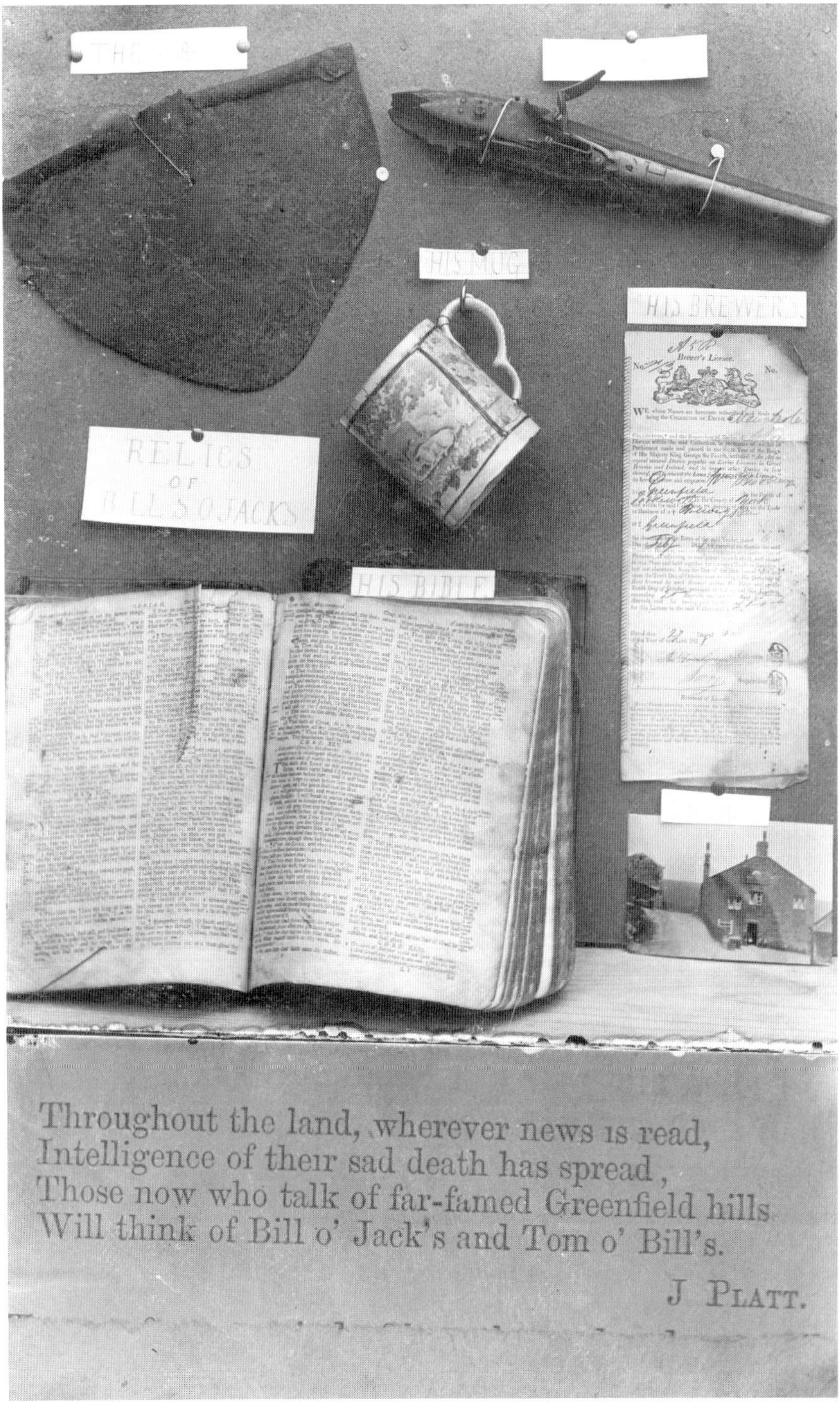

A postcard showing the original display of the items associated with the murder; all except the pistol are now held in Saddleworth Museum. (Courtesy of Saddleworth Museum)

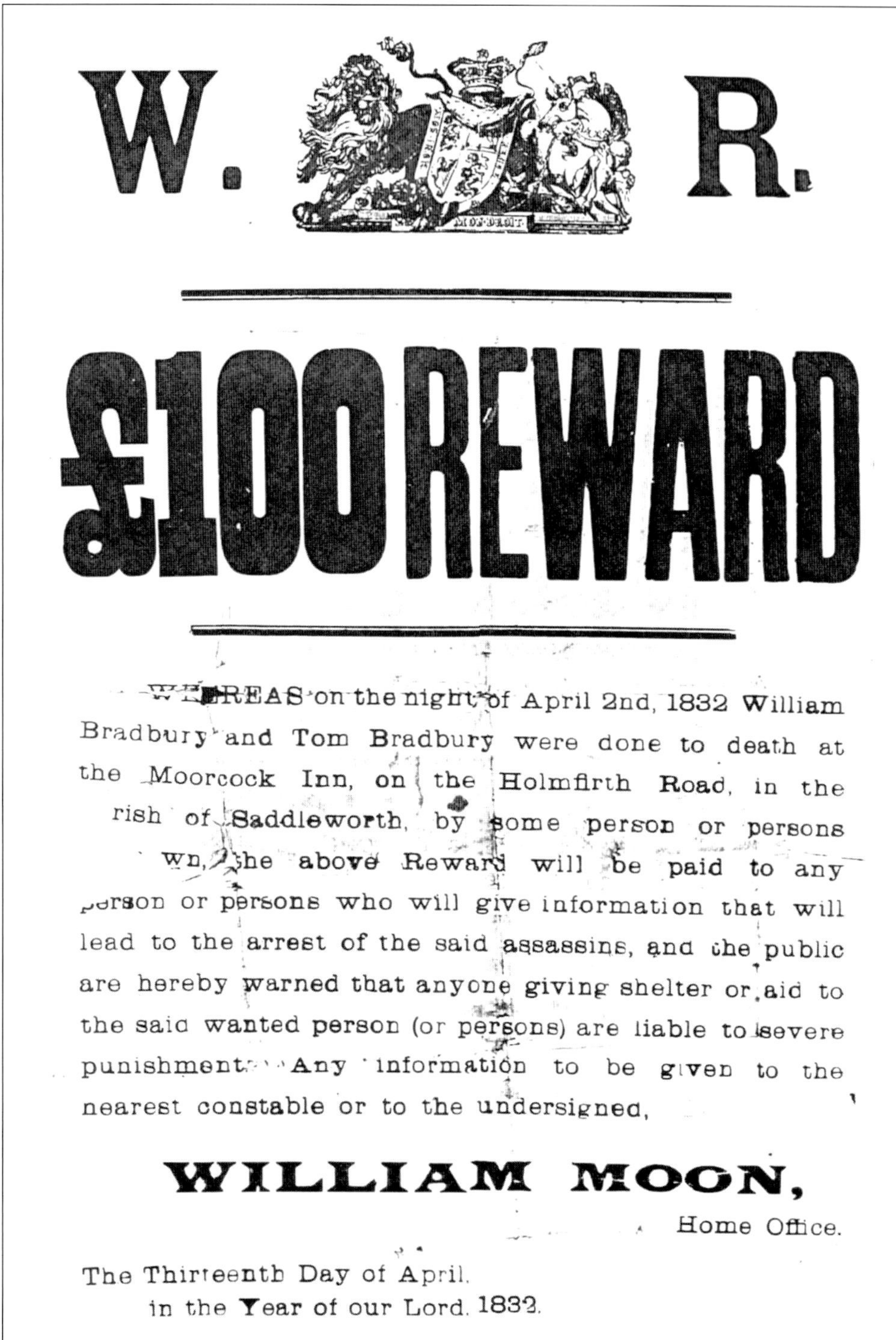
W. R.

£100 REWARD

WHEREAS on the night of April 2nd, 1832 William Bradbury and Tom Bradbury were done to death at the Moorcock Inn, on the Holmfirth Road, in the rish of Saddleworth, by some person or persons wn, the above Reward will be paid to any person or persons who will give information that will lead to the arrest of the said assassins, and the public are hereby warned that anyone giving shelter or aid to the said wanted person (or persons) are liable to severe punishment. Any information to be given to the nearest constable or to the undersigned,

WILLIAM MOON,

Home Office.

The Thirteenth Day of April,
in the Year of our Lord. 1832.

One of the reward posters printed in the weeks after the murders; an earlier version had been printed by Constable Buckley. (Courtesy of Saddleworth Museum)

Sidebank, where Thomas Bradbury's wife and four children lived at the time of the murders. (Courtesy of Saddleworth Museum)

A mug that supposedly belonged to William Bradbury. (Courtesy of Saddleworth Museum)

Bill's o'Jack's and its tearoom photographed c.1900. (Courtesy of Saddleworth Museum)

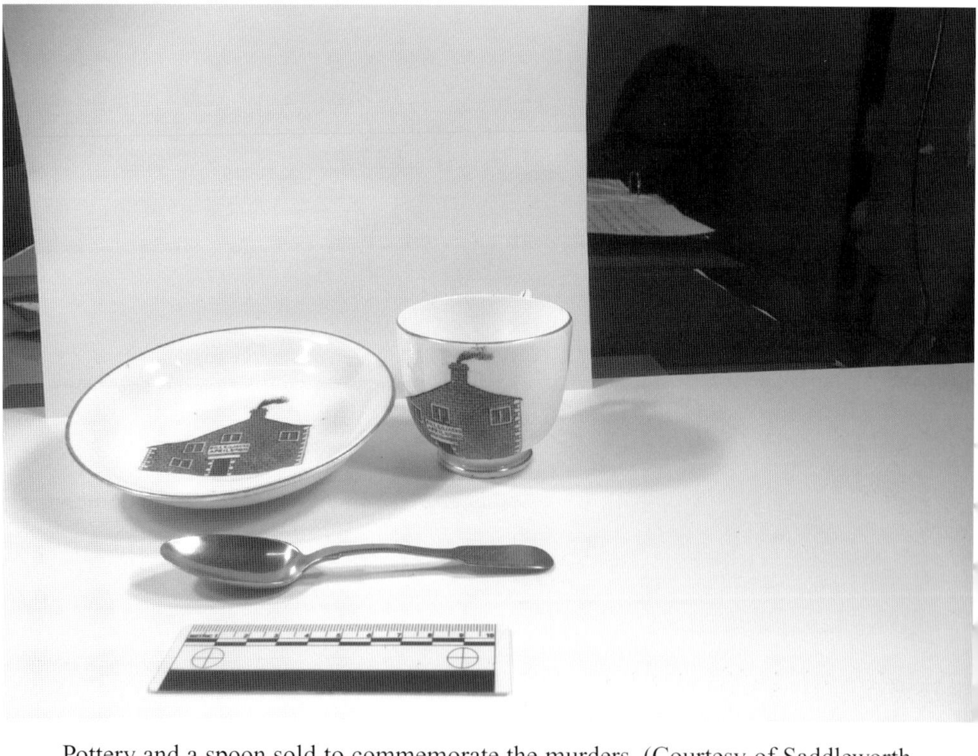

Pottery and a spoon sold to commemorate the murders. (Courtesy of Saddleworth Museum)

Above: The intact grave photographed in the twentieth century. (Courtesy of Saddleworth Museum)

Right: Front cover of William Bradbury's Bible. (Courtesy of Saddleworth Museum)

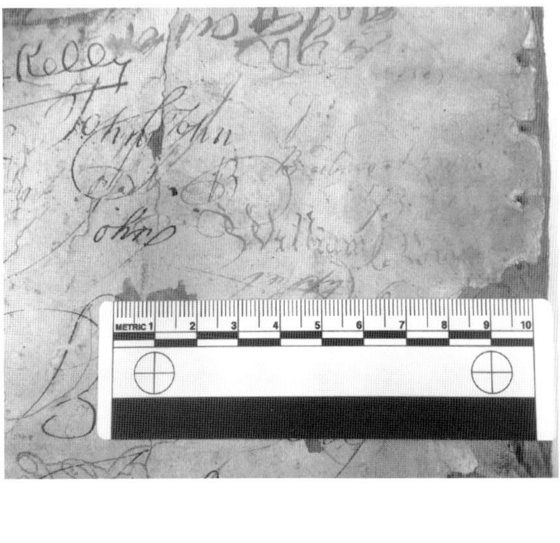

Inside cover of William Bradbury's Bible, featuring his signature. (Courtesy of Saddleworth Museum)

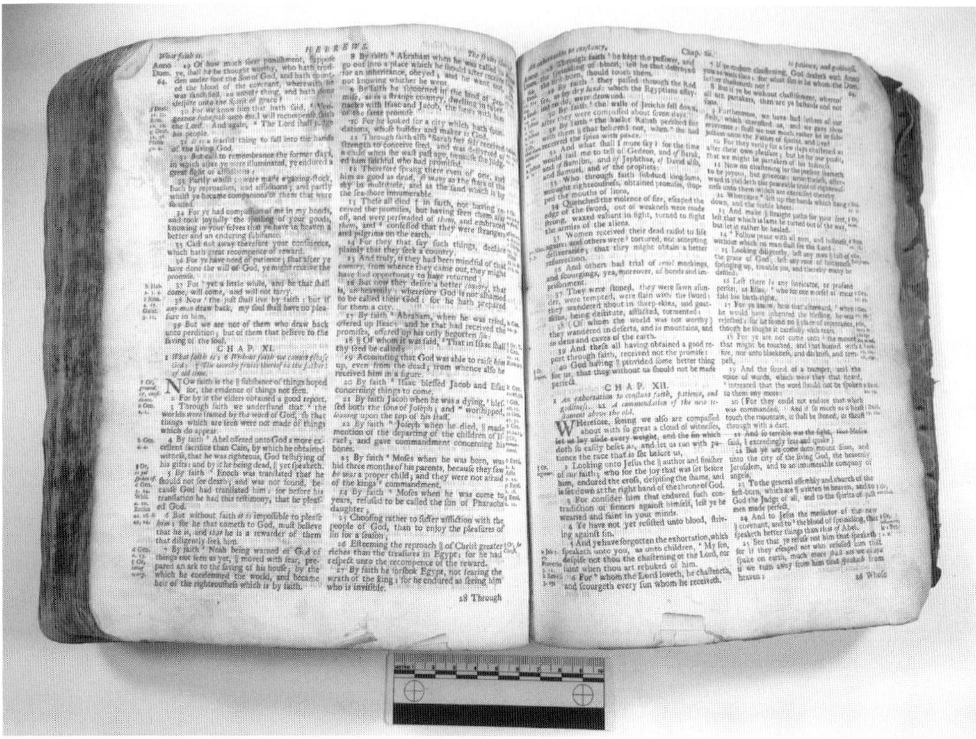

Supposedly blood-stained pages of William Bradbury's Bible. (Courtesy of Saddleworth Museum)

The shovel found at the scene. (Courtesy of Saddleworth Museum)

Above: Sidebank and the area around Alderman's Hill photographed in 2010. (Courtesy of Peter Fox)

Right: Fairbanks, where William Bradbury lived before running Bill's o'Jack's, and where Thomas Bradbury was born. (Courtesy of Peter Fox)

Left: The current state of the Bradbury grave, located in the south-west corner of St Chad's graveyard. (Author's own)

Below: The inscription on the memorial. (Poliphilo/Wikimedia Commons/CC0 1.0 Universal)

The surrounding area of the graveyard where the Bradbury memorial is located; St Chad's can be seen in the background. (Author's own)

The site of Bill's o'Jack's photographed in 2019; on the right is Alderman's Hill and in the centre is Bill's o'Jack's Plantation. The path visible on the right, just below Alderman's Hill, was the road that descended to Bill's o'Jack's until 1937. The water in the background is Dovestones Reservoir. (Author's own)

Finding a Motive

As any prospect of finding the murders faded, the people of Saddleworth turned inward and began to speculate. If they could not say *who* killed the Bradburys, could they at least establish *why*? By the time of the inquest, one theory was growing in strength: that this was a targeted attack, with a motive of revenge. The question of motivation is complicated, but in this case not because of limitations in the evidence. There were a lot of people who might have had reason to be deeply angry with the Bradburys. Were any of them angry enough to kill the two men in an extremely violent attack?

It is easy to imagine, after the funeral and as the frenzy began to fade, people taking a step back and giving serious thought to the events of the previous week. Until then, the two Bradburys had been portrayed – in the press at least – as tragic victims. But those who knew them must have realised that reality was not quite so straightforward.

Perhaps theft – the only motive considered up until then – was not the only possible explanation. The biggest problem with that scenario was the lack of evidence that anything was stolen, and there is just an echo of that realisation growing over the course of the first week. Family members who had arrived in the immediate aftermath of the discovery were reported to have said that money had been taken, but this certainty gradually evaporated. For example, Butterworth had initially written in his notebook that £7 had been stolen, but later crossed out the amount; his edited article (but not the published version) simply said: 'Money, usually in the drawer, had been taken from behind them'.

Journalists writing later in the week were even more cautious. The *Manchester Guardian* said that the family only *suspected* that money was taken, and the amount was largely a guess: 'The booty they obtained in money would, according to the statement of near relatives, not exceed seven or eight pounds'. *Wheeler's Manchester Chronicle*, probably written last, was the least certain: 'It cannot be ascertained whether [the attackers] found any money, but the respectability of the old man and the extent of his custom would naturally lead them to a supposition that he had property. He is stated to have told one of his family that he had laid by £7, which would perhaps do to bury him but at present it is impossible to ascertain whether he had any, and if any, how much money'.

Therefore, no-one – certainly not the family – *knew* that money had been taken. They simply believed William *might* have had around £7 in the house, and its absence would not necessarily signify theft. In fact, there is very little evidence that anything was stolen. Thomas Smith and Ammon Platt described damage to a set of drawers – where Butterworth said the money was kept – in the main room, as if they had been smashed open. Similarly, *Wheeler's Manchester Chronicle* (7 April) said that 'two small drawers, at the top of a chest which stands in the public room, were found broken open'. And when the reporter for the *Manchester Times* accompanied the inquest jury on their inspection of Bill's o'Jack's, he reported: 'The drawers, which had been forced open with the kitchen poker, were also smeared with blood'. So perhaps something might have been taken from there.

This was not the only occasion that initial speculation came to be tempered. As crowds gathered outside Bill's o'Jack's on Tuesday afternoon, they muttered that the place had been emptied. Thomas Smith – in the *Liverpool Mercury* version of his letter – wrote that 'every portable article in the house was carried off'. This was taken even further in the *Manchester Times* (7 April): 'The house was completely ransacked, and everything of value carried away'. This did not come from Butterworth and was probably an extrapolation from Smith's letter. Later in the week, the reporter for the *Manchester Guardian* (7 April) said that, presumably unhappy with the meagre amount of money they found, the attackers 'burdened themselves with the plunder of almost every portable article of value the house contained: such as clothes, bedding, &c'. These are odd items to take, and as the reporter observed, would have burdened any getaway as well as being an obvious sign of guilt.

By the end of the week, this 'plunder' had been narrowed down even further. *Wheeler's Manchester Chronicle* (7 April) said: 'It does not appear that [the attackers] went up-stairs, but from different parts of the house they have taken a black coat and waistcoat, a pair of drab kerseymere trousers, three shirts, two sheets, three bolster-covers, and two India silk handkerchiefs, red and yellow'. The notion that clothing was stolen is further supported by Butterworth, who wrote that 'several suits of clothes and wearing apparel' were taken. In fact it seems that by the end of the week, the consensus is that these items were the only ones definitely taken, which is a long way removed from the idea that the house was 'ransacked'.* And when the family auctioned the contents of Bill's o'Jack's, there must have been plenty left to sell.

Why would thieves break into the house and kill two men to steal a few items of clothing (presumably from the drawers), and never bother to look upstairs? Perhaps a dramatic explanation would be that they sought one particular item. But more prosaically, maybe the attackers were badly injured, and these things were used to stop the bleeding. Or they were intended to replace items of clothing that were unusable after the fight.

In fact the notion of a disturbed robbery as being the reason for the murders – such as outlined in the various 'confessions' – does not quite stand up. Would casual thieves, who were content to steal clothes and maybe a small amount of money, be armed with a loaded cavalry pistol? For example, it is highly unlikely that Reuben Platt's three Irishmen just happened to be armed. To bring a weapon would imply an element of pre-planning, but what would the perpetrator have hoped to find? Perhaps the biggest problem is that such a thief would have had little

* Even this cannot be certain. The list of stolen items must have been generated when the family (who did not live at Bill's o'Jack's) compared what was in the house to what they *thought* was in the house. There is no guarantee that their knowledge was up to date.

reason to inflict severe injuries on the victims. If the robbery had been disturbed, why would the intruder(s) not have fled when confronted by an angry Thomas Bradbury? Why engage in a life-and-death struggle and beat the two men – with multiple weapons – far beyond the point at which they could have easily escaped undisturbed? There are a few possibilities: William or Thomas might have recognised them; or perhaps Thomas trapped them in the house so they had to fight. But none are entirely convincing.

In short, while the scenario of robbery cannot be discounted, there is no conclusive evidence to support it and it does not convincingly explain the prolonged violence towards the victims. Nor was this a statistically likely motive. Homicide associated with burglary was extremely rare in this period and beyond.

If this was not a disturbed robbery, what was the explanation for the deaths? After the funeral, people began to reflect on Thomas's fiery nature. The *Manchester Guardian* stated in the conclusion to its report on the inquest printed on 14 April: 'Tom is said to have incurred the hatred of a number of Irish, who, in summer, visited the moors for the purpose of cutting heath to make into brooms. Whenever he found them, he pretended to have a right to the heath, and demanded an acknowledgement for what they had cut, and if they refused, or were unable to pay him, he would set fire to it, or cut the cords and scatter it abroad. On such occasions they would sullenly depart, vowing deep revenge'.

A similar story appeared in Butterworth's notebook, part of his report on the Red Bredburys, written sometime after 19 April (but before a version appeared in the press on 21 April*): 'An opinion is

* Not every newspaper liked this idea; for example, the *Manchester Courier* omitted these lines when it published Butterworth's article, preferring instead to strengthen the case against the Red Bredburys.

speedily gaining ground that the atrocious murders recently committed in Saddleworth were an act of revenge perpetrated by poachers and other unlawful visitors to the moors, with whom the younger Bradbury always interfered when they took too much liberty with game, gathering bilberries or cutting fern for brooms'. These two stories are sufficiently different to indicate that several accusations were being made against Thomas in the more reflective mood that had taken hold. Perhaps this growing impression was the reason that the Red Bredburys came to be suspects.

Away from the newspapers, the character of Thomas Bradbury was more freely spoken of and people had their own ideas about why he was killed. The unpublished and problematic 'Annals of Saddleworth' by Joseph Brierley contains information from a man called Matthew Marsh, who knew both William and Thomas Bradbury. Some of the relevant details recorded by Brierley date from the early 1890s when the document was written, for example an outline of the suspected case against the Red Bredburys. But Brierley went much further than this well-known story: he suggested that Thomas Bradbury and his cousin, Jamie Bradbury (i.e. one of the Red Bredburys), used to cause trouble together on the moors. Did this information come from Marsh?

There is also a tale, some of which is missing from the manuscript, in which Thomas almost beat a 'besom-maker' to death on the moors. Referring directly to the murder, and apparently either directly quoting or paraphrasing Marsh, Brierley described what he believed to be the cause: 'On the 13th August 1831, Tom o'Bill's was returning home from a stroll towards the Isle of Skye [a public house on Saddleworth Moor]. At that time, a new road from Greenfield to Holmfirth was being made, and the navvies who were Irish had built a house or a hut of sods in which to dwell … This formed a shelter at night for about 12 or 15 navvies engaged in the making of the new road. Tom o'Bill's who was partly drunk … thought he would have an act with the Irish as he returned home, so instead of quietly passing about his own business went and pushed the House of Sods over and nearly the whole mass of dirt and timber fell on the quiet and harmless sleepers. Some were slightly hurt but none badly injured or killed. Three or four of them got away and ran after Tom o'Bill's but were not able to catch him, though they said that they would murder him if they did. They knew it was him who had pushed the hut over, and they vowed to murder him before they left England'.

The vague mention of the Holmfirth road being under construction might indicate the account was written long afterwards, because the road was already complete in 1832. However, the Meltham and Wessenden Head Turnpike was almost certainly still being built at the time, and the Isle of Skye was located at the junction of this road with the Greenfield Road. And the very precise date given for the incident suggests that someone – presumably Matthew Marsh – had made a specific note of the event when it happened, even if the account was written later. Butterworth might even have been alluding to these events in his article. His suggestion that Thomas Bradbury had 'interfered' with people on the moors could be based on information that Brierley attributed to Marsh: that Thomas used to 'boss and dictate to almost everybody' who went on the moors.

However, even these explanations based on revenge as a motive continued to blame the Irish. Why was everyone so convinced of the culprits' nationality? The likeliest explanation – although outright prejudice should not be discounted – related to the last recorded words of William Bradbury: 'Pats, Pats'. Had anyone ever gone to court for the murders, this would have been important; in homicide cases, 'dying declarations' – words spoken by an involved person immediately before their death – were permitted as evidence in court (the only hearsay so allowed). Building a case against anyone would have relied on interpreting William Bradbury's words.

However, this was not entirely straightforward. While 'Pats' was certainly a widespread derogatory term used to refer to the Irish, we cannot be certain of what, if anything, was said. No newspaper report before the inquest mentioned any words spoken by William Bradbury. The magistrates' letter asking for an increased reward from the Home Office and the testimony of Ammon Platt explicitly state that William did *not* speak. Although we know from Thomas Smith's letter (and Butterworth's first report) that it was immediately suspected that Irishmen were responsible, it is impossible to know whether this arose from Reuben Platt's tale or from words muttered by a dying man.

The only definitive contemporary statement that William Bradbury spoke intelligibly came from James Whitehead at the inquest. Most newspapers said that Whitehead claimed to have heard 'Pats, Pats', although the *Manchester Times* had the subtly different 'The Pats, the Pats'. But Whitehead admitted that it was difficult to understand Bradbury (and, further complicating the issue, Butterworth recorded that Whitehead himself was difficult to hear clearly at the inquest because he spoke 'in so low a tone'). Whitehead then asked Bradbury if his son had been there; the latter may have replied 'Aye' (the *Manchester Times* said that Whitehead got no reply to this). However, not every newspaper gives the same wording.

Except for possibly replying 'Aye', did William speak again? *Wheeler's Manchester Chronicle* (7 April) states that the old man was 'repeatedly interrogated by the surgeon and others, but though he betrayed, by muttering, a consciousness of the questions, not a sound escaped his lips which was at all distinguishable'. Only two questionable witnesses – Thomas Smith, who claimed to have spoken directly to Bradbury, and the stonecutter Joseph Matthews quoted in the *Manchester Guardian* on 14 April – ever suggested anything to the contrary, and both should probably be discounted.

Therefore the only evidence for 'Pats, Pats' comes from words spoken quietly at an inquest, not necessarily reliably recorded, when the witness himself made clear that William was hard to understand. Whitehead certainly *thought* he heard Bradbury say 'Pats'; he gave Hegginbottom the impression that the person lying on the floor, whom he believed to be the attacker, was Irish. But Whitehead could, in the circumstances, have been mistaken, and wrongly interpreted noises as words. He could certainly have mis-heard or misunderstood; later writers freely speculated about what Bradbury might actually have been trying to say. Or Whitehead could have been driven by his own prejudices; did he believe that the attackers *must* have been Irish and so heard what he wanted? And because the inquest took place four days after he had found Bradbury dying in his bed, did the rumours swirling feverishly around Saddleworth influence Whitehead's evidence? If everyone was looking for Irishmen, did that affect – consciously or unconsciously – his testimony? Or was everyone aware that Thomas Bradbury had been in dispute with some Irish workers, and these were the immediately obvious suspects?

Quite simply, we don't know. But other people – Irish or not – would also have had several reasons to be unhappy with Thomas and his father.

Although there are several indications that William Bradbury was well-liked in the area, he was hardly a genial, friendly grandfather. In 1830 his landlord had evicted him for refusing to pay rent, but he had refused to leave, instead living in a hut next to Bill's o'Jack's. He had run an illegal 'hush shop' and was happy to operate under a beer licence which required less monitoring from the authorities. There is even a possibility that he was claiming land as part of the enclosure process. What else had he done over the years? Who else had he angered?

Thomas probably had even more enemies. He was well-known for spending time on the moors and killing game – in effect, living as a poacher – and had poisoned hunting dogs a few years before out of a desire for revenge. He was somehow involved in the enclosure process, an emotive subject, and had attended at least one meeting. Possibly he was involved in politics and had been present at Peterloo. Described as a 'wild sort of man' in the 'Annals of Saddleworth' and 'powerful' by George Shaw, he seemingly radiated temper and violence. There would have been no shortage of people who bore a grudge.

There was a much later hint that retribution against Thomas was the reason behind the attack. A Saddleworth man called Joseph Thornton wrote: 'The fact was that there were too many unwilling witnesses, some of whom could have hanged the culprit on their own evidence. Many declined to come forward with substantial facts on account of the unfriendly behaviour of the Bradburys towards those who had to travel on the road from Greenfield to Holmfirth. The gamekeeper [i.e. Thomas Bradbury] was a terror to the pedestrians as well as to the poacher'. Thornton concluded: 'Statements have since been made that if the tragedy had not taken place on the above date, it would have taken place shortly afterwards'.

It is uncertain when Thornton wrote this, but for reasons that will become apparent later, it must have been later than 1871, already long after the murders. It could have been *much* later as Thornton lived until 1924 (the book was published posthumously in 1967). Therefore his words should be treated with caution, but they tally with the scanty contemporary evidence about Thomas Bradbury's behaviour. Perhaps Thornton's writing reflected what had come to be believed: that Thomas Bradbury was a violent poacher who terrorised residents and passers-by on the moor, making revenge a potential motive, one which would explain the extreme violence of the attack.

Overall, there would have been no shortage of people with a personal grudge against William or – more likely – Thomas Bradbury. So rather than theft, was the motivation revenge?

Unlike other scenarios, this theory is firmly rooted in historical circumstances. Suspicion that the murderers were Irish reflected hostility towards immigrants. The workers supposedly angered by Thomas Bradbury were constructing the roads, railways or canals intended to connect Saddleworth to the rest of industrialised England. The hut which he might have overturned was situated on Saddleworth Moor which, for just a little longer, was not yet enclosed; even Butterworth's description of 'unlawful visitors to the moors' is not entirely accurate as the claims had not yet been finalised and its ownership was still being decided. And possibly, just possibly, Thomas had been driven to exploit those moors – through poaching or running what amounted to a crude protection racket – because he needed money. Perhaps he was another victim of the drastic social changes gripping Britain, but his solution set in chain events that led to his death. Looked through these lenses, the murders might have been another manifestation of the turbulence of the late Georgian period. Perhaps someone – whether it was the Bradburys or those who killed them – was making another protest against the direction in which the world was heading.

While lacking evidence, this solution at least provides some narrative satisfaction. But it is nothing more than speculation in a story that already contains far too much.

A final intriguing possibility emerged in the William the Fourth on 7 April 1832, during the first inquest, held before that of the Bradburys. Because Michael Stocks junior was also investigating the death of a new-born girl.

Her body had been found hidden in a privy (outdoor toilet) at Foulrakes, a house in Greenfield belonging to a man called Samuel Wrigley. Her mother, it was quickly established, was Esther Porritt, one of Wrigley's servants. Although they were attending to report on the Bradburys, journalists also wrote about this first inquest. Perhaps they had nothing better to do, but their newspapers were happy to print the stories. Butterworth described Porritt as 'a tall lusty woman' while *Wheeler's Manchester Chronicle* said she was 'a fine-looking woman' and suggested she was around 20 years old. At her trial later in the year, Porritt revealed that she was 26. According to the *Manchester Guardian*, she was 'a native of Chapel-en-le-Frith, Derbyshire' and 'a remarkably fine young woman'. The latter newspaper related that she had lived 'at Mr Garforth's, of Low Side, near Oldham' before moving to live with Wrigley as a house servant earlier in 1832.

Wrigley and his wife had suspected Porritt of being pregnant in February and March, shortly after she began working for them, and reported her to a Saddleworth constable. The *Huddersfield and Halifax Express* account of the inquest stated: 'She was waited upon by the constable of Saddleworth, who had received intimation that she was with child, with a view to remove her to her place of settlement [in other words, her home parish]; but she denied being in that state, and no further measures were taken'.

Around midnight on Sunday, 1 April, while the Wrigleys were away in Oldham, Porritt left the bed she shared with Hannah Woffinden, a fellow servant, and went downstairs for some time. Woffinden heard her moving around the kitchen and confronted her when she returned; Porritt said that she had been extremely thirsty. The following morning (the Monday), Woffinden noticed a significant change in Porritt's appearance and found spots of blood on the kitchen floor. Porritt denied Woffinden's accusation that she had given birth and continued her usual duties. When the Wrigleys returned on Thursday, Woffinden told them of her suspicions. The house was searched and on Friday, 6 April, Woffinden herself discovered the dead child in the drain of the privy behind the house (some accounts of the inquest implied that Woffinden effectively carried out the search alone). Porritt admitted giving birth but said the baby had been born dead; she had hidden the body to conceal that she had been pregnant.

A constable was called and Porritt was detained until the inquest the following day, where she continued to say that the girl was stillborn. Two surgeons who had examined the body on the morning of the inquest were uncertain, but according to the *Manchester Guardian* 'both pronounced an opinion, though very guardedly, that the child had breathed after birth'. The inquest jury gave a verdict of 'wilful murder' and Porritt was sent to York where she would be held in custody and tried.

In September 1832, at the summer sessions of the York Assizes, Esther Porritt was sentenced to six months hard labour for 'concealing the birth of her infant'. The *York Herald* reported on 8 September: 'The prisoner had been committed for the wilful murder of the child, but the Grand Jury ignored the bill, there being no evidence that the child was born alive'. Such hesitancy on the part of juries to find mothers guilty was common in cases like Porritt's; infanticide – the murder of newly born but illegitimate children for the purposes of concealment – was not unusual in this period, but convictions were rare.

Although sad, there was nothing apparently remarkable about Porritt's story. However, a different picture emerged in the pages of the *Manchester Guardian.* Having given a thorough account of the Porritt inquest, the writer added more detail, without specifying his source: 'This same woman, some time since, bore a child by Thomas Bradbury, the particulars of whose murder we have been detailing; she then lived at a public inn, at Ashton-under-Lyne, and, probably, removed from Low Side to Foulrakes, in order to be again in his neighbourhood. The child, as she confessed, was born on the night of Sunday the first of April, and she might probably conceal it in order to prevent Tom from knowing she had again been pregnant. But a catastrophe still more dreadful cut him off from all knowledge of the circumstances, his murder having taken place on the night following'.

No other contemporary account linked the child who died with Thomas Bradbury. Perhaps at the inquest Stocks had asked newspaper reporters to be discreet and omit any mention of a connection between Porritt and Bradbury; maybe the *Manchester Guardian* was the only publication not to co-operate. On the other hand, it could have been reporting gossip – either from the inquest itself or given to the *Manchester Guardian* journalist separately. It might not have been a coincidence that Butterworth, after his account of the inquest, wrote in his notebook: 'Rumour, with her thousand tongues, has spread around a multitude of unfounded assertions and in this mass of falsehoods it is difficult and vain to cull out the truth, and though it is generally mixed up with error both are inseparable'.

But it is notable that the author of the *Manchester Guardian* article chose his words very carefully. The background was expanded *after* the events of the inquest, as if it was a later addition to the piece. He twice specified 'probably' and never stated outright that *this* child was Bradbury's, only saying definitively that he and Porritt had *previously* had a child. Does this caution make the claim stronger? The writer clearly differentiated between what he regarded as fact and conjecture.

But there is no evidence that the claimed connection between Porritt and Bradbury was made at the inquest, let alone that it was accurate.

Can anything be corroborated? Not really; although there is nothing to refute the idea, there is nothing to support it either. If Porritt's age given at the trial is correct, she was born around 1806; if the *Manchester Guardian* reported accurately, she was from Chapel-en-le-Frith. The closest candidate was a girl called Esther Porritt, baptised at Chinley in 1805, the daughter of Jonathan and Malley Porritt; Chinley is close to Chapel-en-le-Frith.* Perhaps this was her. But no definitive trace of Porritt appears on the 1841 census nor any later ones.† As there was no legal requirement to register marriages or deaths until 1837; she could have married or died before that date, leaving no surviving record. Or she could have moved somewhere else where she became untraceable.

There is just one possible hint to back up the claims of the *Manchester Guardian*. At Ashton-under-Lyne, where the newspaper said that Porritt lived for a time, a child was baptised in 1826: James Bradbury, the son of Esther Bradbury, a spinster of Stalybridge. No father is named. The location, date, the first name of the mother and the surname Bradbury fit the rumour. As so often in the story, there is no clear trace of any of these people afterwards. If this was Esther Porritt and Thomas Bradbury's child, there is no way to prove it. However, there is one interesting coincidence; Thomas and Ann Bradbury's youngest child was born in 1826, suggesting that their marriage broke down soon after this date (when, at the age of 33, Ann could have had more children before Thomas's death). Do these events explain why Thomas was not living with his wife at the time of his death? Did he move in with his father after having a child with another woman? But why would Bradbury have been in Oldham or Ashton-under-Lyne in 1826?

---

* Incidentally, George Shaw, the local man who mentioned the Bradburys in his diary, learned of their murders from newspapers in Chapel-en-le-Frith on 8 April, the night before he returned home.

† A woman called Esther Porritt died in 1875 and was buried in Chapel-en-le-Frith, but she had been born around 1823.

Another possibly supportive piece of circumstantial evidence concerns the location of Porritt's workplace, Foulrakes. The house was very close to Road End, along Kinders Lane; this rather isolated road leads up to a place called Tunstead, from which several paths travel back down the hill to the Holmfirth Road, very close to Sidebank where Thomas Bradbury's wife lived in 1832. Does the location of Foulrakes corroborate the claim in the *Manchester Guardian* that she moved 'in order to be again in [Thomas's] neighbourhood'? Did she want to be near the father of her unborn child?

And of course, the timings are quite a coincidence. Porritt gave birth either late on Sunday night or early on Monday morning. On Monday evening, Thomas Bradbury parted company from Reuben Platt at Road End (by the William the Fourth), at the end of Kinders Lane, just over a hundred yards from Foulrakes. Bradbury was attacked some point between then and the following morning. But of course, it could have been just such coincidences that inspired the writer for the *Manchester Guardian* – or the local gossips – to manufacture something to connect the two events.

It was not until 1926 that anyone resurrected in print the claim from the *Manchester Guardian*. An Oldham councillor, A. J. Howcroft, wrote a romanticised account of the murders which explicitly named the dead girl as the child of Thomas Bradbury and suggested that the outraged father of Esther Porritt had murdered the Bradburys. And in their analysis of the story in 1987, Neil Barrow and Terry Wyke observed that if the story was true, it was possible that the relationship with Porritt could have 'soured' or that Bradbury could have argued with Porritt or, more likely, a friend or family member. They also suggest that this might account for the extreme violence inflicted on Bradbury.

To go this far, we need to produce a chain of circumstantial evidence and make a dangerous number of assumptions. The biggest is that Thomas Bradbury was the father of the child who died around thirty-six hours before he did. Not even the *Manchester Guardian* went quite as far making that explicit claim (although the hint was strong enough). And yet, in truth, we have little idea where Thomas Bradbury went after leaving Reuben Platt. He went to the shop, but what if he headed home along Kinders Lane? Perhaps he called at Foulrakes to see Esther Porritt. As with so many aspects of this story, there is insufficient evidence even to assess the likelihood of a relationship between the two. Almost anything is possible.

Thereforc, as the people of Saddleworth gradually seemed to realise, there was no shortage of possible motives for the murder. Was it a robbery gone sour? Anger? Revenge? A poaching dispute? Or something else entirely, masked by our ignorance regarding so many aspects of the victims' lives?

Although the murders have continued to fascinate for almost two hundred years, many of these potential theories were forgotten and writing came to focus on one or two suspects to the exclusion of all else. Subsequent retellings focussed on facts and interpretations nowhere to be seen in 1832. In fact, almost every word written in later years was influenced to some extent by an extremely popular but unreliable account which completely reframed the story. The nominal author inadvertently changed the course of the legend and in doing so, accidentally became one of its dominant figures.

Joseph Bradbury was born in Saddleworth on 7 May 1838, six years after the deaths of his unrelated namesakes. His father, also called Joseph, was a clothier who died around two weeks after his son's birth. As he grew up in Dobcross with his mother Hannah and sister Elizabeth, young Joseph would have heard tales about Bill's o'Jack's, which continued to retain a grip on local imagination. Occasionally, the story had even returned to the pages of newspapers and the building in which William and Thomas had died remained a local attraction; it is likely that Joseph visited as it was less than two miles from his home.

In his youth, Bradbury lived in an area of Dobcross known as Woolroad, just north of Uppermill and close to Saddleworth Railway Station, which opened in 1849. Perhaps he spent time in the King's Head, where Charles Mullen had been held in 1832. At the time of the 1861 census, he still lived with his mother (by then a 'landed proprietor') at Dobcross; by then Bradbury was a medical student and soon after he qualified as a doctor.

Little else is known of his early life; he certainly moved away from Saddleworth, probably not long after 1861. In 1871 he married Annie Smalley in Essex and spent the following years travelling around, spending time in Essex, Cheshire, London and France. But as well as being a doctor, Bradbury had ambitions as an author. And it was his entry into this world that had a considerable impact on the story of Bill's o'Jack's, transforming it into a legend populated with stereotypical villains. However, that was never his intention and the fault – if blame is to be apportioned – did not lie with him.

Sometime in the winter of 1870, Bradbury had been suffering from what today would be termed as stress but which he described at the time as 'a period of length and arduous toil, and more than usual mental anxiety' which had caused 'over-burdened nature' to 'begin to give way'. His remedy was a visit to the places of his 'happy childhood'. As a starting point, he chose Bill's o'Jack's, which he remembered well, particularly 'the horrid catastrophe which has made the place so notorious'. Therefore, he arrived one winter morning by train at Greenfield station (opened in 1849) and began walking down the hill towards Road End to begin his explorations of the area.*

Whether his intention was always to write about his travels or whether the idea occurred to him once he arrived, the result was a series of weekly articles under the heading 'Saddleworth Sketches' which appeared in the *Oldham Chronicle* (under the pseudonym 'F. D. M.') over the winter of 1870–71. The first two were about his visit to Bill's o'Jack's. It was probably this particular subject matter that interested the editor of the *Oldham Chronicle* and guaranteed the success of Bradbury's series.

The opening two pieces, entitled 'Bill's o'Jack's and Greenfield', were largely about the 'horrid catastrophe'. After detailing his reasons for the visit – and making an immediate link to the murder from thirty-eight years earlier – Bradbury described how after leaving Greenfield Station, he encountered an old man who gave his name as 'Owd Kedlock'.

The opening of the article had already made plain Bradbury's literary intent, and when he wrote about 'Owd Kedlock', he used the fashionable device of writing in local dialect. This trend had begun in earnest around ten years earlier; often of working-class origin and aimed at locals who spoke that way, dialect writing encompassed prose, ballads and poetry. The style could evoke humour, sentiment or nostalgia depending on the intended purpose.

* The author, incidentally, ate breakfast at the Clarence Hotel, whose landlord was 'Gustus' Bradbury, the eldest son of Thomas Bradbury.

Bradbury wrote several pages of dialogue in which his new friend's speech was written entirely in dialect. 'Owd Kedlock' – who apparently had 'a peculiar whining voice, half guttural and half nasal' – greeted him 'Neaw mester! Houd on a minute, un let's be company if yore be own moi gate'. This added little to the narrative, was written purely for effect, and made the words almost impenetrable to all but dialect speakers. Nevertheless, 'Owd Kedlock' played a key role in the story.

During their conversation, Kedlock revealed that he had some old papers, which had come to him through his father and some neighbours, about the Bill's o'Jack's murders, including some 'inquest pappers' [*sic*] and various other items. In exchange for food at the establishment by then called the Moorcock— but still better known as Bill's o'Jack's – Kedlock offered to bring the papers for Bradbury to look at. At this point, there is an interlude in the narrative in which Bradbury described his journey up the hill, a passage far more representative of the form that most 'Saddleworth Sketches' would take. But the article eventually reached the point at which he arrived at the Moorcock, and Kedlock showed him the papers.

These consisted of a packet of 1832 newspaper articles taken from the *Manchester Courier* and handwritten manuscripts which were 'old and faded', dated 'about the time of the murder'. Bradbury reproduced the *Courier* reports in 'Bill's o'Jack's and Greenfield', but omitted the manuscripts as there was 'no material difference' in the different accounts. The extracts stretched over the first two articles in the 'Saddleworth Sketches' series, breaking off after the entries from 7 April 1832 and resuming a week later with the inquest reports.

After some brief comment on the case, and reproducing the inevitable verses from the famous grave, Bradbury wrote about his onward journey. The text was a mix of scenic descriptions, extracts from poetry and some local history. The other pieces that he produced for the *Oldham Chronicle* followed a similar pattern and while they probably appealed to a local audience, they would almost certainly have been forgotten if Bradbury had not opened with that discussion of the murders.

Continued interest in the case inspired someone – possibly Bradbury but more likely a person connected to the newspaper – to collect Bradbury's articles in a book. The resulting *Saddleworth Sketches*, published in 1871, comprised twenty-three 'sketches' which, according to the publisher's preface, had been 'to some extent condensed, and the whole carefully corrected, so that it is hoped errors in circumstances and dates have been minimised'.

But crucially for the growing legend, the biggest changes to Bradbury's original work came in his account of the Bill's o'Jack's murders.

The publisher's preface promised that 'the original idea of their writer, Mr Joseph Bradbury, has been adhered to, but, in consequence of his prolonged absence from Oldham, he has not been able to undertake the revision'. Among the 'additions for which Mr Bradbury is not responsible' were four chapters at the end of the book, comprising just over fifty pages. And, the publisher casually noted, there had been 'considerable additions' to the opening chapter, 'Bill's o'Jack's and Greenfield' – seventeen pages of 'additional facts and speculations'. The changes were probably commissioned by the editor of the *Oldham Chronicle* who realised that content about the murders would generate more sales.

On a more prosaic level, Bradbury's original two 'sketches' were combined to form the opening chapter but were otherwise faithfully reproduced until the insertion of the seventeen pages, just before the part that quoted the epitaph. After the additional section, the chapter reverted to Bradbury's text. The switch in style was jarring and gave the book a very odd shape; certainly nothing else in its 259 pages compares to that expanded section. Yet it was this part which attracted enormous attention, making the book – and Joseph Bradbury – very famous, even if he was not responsible for the words that were extensively quoted. In fact, the additional pages dominated all subsequent retellings of the story.

The new section provided some apparently fresh information about the murders but cannot be taken at face value. First, the author is unknown; it was certainly not Bradbury and could have been the work of several people given that there were internal contradictions. Perhaps the most likely candidate was Jonathan Hirst, the editor of the *Oldham Chronicle*, who was born in Holmfirth in 1818 and lived for years in Saddleworth; he would presumably have been very familiar with the story of the murders. He had also worked for the *Huddersfield Examiner* between 1854 and 1856, just after the 'confession' from Australia was printed in the rival *Huddersfield Chronicle*, when the story was certainly in people's thoughts. A second, larger issue is that the information was published almost forty years after the murders. Although there was much convincing-looking new detail, it cannot be verified and is likely to be an accumulation of four-decades-worth of gossip – polished and refined, but still gossip.

Finally, the biggest problem with the published version of *Saddleworth Sketches* is that the anonymous author – for ease of reference, we will assume this was Hirst and use his name – had access to just one printed source: the 1832 newspaper reports in the *Manchester Courier*, as reprinted in Bradbury's original article. Nor did he quite have the original version of the *Manchester Courier*. Bradbury, either by accident or design, did not stay completely faithful to the 1832 texts. For example, he included the letter from Thomas Smith as published on 7 April 1832, but where the *Manchester Courier* originally printed 'six Irishmen', Bradbury gave the number as five, perhaps to match the number supposedly given by William Bradbury. Secondly, maybe for reasons of space, Bradbury omitted the address of Thomas Smith – 'No. 16, Maskill-street, Chorlton Row' – which had been included in the *Manchester Courier*. But Hirst, unaware that the address had originally been part of the letter, drew attention to its absence, arguing that Smith had deliberately not given it to avoid being questioned or called as a witness.

Hirst also made his own alteration to the text, where it referred to the girl who discovered her dying uncle. Bradbury's original article accurately quoted the *Manchester Courier* report on the inquest (from

14 April) and called her Amelia Winterbottom. But when this was incorporated into the book, her name was altered (without comment) to Mary Winterbottom both in the quoted report and in the text added by Hirst. If the girl's real name genuinely was Mary – which is highly likely – Hirst might have corrected it for the sake of accuracy; in which case, he had at least one very good source in Greenfield. The name Mary had certainly never been written down elsewhere. This was not the only occasion in which Hirst twisted the narrative in the *Manchester Courier* to match what he believed to be the reality.

Although in terms of understanding the murder, Hirst's additions to *Saddleworth Sketches* must be treated with caution, they *do* provide good evidence of what was being said about the case in later years. Hirst could have personally heard these stories because he lived in Saddleworth; in 1871, his residence was Grasscroft, which is very close to Greenfield and Uppermill.

And it is indisputable that Hirst made some effective points, such as his suggestion that the letter by Smith 'must have drawn very largely on his imagination for his facts, and … penned as matters within his own knowledge what was the merest hearsay, loosely floating about the crowd at the inn, swayed by horror, and in wild excitement making random guesses at the perpetrators of the appalling crime'. He also argued that the three Irishmen seen the night before (whose existence he doubted) could not have been the murderers as they would have completed their robbery long before Thomas Bradbury returned home unless they walked an implausible distance along the Holmfirth road before turning back: 'They would have completed their diabolical crime quickly, and have been far away with their plunder long before half-past ten o'clock'. Nor would they have had a particular reason to harm William Bradbury.

But Hirst also made mistakes, such as his dismissal of the notion that 'Mr S. Lavender', to whom Smith's letter was addressed, was the deputy constable of Manchester. Instead, he tentatively (and incorrectly) identified the recipient as the deputy constable of Saddleworth and noted that 'at that time a man named Lavender, who took considerable interest in the tragic circumstances, resided in the neighbourhood of Shaw Hall'.* His reliance on the *Manchester Courier* also caused omissions in the story. For example, there was no mention of the well-known faults of William and Thomas Bradbury that had been reported in other newspapers in 1832 (and which had been removed from Butterworth's article before it was printed in the *Courier*). Indeed, Hirst legitimised Thomas in describing him as a 'gamekeeper'; at best, he might have been a kind of watchman for certain areas on the moor.

And given that they were never mentioned by the *Manchester Courier*, the 'broom collectors' and Esther Porritt played no part in Hirst's narrative nor in his theories about the murders. Does this mean these elements of the story, which circulated in 1832, had not been included in the ongoing legend recorded by Hirst? Possibly, although there is no way to be certain; we cannot tell how much of Hirst's writing came from his own imagination, and how much had been passed around as gossip in the houses, pubs and streets of Saddleworth.

But the overall effect was that Hirst only had a partial picture of the events of 1832. And, unfortunately, later writers chose to follow *Saddleworth Sketches* unquestioningly, not realising these limitations.

This might not have mattered except for the identities of the suspects offered by Hirst. Assuming that he had no ulterior motive that has been lost to us, and if his writing accurately summarised what people were saying about the murders forty years later, in the intervening period all attention and all suspicion had come to focus on just three people.

* Stephen Lavender, the Manchester deputy constable, died in 1833 so can hardly have taken much subsequent interest in the case.

Other potential candidates – the three Irishmen, Charles Mullen, the men at Hooley Hill, the broom collectors, the workers at the Isle of Skye, the various 'confessors' – had all been forgotten. Instead, Hirst focussed on some familiar names: the Red Bredburys and, implausibly, Reuben Platt.

It is possible that Hirst fancied himself as an amateur detective and constructed his own convoluted theories to explain the murders, in which case *Saddleworth Sketches* has little to offer the historian. But perhaps a more likely scenario is that he was recording what he had heard while living in Saddleworth. This would also explain some of his more eccentric interpretations of the *Manchester Courier* articles – he was attempting to skew the facts to fit the gossip; to reframe the newspaper account to match the story being told by his contemporaries in Saddleworth. If that was the case, however, he did not do a very good job.

The first suspect presented by Hirst was Reuben Platt. Hirst's case against him was built around one simple detail: the words supposedly muttered by the dying William Bradbury. As the *Manchester Courier* had accurately recorded, James Whitehead said at the inquest that William had mumbled 'Pats, Pats' when asked who was responsible. Everyone at the time, including Whitehead himself, had assumed Bradbury was referring to Irishmen.

But Hirst offered a very different interpretation: 'It was much questioned at the time in the neighbourhood whether the words were 'Pats, Pats', or 'Platts, Platts'. The old man could only speak with extreme difficulty, and very indistinctly, so that the bystanders might easily mistake the one for the other'. In other words, Hirst argued that William Bradbury might have been trying to say that he had been attacked by at least one man whose name was Platt. But Hirst – or the people of Saddleworth who made this leap – seemingly waved aside considerations of whether the dying man understood what he was being asked or if he had been heard properly. He continued: 'This idea has not yet died out in the district, and strong suspicions, founded mainly, if not solely, upon that slight hypothesis, were directed towards Reuben Platt'.

This interpretation was certainly not made in 1832. Had Hirst been able to read other newspapers, he would have realised that Platt had been consulted several times by constables and magistrates, which would hardly have been the case if there were any doubts about him at the time of the murders. Assuming that he was correct in saying that 'strong suspicions' had been expressed against Platt, these rumours must have come from a later date. The suggestion might be circumstantially supported by the line 'the "thousand and one" dark insinuations which are aimed at certain families in the locality' from the 1853 'confession' report in the *Huddersfield Chronicle* (with which Hirst might have been familiar). This most likely refers to the Red Bredburys, but the use of 'families' plural might mean that Platt also faced 'dark insinuations'.

Yet a few pages later, Hirst seemingly demolished the very heart of the argument. When dismantling the credibility of Thomas Smith's letter, he wrote:

> 'Had [Smith's] details [of William Bradbury speaking] been correct, or even partly trustworthy, many other persons who flocked to the place on hearing of the catastrophe must have heard the old man speak, but not one of them has affirmed that the dying man could answer any question, or do more than mutter indistinctly the word Pats or Platts. Not a few of them are living at the present time (1871), and they agree in denying the old man's ability to converse or answer any question put to him'.

The author goes on to cite someone who was present as saying that William 'could not speak when found, and that he never spoke as to be understood up to the moment of his death. His lips moved as if he was trying to say something, and a feeble mutter was detected, but no well-defined word passed his lips, so that those who alleged that he had made use of the words "Pats, Pats", several times might well be mistaken'.

The contradictory nature of these two sections – the words attributed to William Bradbury being indications of Platt's guilt *and* possibly never spoken at all – could be explained if they had different authors, which is certainly possible if the expansion was the work of several people. On the other hand, it is very likely that Smith's part in the story had been forgotten and so when his letter was reprinted in the *Oldham Chronicle*, most readers were seeing it for the first time. Therefore the analysis of the letter might have been Hirst's own interpretation of 'new' evidence, which inadvertently undermined the popular argument against Platt.

But the *Manchester Courier* articles – like all those printed in 1832 – contained nothing which incriminated Platt in the slightest. Therefore Hirst, possibly trying to weave it into the legend that blamed Platt, was forced to twist what it said, accentuating some parts and dismissing others. Over several pages, he built that argument.

Part of his problem was that the *Manchester Courier* made plain that in the immediate aftermath of the murders, all suspicion had fallen on the three Irishmen seen by Thomas Bradbury and Platt; this did not fit with the idea that Platt was to blame and so had to be explained away. Therefore Hirst concluded that Platt had invented the trio to offset the suspicion that William Bradbury had said 'Platts'. For example, because no-one appeared at the inquest to corroborate their existence, 'it is, therefore, tolerably evident that if the three Irishmen were not a myth, the testimony of Reuben Platt alone established their presence in the neighbourhood'. Where the *Manchester Courier* offered any evidence to the contrary, Hirst disparaged it. The line in that newspaper about others having seen the three Irishmen in the area that night was dismissed as 'merely one of those flying reports engendered in a neighbourhood whenever events of a startling and mysterious character take place'. But other newspapers had made clear that there had been plenty of sightings of the men on Monday night; they undoubtedly existed, no matter how inconvenient that was for the legend that Platt was responsible. Additionally, the idea that the killers were Irish had first been expressed by James Whitehead, when he told Samuel Hegginbottom that an Irishman was lying on the Bradburys' floor; it had not originated with Platt.

Hirst interpreted the inquest as an investigation into Platt, overlooking that his presence there was simply to establish whether

Charles Mullen was one of the three men. As such, Hirst was critical of the coroner's conduct, arguing that he should have called more witnesses or questioned Platt more closely. And Hirst tried – none too convincingly – to dismantle his suspect's testimony. He said that Platt had attempted to stoke up suspicion against the men, for example by claiming that one kept his face hidden (which Hirst argued, rather implausibly, merely meant that he was looking in the direction he was travelling). Platt's description of the men as 'skulking' – which actually came from Butterworth's pen, was not used in any other inquest reports, and was probably not a word directly used by Platt at the inquest – was intended to incriminate them (other witnesses agreed the Irishmen walked slowly). And Platt must have invented Thomas Bradbury's statement that one of the men had previously stolen from Bill's o'Jack's because had it been true he would have questioned his friend extensively owing to 'the characteristics of the class to which they both belonged'.

The criticisms of Platt mounted up to the point of ridiculousness as Hirst tried to find anything in the *Manchester Courier* that cast doubt on him. Platt should have told the coroner more. Platt would have known that William Bradbury was alone and an 'easy victim'. Platt took a suspiciously circuitous route home to Primrose which might have allowed him to double back to attack the old man. (Why bother to accompany Thomas if that were the case? And the route was easily explained by his admitted visit to another public house on his way home.) Hirst concluded that Platt's account 'appears to be thoroughly untrustworthy in its details, as well as its main features', and was put together perhaps to divert attention from Platt himself. He noted, in passing, that the 'facts' which contradict Platt were 'well known in the district'. But unless everyone had access to the *Manchester Courier* article, how would they have known about the evidence given at the inquest? Through the insignificant figure of a weaver known as 'Owd Kedlock'? Or did Hirst mean that everyone had their reasons for suspecting Platt, and these 'facts' did not match the newspaper reports from 1832?

And nowhere was there even the slightest hint of an answer to the most important question: *why* would Platt have wanted to murder the Bradburys? All that was offered – by Hirst or 'the district' – was a desire for 'plunder', which even Hirst noted was 'inadequate' as a motive.

The only potentially valuable information (which was not in the *Manchester Courier* and therefore must have been part of the stories Hirst had heard) concerned Thomas's movements on that night – he spent time with his family, as was his custom, and would have left no earlier than 10 pm. The only contemporary newspaper to mention a visit by Thomas to his family was *Wheeler's Manchester Chronicl*e (which gave a departure time of 8:30 pm). But even this apparently important evidence was deployed against Platt – he would have known Thomas's routine and therefore would have been able to take advantage of his absence from home. Hirst also mentioned the candles that Thomas bought from the shop – which are not present in the *Manchester Courier*, so Hirst must have learned of them through his local sources – although he mistakenly says they were scattered on the floor when they were actually found crushed in Thomas's pocket.

Hirst conceded that 'whether Reuben Platt was engaged in the crime or not will never be known', and that the suspicions against him were based on little more than 'the old man's indistinct mutterings', but 'some people thought hardly of him as long as he lived'. At this point, he finally left Platt alone after nine pages of slightly rambling and convoluted discussion. Later in his narrative, when discussing the Red Bredburys as suspects, Hirst once more returned to Platt, suggesting that he had told them that William Bradbury was home alone.

These doubts about Platt seem absurd, but they proved very influential. Almost every subsequent writer about the murders cast Platt as a prime suspect, purely because of what was assumed to be Joseph Bradbury's conclusion. None of the criticism of Platt's evidence stands up to scrutiny and Hirst could offer no hint of a motive for Platt to attempt robbery or murder. Nor did he display any sign of being in a fight as he told everyone his story in the days after the murder. It is extraordinarily unlikely he was involved.

But if Hirst can be believed, local gossip strongly connected Platt with the murders in subsequent years. Such rumours would have paid little heed to actual evidence, especially as memories faded. Hirst's attempts to twist that evidence to match the stories might have been an attempt to overcome the problems encountered when the case against Platt was examined in any depth. Perhaps his expansion of Joseph Bradbury's articles was even driven by the reaction in Saddleworth when they appeared in the *Oldham Chronicle* in 1870: an outraged but irrational insistence that the *Manchester Chronicle* articles did not tell the real story.

Hirst told another story that had been passed down but had not been mentioned in any contemporary account. He suggested the initial reported number of five Irishmen in the *Courier* version of Smith's letter might have arisen because 'people from about Nook Steer were amongst the earliest visitors to the place after the alarm had been made', and some of them had seen five men the previous evening. The men had been passing a game of pitch-and-toss when one was accidentally struck by a coin and refused to return it. An angry confrontation resulted, which was still taking place as Bradbury and Platt passed by. According to Hirst: 'The five men – whether Irishmen or not does not seem to be certain, but they would be likely enough to be regarded as such merely on the ground of being strangers – passed on in the opposite direction, as if going to Holmfirth, along the road leading nearly past Bill's o'Jack's. They had called at an alehouse at Road End, then kept by a person named Hinchcliffe, where they had a pint or a quart of beer'.

Hirst suggested that the 'earliest visitors' from Nook Steer might have begun the rumours that Irishmen were involved which he admitted would weaken the case against Platt as it might have explained the origin of the notion that William Bradbury said 'Pats' and rule out 'Platts'. (Again, he was unaware that it was James Whitehead who first said that the culprits were Irish or that the very early versions of the story, as told by Thomas Smith, blamed Irishmen, even before the idea that William said 'Pats' was widely known.) And at this point, Hirst also reluctantly retold the story (which originated from Butterworth) of how three men had supposedly been seen at Hooley Hill; but in his last attempt to buttress the story against Platt, he argued that the men could not have been those seen at Bill's o'Jack's as it would have been too far to travel in the time between sightings.

Whether these five men and their argument over pitch-and-toss existed, whether they were a distorted memory of Platt's three Irish workers, or whether they were an invention, their story should not be taken too seriously as its first appearance in print was not until 1871. It does not provide any evidence to untangle the events surrounding the murders. Instead, it is another indication of the gossip that continued to circulate almost four decades later.

Having finished with Platt, Hirst moved on to the other main suspects: the Red Bredburys. In this case, he was building on what Joseph Bradbury had already written.

Bradbury's original 'sketch' had some details about the Red Bredburys which had never been published before and which apparently came from the written manuscripts in the possession of 'Owd Kedlock'. These included an account of the trial of 'Red Tom Bredbury': 'It is asserted that upon the adjournment of the first trial, 'Red Tom' spoke out boldly in public, and said that Tom o'Bill's o'Jack's would not appear against him at the sessions; and the sequel proved him right'. Joseph Bradbury then made his only real comment regarding the murders: 'Whether or not "Red Tom" instigated the Irishmen to commit the murder we have no means of knowing, but the Saddleworth people even yet associate them together, and it is said that when "Red Tom" departed this life, near Holmfirth, some years since, he died in extraordinary agony, and constantly mentioning the murder of the two Bradburys. Whoever committed the crime they still remain undiscovered and the murder of Bill o'Jack's will probably remain one of the mysteries of the age'.

This was the first published suggestion that one of the Red Bredburys had openly threatened Thomas Bradbury beforehand and that one of them 'died in agony'; no previous account, including the 1851 article in the *Huddersfield Chronicle*, mentioned this. But it was a cautious summary by Joseph Bradbury, perhaps based on what the manuscripts said. It also contradicted the *Huddersfield Chronicle*, which said that the suspect was called James Bradbury, not 'Red Tom'. And, of course, because the contents and author of the manuscripts are unknown, little credence can be attached to the claim.

Hirst considerably expanded on this in *Saddleworth Sketches* but named different people. His version said that the Red Bredbury suspects, unrelated to the victims and living in Hoowood, were the son and grandson of 'Red Tom': James (known as Jamie) Bradbury and his son Joe. The former had a reputation as a 'desperate poacher' who had a hostile relationship with the gamekeepers on the moors. Hirst described him as 'a strong, powerful man, rough, rude and uncultivated, a hard drinker, a hard hitter, and an implacable foe'. In contrast, Joe was 'silent, strong, dogged, ignorant, and capable of being led into any kind of mischief by one who, like his father, had ascendancy over him'.*

Hirst's version of the case against the Red Bredburys combined the account of Joseph Bradbury with the story in the *Manchester Courier* but added some new details that probably reflected what was being said in Saddleworth afterwards. He admitted that there was no direct evidence against them but outlined the circumstantial account.

* The 1841 census records a man called Joseph Bradbury, born around 1806, living in Austonley. There is nothing to prove or disprove a connection with the Red Bredburys. However, a baptismal record for a Joseph Bradbury at Holmfirth in 1807 names his father as Lot Bradbury. The biblical name Lot *might* indicate a connection with Job Bradbury and a *possible* connection with the Red Bredburys, but would establish that this Joseph was not the son of James Bradbury.

The Red Bradburys had been seen at the public house by St Chads on the Monday night. The following day (which Hirst inaccurately stated to be the first day of the Sessions), Jamie Bradbury set out for Pontefract, but on the way passed through Meltham before eight o'clock in the morning, and while in that village he was heard to declare that Tom o'Bill's would never appear against him at Pontefract, supplementing it with the remark that 'he believed he was in hell by that time'. This story had never previously appeared in print and was clearly a legend from years later; if there had been a witness to this in 1832, the magistrates would not have freed the Red Bredburys.

In Hirst's version, Thomas was to have been the prosecutor (which was not mentioned in any of the 1832 reports), an unlikely state of affairs given his own uncertain reputation and the lack of an incentive for him to take a fellow poacher to court. Hirst argued that the Red Bredburys would have had a strong motive for murder as they would have received considerable punishment had they been found guilty of poaching.

He added more rumour that had attached itself to the tale: 'It was also believed in the neighbourhood by many people that when they returned home, sometime after midnight [early on Tuesday 3 April], their blood-stained garments were washed by Jamie's eldest daughter, and it was remarked that the coat which her father had worn on the day of the murder was never seen again by any of the neighbours'. This was not the only part supposedly played by the daughter; she also provided an alibi: 'She was ready with her testimony, of course, to the effect that she saw nothing suspicious about them when they came home on Monday night, the 2nd of April, and no doubt she was equally confident that the hour at which they reached Hoowood was only just late enough to enable them to travel from the Church Inn, in Saddleworth, without stopping anywhere'.

When Jamie and Joe were acquitted, owing to an absence of evidence, they and their 'party' were 'jubilant at the result, and their journey home from Huddersfield had some of the features of a triumphal procession. The reader may be quite certain that they did not forget to call at every public house on their road from Huddersfield'.

Hirst concluded his tale by echoing the rumour reported in the *Huddersfield Chronicle* saying that Jamie never set foot in another public house, the implication being that he was afraid of giving himself away while drunk. Also, 'it was rumoured strongly in the neighbourhood that when one of the "Red Bredburys" was on his deathbed he was anxious to confess his crimes, but that the family would not on any account allow anyone to enter the room where he lay'.

The case as presented in *Saddleworth Sketches* against the Red Bredburys was a strong one, but it was far removed from reality. The numerous additions and embellishments were probably the result of years of gossip, and might have featured some exaggeration on the part of Hirst or his local sources. Unlike the theory about Platt, the case against the Red Bredburys had apparent support in the pages of the *Manchester Courier*. But the relevant article about those suspects had been sensationalised in 1832; the original caution in the story as written by Butterworth had been removed by the time it was published.

But the crux of the argument was that the Red Bredburys – in this version in the person of Jamie Bradbury – could not have known of the murders by the time they reached Pontefract on Tuesday morning unless they were the guilty parties. In reality, they never appeared at those Sessions and the magistrates learned of the murders via a different route. In the face of these simple facts, no matter how much the story was embroidered afterwards, the case against the Red Bredburys – whether that was Tom, James, Jamie, or Joe – evaporates.

If the tale of the Red Bredburys that appeared in *Saddleworth Sketches* had little actual value for anyone hoping to solve the murders, it does provide evidence of the survival of those long-lasting rumours first reported in the *Huddersfield Chronicle* in 1851. The writing of Hirst and Joseph Bradbury cemented those rumours as virtual facts and no subsequent account of the murder would be complete without the Red Bredburys as the lead suspects.

One important but little-known later work, written around twenty years later, was the unpublished 'Annals of Saddleworth', written by Joseph Brierley in the 1890s, which also featured the Red Bredburys.

However, their inclusion in the 'Annals' is complicated. Brierley openly attributed some of his tale to *Saddleworth Sketches* (although he dismissed the notion that the Red Bredburys would have proclaimed their guilt for all to hear.) But he also presented information that had never appeared elsewhere. We know that *some* of his information came from a man called Matthew Marsh, a contemporary of William and Thomas Bradbury, but it is unclear which parts come from Marsh and which from Brierley. Therefore what Brierley had to say about the Red Bredburys could have been written contemporaneously with the murders*, or it could be gossip accumulated from various sources and recorded many years after.

Brierley wrote that Thomas and his cousin Jamie Bradbury (the familial relationship was explicitly made) used to cause trouble together on Saddleworth Moor but both were pseudo-gamekeepers/watchmen for small areas of privately owned land. Jamie had been warned by Thomas to keep off the land for which he was responsible, but had been ignored by his cousin. Thomas therefore reported Jamie, but for trespass rather than poaching. This sounds plausible and would explain where the idea of a revenge killing originated, but the provenance of the story is too uncertain to make it a reliable source.

Suspicion certainly lingered around the Red Bredburys because they feature in Joseph Thornton's *New Saddleworth Sketches* (published posthumously in 1967). It is not clear when these sketches were written (the author lived from 1846 until 1924) but Thornton mentioned how the murders had been discussed for 'many generations'. As he referred to his own work as 'sketches' (not just in the title), he must have been writing after Joseph Bradbury's book had been published in 1871.

* As Marsh apparently recorded an exact date of 13 August 1831 for Thomas Bradbury's encounter with the workers in the hut near the Isle of Skye, some of the information in the 'Annals' could even pre-date the murders. But we do not know which parts of Brierley's account originate with Marsh, nor even when Marsh recorded the information used in the 'Annals'.

Discussing a motive for the murder, Thornton said: 'Seemingly, it was the sequel to a poaching affair which occasioned one Jamie Bradshaw [*sic*] and another to be summoned to appear before the magistrate on the following court day. This action aroused great interest among pleasure-seekers, moorland ramblers, and lovers of game… In a taproom full of company Bradshaw proposed to lay any amount of money against any person in the room that neither Bill o'Jack's nor Tom o'Bill's would ever appear against him, and this statement proved to be true. Is it not strange that nothing more definite was done in connection with it?' Thornton had confused the names of the suspects, and appeared unaware that they were examined by magistrates and released. Clearly he was not using *Saddleworth Sketches* as his source, so he must have been referring to a different version of the same story still in circulation when he was writing. And the confusion over the name of the suspects could have arisen easily enough because Brierley, in his 'Annals', noted that Jamie Bradbury was also known as 'Jammy o'Bradshaw's'. Perhaps Thornton knew of this name and mistook Bradshaw for a surname.

If we cannot be certain of the reliability of any of these stories, they do reveal one important fact: there clearly were several alternative sources of information about the Red Bredburys. The version recorded in *Saddleworth Sketches* was not the only one, even if it subsequently became dominant. And these variants survived long enough to be recorded in the 'Annals of Saddleworth' in the 1890s and by Thornton before 1924. Once again, the legend was clearly thriving long after the events upon which it was based.

And Hirst provided more evidence of the way the legend had grown. In the last part of his expanded section, he dismissed other rumours he had heard. For example, Thomas was so strong that there must have been at least three men involved in his killing; Hirst countered that the Red Bredburys were strong enough to manage both Thomas and his father, particularly with the element of surprise. Another suggestion was that there were traces of blood leading from the inn along the moors which came from one of the attackers wounded in the fight. This had grown to incorporate the notion that the wounded man had been killed by his fellow murderers and buried in secret on the moors to facilitate a more rapid escape. But Hirst noted that there was no reliable authority for either version. There had also been rumours of confessions: that a man had confessed in Ireland (which Hirst said had 'proved to be a baseless story' upon investigation); that one of the Red Bredburys had made a deathbed confession in Australia (Hirst dismissed this because neither man went to Australia, although he said that the daughter who had provided the alibi had emigrated there after her marriage; in reality this was probably a distortion of the 1853 'confession' story). Although these stories must be discounted as reliable evidence, they show the changing nature of the legend and how it had developed since 1832.

With the end of Hirst's section, *Saddleworth Sketches* jarringly resumed Joseph Bradbury's gentle wanderings through the region. Despite the warning in the publisher's preface, subsequent writers were too excited by the evidence and interpretation offered by Hirst to notice the discordance in style and intent, and Bradbury was credited with making a great contribution to the case. In reality, he had written little of the relevant chapter but the changes made his book extremely popular and lent it a kind of immortality. Nevertheless, his own writing proved valuable for later historians of Saddleworth because of his descriptions of the area. Jonathan Hirst died in 1876 and if he was indeed the author of those seventeen pages, never received any credit for his contribution to the legend of Bill's o'Jack's.

Another man with a passing association died the following year. 'Owd Kedlock' had achieved a degree of local fame following his appearance in 'Bill's o'Jack's and Greenfield'. In a later one of his original articles, Joseph Bradbury visited 'Owd Kedlock's' house ('Kedlock Ho'), and discovered that Kedlock had read the article in which he starred. Although coming across as something of a cliché, not least for Bradbury's decision to write his speech in dialect, 'Owd Kedlock' did exist. His real name was James Horsfall, but he had been known as 'Owd Kedlock'* since he and some friends had formed the 'Kedlock Club' in the 1830s or 1840s as a mock-political society. Before that, Horsfall/Kedlock had been known as 'Lung Yers' (Long Ears). Born in Saddleworth sometime between 1795 and 1805, he had worked as a weaver in Deanhead all his life until he achieved a certain degree of fame through the pen of Joseph Bradbury. It did not help him much; by the time *Saddleworth Sketches* appeared, Horsfall's children were dead and around that time he moved in with a grandson of doubtful character in Diggle. His life savings were used up by this man and Horsfall was taken into Saddleworth Workhouse, where he died in 1877.†

But 'Owd Kedlock' played an important role in the reinvention of the story for *Saddleworth Sketches*. By providing copies of the *Manchester Courier* articles to Joseph Bradbury, he accidentally made that newspaper the dominant source in all future retellings and shaped the case argued by Jonathan Hirst.

Kedlock and Hirst, although it was probably not their intention, also launched Bradbury's career as a writer. The success of *Saddleworth Sketches* – even though the most famous parts were by someone else – allowed Bradbury to spend the next twenty years writing fiction. By the mid-1870s, he had contributed to various magazines and published several long-forgotten novels such as *The Terror of the Peak, The Ardernes of Arden Hall,* and *The Honour of his House or the Knight of Heywood Hall.* In 1874 he relocated to the Isle of Man and settled in Laxey, where he was the only doctor. His literary interests switched mainly to local history; he researched ancient remains on the Isle of Man and became a member of the Antiquarian Society but continued to write

* 'Kedlock' or 'skedlock' was the local name given to ragwort; 'skedlock carts' were a form of wheelbarrow or small wagon used by children to collect rushes and plants.

† His burial record says that he was 82 when he died in 1877, but census records give a birthdate of 1805. On the 1851 census, Horsfall and his family lived at Fairbanks, where William Bradbury had once worked.

fiction, including *A Lost Name*, *Grace Barton*, and *Juan Beg, the Laxey Miner*. The 1881 census records him living in Laxey with his wife Annie and a servant; by 1891 he and his wife had taken in an eleven-year-old 'waif' called William Thomas Soar.

Bradbury's last book, published shortly before his death, was *First Davenport of Bramhill*, a novel about a knight, set in the fifteenth century. It is the only one of Bradbury's books – other than *Saddleworth Sketches* – for which any contemporary reaction survives. The *Saturday Review* in 1894 slammed it as 'a story of portentous dullness at considerable length', full of clichés and containing characters who 'behave as no human beings ever could have behaved'. For those wondering if such harsh words were warranted, the opening paragraph of the book gives a flavour of Bradbury's style:

> 'The bell in St Mary's tower had just struck the hour of curfew; the darkening night was drawing on apace; the last beams of the setting sun had just forsaken the heights above the Mersey on an eventful evening in the early part of the winter of the year 1460, when two pedestrians of very dissimilar appearance were observed to be winding their slow and gradual course along an ancient and in some parts well-sheltered footpath which led from the elevated and scattered hamlet of Heaton-Mersey to the banks of the river below, and so forward into the town of Stockport.'

Whatever his merits as an author, Bradbury was highly regarded in Laxey, not least for his reputation for taking care of the poor. The *Isle of Man Times* recorded that Bradbury died on 1 May 1895. An accident in the frosts of the previous January had left him housebound and 'not being in robust health', he became ill in the cold of that winter. His 'ailments were chiefly of a bronchial nature' and eventually he died from them. But even then, Bradbury was still chiefly known as the author of the extremely successful *Saddleworth Sketches*, published twenty-four years earlier.

That remains the case today, even if he never wrote the words which altered forever the way in which the story of Bill's o'Jack's was told.

What was it that *Saddleworth Sketches* achieved? Assuming Hirst did not invent everything through some inexplicable vendetta against the memories of certain individuals, he told us what people had been saying: the rumour that had hardened into suspicion that either Platt or the Red Bredburys were responsible. Perhaps that is the value of the book – Hirst was recording the shape of the gossip. But until he wrote it down, and tweaked it using the sources provided by Joseph Bradbury and 'Owd Kedlock', it had been local gossip, likely unfamiliar to anyone outside Saddleworth. Like all such stories spread by word of mouth, it was fluid, easily altered, and transmutable; we can even occasionally see how, when and why it changed. Afterwards, the rumour might as well have been set in stone. One particular version of the tale was transmitted and informed opinion and theory for all those who were to tell the story in future, long after the gossipers had died.

Such an outcome was not planned by Bradbury nor by Hirst, who probably just wanted to sell as many books as possible and was not too concerned by the accuracy of his work. But when the book came out to considerable acclaim in 1871, the families of Thomas Bradbury and Reuben Platt still lived in Saddleworth. For some, the book might have produced one or two uncomfortable moments. But the landlords of Bill's o'Jack's, still doing healthy trade, must have rubbed their hands with glee.

'Morbid Pilgrimage'

The story of the killing of Bill o'Jack's and Tom o'Bill's far outlived every one of the characters whom it touched. There are a few surviving traces of the people involved in the events, but their fates are largely unknown. For example, it is uncertain what happened to Amelia Winterbottom after her part in the proceedings ended. We have no way of knowing if she was affected by what she had seen, but assuming that her real name was Mary, she continued to live with her mother Nancy at Fernlee until the latter's death in 1863. In the 1850s she gave birth to two children, Henrietta (1852) and Benjamin (1858), but never married; we do not know the identity of their father. Mary probably – but not certainly – died at the age of 49 in 1869, and her children continued to live with her father.

Of the other early witnesses, James Whitehead still lived at Binn Green when the 1841 census was taken, at which time he was around 60 years old, with his wife Betty and four children: Henry, Joseph, Esther and William. Butterworth's account of the inquest had described Whitehead as an old man who was hard to hear when he spoke, but he was only 52 at the time. He died in 1850, aged around 70. And Samuel Hegginbottom, the surgeon, died in 1845 at the age of 52.

Edwin Butterworth, whose reporting of the murders proved so influential, continued to work in journalism until the 1840s. His attempts to establish contacts with newspapers in York and London were unsuccessful; work began to dry up as his local stories attracted less interest. Following the failure of the family business that he had taken over, he became increasingly impoverished and his health began to fail. As he also became less reliable in submitting reports, editors cut him loose; for example, his contract with *Wheeler's Manchester Chronicle* was terminated in April 1848. Just a few weeks later, he died from typhus.

And what of Reuben Platt, a man whose reputation seems to have suffered even if he was unjustly suspected? By the time of the 1841 census, when he was around 50 years old, he still lived at Primrose with his wife Alice. Several other Platt families lived in nearby houses. He and his wife had at least three children (one of whom died young), but none lived with them in 1841. Platt died in 1849, aged 59, and was buried in the same churchyard as the Bradburys. His widow moved to Uppermill, where she ran a lodging house according to the 1851 census. She lived alone at the time of the 1861 census, and in 1871 her address was St Mary's Gate, Uppermill; this is next to what is now Uppermill Library. She died in 1874 at the age of 82. She had lived long enough to read *Saddleworth Sketches*; if this book accurately described suspicion against her husband, she had endured forty years of rumours and whispering. At the very least, she must have received a few questioning looks after the unlikely theories began to circulate once again in 1871.

The Bradbury family are easy enough to trace. Nancy Winterbottom, who died in 1863, was the last-surviving child of William Bradbury; her siblings William* and Mary died in 1854 and 1860 respectively. All three of Thomas's brothers and sisters had lived into their eighties like their father.

The family of Thomas Bradbury continued to be associated with Bill's o'Jack's for some time. After the death of William, the beer house was run by a man called James Woods but around 1840, Thomas's eldest son Augustus Bradbury took over. Not long after, he successfully applied for the full licence that his grandfather had lost, and it was around this time that Bill's o'Jack's changed its official name from

* William and his wife were interred with the two murder victims in St Chad's churchyard.

the Cherry Tree to The Moorcock, by which it was known until its demolition.

It is worth spending a little longer with Augustus. He had married Sarah Ann Bradbury (from another of the many Bradbury families in the area) in early April 1836; two months later, his first child, Sarah, was baptised, offering echoes of the hurried marriage of his own parents. Sarah died at the age of 3. The couple had seven other children who survived into adulthood.

One interesting snapshot survives of life at Bill's o'Jack's with the Bradburys. In October 1855, an article was published in *Household World*, a magazine edited by Charles Dickens. Written by the novelist Geraldine Jewsbury, the piece was about her visit to the Great Saddleworth Exhibition. She wrote of the slightly oppressive atmosphere at the edge of the moors: 'The changing shadows on the hills and the deep clear purple mist that filled the valley did not hinder the view, but gave it a strangely solemn aspect. No human life or human bustle seemed able to assert itself – the silence of nature swallowed it up'.

The trip incorporated a meal at Bill's o'Jack's; the disappearance of all signs of life as her group approached the building, and the nature of the hills surrounding it made her describe the place as 'the very spot where a murderer might take refuge to hide himself'. She gave a condensed and inaccurate account of the murders from twenty-four years previously – for example she said that William was found 'dead upon the kitchen hearth' – and explained that the inn was still run by the same family. Jewsbury was greeted by Ann Bradbury (unnamed in the article) who lived there with Augustus and his wife. Ann was 'now an old woman, but erect and alert. She was extremely kind and friendly; but I fancied that she looked as if she had seen a horror which put a separation between her and the rest of the world'. The inn was busy at the time of Jewsbury's visit as 'parties of country holiday-makers' were there, but the author was impressed by the food and hospitality, even though she 'could not suppress a shudder' at being so close to the site of a murder, although 'no traces of the tragedy were visible'.

Ann Bradbury died in 1864 at the age of 73; she was buried alongside her husband in the famous grave at St Chad's.

Augustus's son opened his own establishment, the Clarence Hotel, in 1861. Augustus and his family moved there shortly afterwards, and Augustus took over as landlord; it was through this position that he was mentioned by Joseph Bradbury in the pages of *Saddleworth Sketches*. How many of the rumours in that book had he heard? How many of those stories had been passed around the various public houses that he ran? And what did he think of it all? He lived until 1885, when he was 74 years old. With the death of Augustus's brother Francis in 1895, everyone from the family who had been alive at the time of the murders was gone.

One of the central characters in the story, however, lived on for some time. Although memories faded, a very solid reminder lingered on the road to Holmfirth: Bill's o'Jack's itself. In the years after the murders, the interior was extensively remodelled with an extension added, although the 'murder room' was untouched. The staircase was moved and a living room, inaccessible to the public, created.

The visit of Jewsbury is a good indicator of the changing reactions to the surrounding scene; what had been a romantic spectacle in Georgian times had come to be viewed as wilder and intimidating by the middle of the nineteenth century. And yet visitors continued to come to Bill's o'Jack's, drawn not only by the location but also by its gruesome reputation. A locally born woman called Betty Beaumont, who moved to the United States but came home to visit in the 1860s, wrote that hundreds of people visited each summer 'with as much interest as if the sad occurrence were a thing of yesterday'. The landlords – including Augustus Bradbury – continued to expand the premises, exploiting the growing phenomenon of tea gardens as a tourist attraction by adding an outbuilding which doubled as a tearoom and dancing shed; entertainments included outdoor quoits and wrestling. Coaches and, later in the century, railways helped to attract the crowds.

But the biggest attraction continued to be the events that had taken place in 1832. Even publications such as *Pigot's Directory* in 1834 and *Slater's Directory* in 1851 mentioned the notorious murder in their entries for Bill's o'Jack's. As late as 1899, a visiting journalist noted the abiding popularity of the story: 'It still obtains as a favourite fireside story for many miles' radius around Saddleworth'. The contemporary landlord, Alfred Schofield, told the journalist that the inn had been unchanged since 1832 – which was not true, unless he meant the murder room – and the latter ate his lunch sitting at a bench supposedly from the time of William Bradbury. For those who were sufficiently interested, Schofield sold an eight-page booklet for a penny that told the story of the murders. A similar leaflet was also on sale in 1912.

In fact, the various landlords were happy to cash in on the interest. For example, souvenir plates and jugs, with images of the house – labelled 'Bill's o'Jack's April 2nd 1832' – were produced. Stains were ascribed to blood from the two murdered men (for example when a writer for the *Ashton Reporter* visited in 1855, he declined an invitation to see them) and landlords retold the story to any interested party. Postcards were printed that featured artefacts related to the crime: the blood-stained family Bible, the murderous spade, a mug supposedly belonging to William Bradbury, the brewer's licence from 1828 and the remains of the pistol.

If business was helped by the legacy of the murders, the location soon became an increasingly famous holiday resort in its own right. An outing to Bill's o'Jack's had developed into a local tradition and a constant stream of visitors came to enjoy the sights, the facilities and, of course, the backstory. Parties came from as far as Manchester, whether these were Sunday school outings or holidaying factory workers. Some groups were very large indeed. For example in 1857, hundreds of members of secular societies travelled from nearby towns including Hyde, Rochdale, Honley and Huddersfield; in 1868, over three hundred students and teachers came from Meltham. Even these numbers were dwarfed in March 1894 when over 3000 people – most of whom called at the famous public house – travelled by train from Oldham to Greenfield.

Many of these visitors brought food, but others were served at Bill's o'Jack's; sometimes they brought their own entertainment such as brass bands. Joseph Bradbury, in the section of *Saddleworth Sketches* that he *did* write, observed that at the height of its popular season, 'this lovely inn' might receive on any one day 'fifty or sixty conveyances of all kinds, shapes and colours and laden with happy pleasure parties'. And a report in 1889 described Bill's o'Jack's as 'a famous place for ham and eggs and creature comforts'. Easter was the busiest time; takings from that period could sometimes meet expenses for the rest of the year. And it was always a popular destination for walkers and, in later years, cyclists.

Bill's o'Jack's also played a large role in the Saddleworth Wakes, an annual holiday week that took place each August, in which textile mills and other industrial places of work shut down. The wakes had a religious origin and similar traditions were celebrated throughout the north-west. Festivities included games, dancing and drinking. There was also a much older tradition of having hand-drawn rushcarts (known locally as a 'skedlock' or 'kedlock' carts, from which 'Owd Kedlock' took his name), to transport fresh rushes. Originally used to cover the church floor, by the 1870s, these were sold to landlords of public houses or for horse bedding. At least some form of these celebrations took place before the murder of the Bradburys, but the Saddleworth Wakes really took off from the 1850s. Many of the events incorporated Bill's o'Jack's; it was even noted in 1857 that on the Sunday of Saddleworth Wakes, hundreds of people were solemnly reading the epitaph over the grave of the two Bradburys. By 1860 the final day of the festivities had become known as the 'Bill's o'Jack's Wakes'; events were held in and around the famous public house and drew enormous crowds each year.

In short, the venue had become so well-known that newspaper coverage often described it as 'far-famed Bill's o'Jack's'. No better summary can be written than that provided by a journalist who visited in late 1899. He described it as a 'paradise' for anyone wanting a picnic and noted that its main patrons were 'the toilers in the cotton factories' and people from larger towns in other counties; because of the scenery, 'no other outing is anything like so popular with the lower and middle-class orders'.

The popularity of the venue – and its association with the murder – survived even after the Bradbury family finally left. Augustus Bradbury was still the licensee of Bill's o'Jack's at the time of the 1861 census, but in 1862, it was taken over by Joseph Waterhouse. Perhaps there is a hint of something else going on; Waterhouse was fined in 1863 for opening on a Sunday, when twenty people were found in the dancing shed and more in the parlour. And Joseph Bradbury stiffly observed in 1870 that 'the large dancing *"shed"* is a disgrace to the establishment'. Joseph Waterhouse died in 1864 and his widow took over; on the 1871 census Martha Waterhouse is listed as a licensed victualler and a farmer of ten acres.

In 1875, Bill's o'Jack's was bought by the Ashton and District Water Board, which was in the process of building reservoirs in the area; the Yeoman Hey Reservoir, located very near to Bill's o'Jack's, was completed in 1880. Martha Waterhouse was still the licensee, and her business continued to be good. For example, around one hundred gamekeepers and drivers from a nearby estate had a seasonal meal and celebration there in January 1876. By 1878, James Schofield had taken over.

Yet Bill's o'Jack's continued to operate on the fringes of the law and respectability. In 1878 there were several violent confrontations between English and Irish workers who were involved in constructing reservoirs; Schofield had to confine each nationality to separate rooms to avoid trouble. The following year, police discovered Schofield serving men late on a Sunday night. And Schofield's widow – who took over after his death in 1883 – came to the attention of the authorities in 1888 when police interrupted a cock fight on the grounds. She had neither organised nor watched the event, but her establishment went on a watchlist. And these were not the only concerns; in the 1890s the house became known as a place for poachers to gather, leading to concerns from local gamekeepers.

Although Bill's o'Jack's changed hands several times over the following years and continued to do good business, the Water Board had plans to demolish the building as early as 1901. Only its popularity saved it. Similar plans were aired in 1915 before once again being halted by an outcry. But by 1937, the Board claimed that the sewerage system from the building had begun to contaminate the Yeoman Hey Reservoir; not everyone was convinced, and no evidence was ever publicly presented. In addition there were concerns from the Board that users of the public house were trespassing on its property. Therefore Bill's o'Jack's closed for the final time on 21 April 1937 – the final landlord being a man called Charlie Haigh – and it was demolished that July. Even in those last years, as a flurry of newspaper articles appeared to mark the end of an era, it was still remembered for what happened in 1832; one article described it as having 'long been the "Mecca" of a morbid pilgrimage by people eager to see the spot'.

It was not just the building that served as a reminder of what happened. Violent events – such as an attack on the landlord of the Royal Oak in Delph by burglars in 1856 – were compared to the events of 1832. As late as 1912, the discovery of the body of an excise officer on the moors (an apparent suicide) reminded one writer of the Bill's o'Jack's story. The murders maintained their hold on the imagination of locals even after the setting had been demolished. The William the Fourth public house, where the inquest had been held, continued to display a bloodstained plank which supposedly came from the bed of William Bradbury; the Victoria in Holmfirth had what it described as an axe used in the killing.

Writing in 1932, George Halstead Whittaker mentioned that 'relics' were held by 'various families' in the area and occasionally gathered together; he also knew of the postcard photograph taken of these items. An article marking the centenary of the killings mentioned that the bloodstained Bible was believed to be in the possession of the descendants of the victims in Greenfield. Except for the pistol, the fate of which is unknown, all the 'relics' are currently kept in Saddleworth Museum, although no-one is certain how they came to be there.

But by the time Whittaker was writing, a century after the murders, the story had become detached from its physical remains and continued to drift further and further from the evidence. Having been sent on its way by a firm push from *Saddleworth Sketches*, Bill's o'Jack's had entered the realm of legend. In the years that followed, there was no shortage of strange theories about who had killed the Bradburys.

'Such interest did their tragic end excite'

The biggest problem for anyone attempting a serious history of the Bill's o'Jack's murders has always been the lack of reliable new evidence after April 1832, putting aside the dubious 'confessions'. The only apparently fresh material was that within *Saddleworth Sketches*; because readers would have been unaware that it had been culled from speculation and gossip, it was accepted unquestioningly. Perhaps even more damagingly, those newspaper articles provided by 'Owd Kedlock' became the only sources in wide circulation; the slight distortions and shifts in emphasis made by the editor of the *Manchester Courier* in 1832 had become part of the definitive account.

But not everyone wanted history. The association of murder and fiction was already well-established when the Bradburys died. Writing about crime had become fashionable, part of the wider phenomenon mocked by Thomas De Quincey's 'On Murder Considered as one of the Fine Arts'. Famous murders were retold in cheap novels; penny fiction had become increasingly popular, in particular 'Penny Bloods' which romanticised famous criminals – such as the highwayman Dick Turpin – and recast stories as melodrama. Eugene Aram, hanged in 1759, was a particularly 'popular' murderer around the time the Bradburys died. In reality a petty criminal who had killed a man in Knaresborough over debts, Aram was transformed in verse and prose into a tragic figure grappling with his own sinful nature. In 1828, he was the subject of a ballad, *The Dream of Eugene Aram*, by Thomas Hood. And in 1832 his story was told both in a melodramatic novel, *Eugene Aram*, by Edward Bulwer-Lytton, and a supposedly factual book (actually based on Bulwer-Lytton's novel) called *The Trial and Life of Eugene Aram*. It was against this backdrop that Bill's o'Jack's became an inspiration for art and entertainment.

Almost immediately, the murders were transformed into a play. There were many precedents for such a rapid adaptation; the Radlett and Red Barn Murders, for example, were dramatised on stage many times, in some cases even before the accused had been on trial. So it was probably not an enormous surprise when, in May 1832, *The Greenfield Tragedy, or the Unknown Assassins** was performed at Oldham Theatre. Three groups of suspects were presented: three Irishmen, three 'gypsies' and three poachers, all of whom were at the inn on the night of the murders; the actual murder was completed with the stage darkened so the audience never saw who did it. *Wheeler's Manchester Chronicle* described the performance as 'a solemn tragedy, with new and appropriate scenery, machinery, dresses and decorations' but complained that 'the cast of characters is rather inappropriate, so far as exterior is concerned. The unfortunate Tom o'Bill's, who measured about seven feet, is represented by a *three-feet* votary of the sock and the buskin' (i.e. an actor). The play was never submitted to the Lord Chamberlain for approval so was technically unlicensed and illegal. Around the same time, a dramatised version of the murders was performed at the Saddleworth Wakes.

The story influenced other art forms too. Part of the reason John Mitchell was arrested in 1845 was that he had reminded someone of a song about the murders. There were doubtless many other songs, and other artists were likewise inspired. Poets writing about the spectacular scenery around Greenfield added lines about the perceived 'sickness' or 'terror' of the crime, and the associated loss of innocence.

* *Wheeler's Manchester Chronicle* gave the title as *The Greenfield Assassins, or Murders of Bill o'Jack's and Tom o'Bill's.*

Perhaps the most famous poem was that carved onto the Bradbury memorial in St Chad's churchyard.

Throughout the land wherever news is read
Intelligence of their sad end has spread.
Those now who talk of far-famed Greenfield hills
Will think of Bill o'Jack's and Tom o'Bill's.

Such interest did their tragic end excite
That, ere they were removed from human sight,
Thousands on thousands came to see
The bloody scene of catastrophe.

One house, one business, and one bed.
And one most shocking death they had.
One funeral came, one inquest past.
And now one grave they have at last.

In some ways, the poem on the gravestone – reproduced countless times in writing about the murders – has become just as famous as the events it describes, but it is not clear how or when it was written. The author was a local poet called James Platt, born around 1791. In *Saddleworth Sketches*, Joseph Bradbury was slightly equivocal in naming Platt as the creator, merely noting that he 'claimed authorship of the epitaph … but it is not inserted amongst his works published since his death'. However, Platt was not a prolific author, and those 'works published since his death' consisted of a single, posthumous, 393-page volume of writing from 1865, most of which was heavily religious in character. He also produced unpublished reports for the Saddleworth Branch Bible Society. When he was not writing, Platt worked as a schoolmaster at Boarhurst School from 1814 until the 1830s; there are hints in later writing that he was not a terribly popular teacher, whose 'awful rule' consisted of 'swaying the birch'. From 1840, he was elected to the Board of Guardians for Saddleworth Workhouse, located near Dobcross and in 1854 he became clerk to the Board of Guardians, a role he held until his death in 1864.

Platt wrote the famous epitaph while working as a schoolmaster, which would suggest a date before 1840; perhaps even very soon after the murders. Later stories suggested that Platt used to force his pupils to memorise the lines. A report from 1852 said that he omitted a fourth verse from the gravestone, as it 'did not meet the approbation of the friends of the deceased':

For suffering thus were they the vilest then?
This foolish notion reader do not cherish.
Hear what the Saviour still proclaims to men:
Unless ye all repent, ye too must likewise perish.

The Bill's o'Jack's murders also inspired other forms of writing. Perhaps the strangest was a 12-page book published anonymously in 1860, laboriously titled *Bill O'Jack's: A Conversation Between Dick the Carder and John the Slubber, on Sunday Afternoon, about William Bradbury and Thomas his Son*. It consisted of an imagined conversation between two men in which one man criticised another for his non-attendance at church, but which digressed into a discussion of the murders. Because the focus was religious instruction rather than solving crime, the only conclusion drawn by the two participants in the conversation was that the unknown murderers would one day face judgment from a higher authority.

It did not take long for newspapers to revisit the murders. The story was mentioned in passing relatively frequently, for example after the 1856 burglary at the Royal Oak in Delph, but sometimes it was retold in full. One of the earliest such examples was an 1852 article in the *Huddersfield Chronicle* that presented the main details of the murders without offering any solutions, and summarised the original articles from the *Manchester Guardian*, with some additional colourful description. Reuben Platt's evidence and William Bradbury's utterance of 'Pats' were completely omitted. However, two details were included – that the items Thomas bought at the shop were 'strewed about the house in all directions' and that 'the pistol had previously belonged to the Bradbury family' – which contradicted earlier accounts and were probably dramatic inventions.

Following the publication of *Saddleworth Sketches*, the emphasis altered considerably. For example, an account in the *Manchester Courier* in 1887, part of a series entitled 'Lancashire Episodes: Historic, Romantic and Tragic', was almost entirely based on *Saddleworth Sketches*. The author made accusations against Reuben Platt and the Red Bredburys, was dismissive of the effectiveness of the inquest and repeated several accusations from the book. The article ended with a dramatic poem, which perhaps indicates the intended effect.

Saddleworth Sketches was also the basis for a curious hybrid account of the murders – part history, part novel, part educational instruction – published in 1902. This was a serialised story entitled 'Bill's O' Jack's', written by the journalist and socialist politician Joseph Burgess, which appeared in sixteen weekly instalments within the pages of the *Cotton Factory Times*. The solutions offered in this fictionalised account by Burgess, who had written many tales with industrial settings, largely followed those presented by Jonathan Hirst in *Saddleworth Sketches*, settling on Reuben Platt as a suspect and the Red Bredburys as the most likely culprits. But the story was set against a historical background which included factory reform; Burgess's intention was not just to revisit a still-famous murder, but also to illuminate socialist history. If we can believe the claims in advertising for the *Cotton Factory Times*, the story was an 'enormous success'.

The next substantial shift in the legend was the result of another fictionalised reimagining. In 1912, a novel was published called *Miriam: A Tale of Pole Moor and the Greenfield Hills*, written by D. F. E. Sykes, a Huddersfield author and historian who died in 1920. The somewhat melodramatic story, 'narrated' by a fictional character called Abel Holmes, is not especially relevant, but the murder of the Bradburys played a crucial role. Briefly, Holmes saved a girl called Miriam from the malign interest of Thomas Bradbury and had several subsequent encounters with the father and son before their murder, which occurred during Miriam's rescue from Bill's o'Jack's, where she was held after being kidnapped by another character.

The non-fictional details of the killings in *Miriam* largely followed *Saddleworth Sketches*, aside from the curious error – also expressed by Geraldine Jewsbury in 1855 – that William Bradbury had died in the kitchen. Although neither the Red Bredburys nor Reuben Platt made a direct appearance in *Miriam*, the rumours against these chief suspects were acknowledged. And yet the author took a very different view of the two victims than *Saddleworth Sketches*, making *them* the villains of the story:

> 'I saw the two well-known gamekeepers that all the countryside knew as Bill o'Jack's, and Tom o'Bill's, William Bradbury and Tom, his son, men of bad repute, wenchers and ale-bibbers, and never so happy as when they could get some poor devil of a weaver into trouble with his betters for snaring a rabbit or bagging a bird. Tom was a fine upstanding fellow enough, but his father had an evil face, full of malice and guile. It was a common saying that Bill made the bullets and Tom shot them.'

Such a negative view of the Bradburys had not been expressed in print before then, although it strongly resembled the description of Jamie and Joe Bredbury in *Saddleworth Sketches*.

Although the story itself was not especially original, the identity of Miriam offered a new scenario to explain the murder: she was one of the 'Burnplatters', an almost mythical people who lived in an area near Slaithwaite known as Burnt Platts or Burnt Plats. Various theories explain the unusual name of the region, of which the most plausible is that it arose from the practice of clearing the moors through regular burning.

Sykes managed to link the Burnplatters to the death of the Bradburys through some creative use of William Bradbury's supposed last words as recorded in *Saddleworth Sketches*:

> 'As a neighbour bent over [William Bradbury] he had been heard to mutter with his last breath: "Pats, Pats", or was it "Platts, Platts"?
> And which that neighbour could and would not say.
>
> Many and many a time as the years rolled by have Jim and I pondered and talked over poor old Bradbury's effort to tell who had done him to death. There was in both our minds the same thought: not Pats, not Platts, but "Burnplatts", old Tom [*sic*] had tried to gasp as he lay a-dying.'

Sykes can perhaps be forgiven for artistic licence in giving the well-worn valediction of William Bradbury yet another twist which had little basis in reality. His story was a romance in which the murder was simply a plot device; his real fascination was with the Burnplatters themselves.

In fact, he had written about them before in his 1906 *History of Huddersfield and the Valleys of the Colne, the Holme and the Dearne*. Most of his section on Burnplatters was derived from one source, an 1847 article for the *Bradford and Wakefield Observer* by George S. Phillips, part of a series called 'Walks Round Huddersfield'. Writing about 'Burn Platts', Philips said:

> 'A few years ago the inhabitants of the Platts were literally savage, living in log huts thatched with sods, and paying neither rent nor taxes. They were a community to themselves and had their own wild laws and government. They were the terror likewise of all wayfarers, and it was dangerous for any man to go amongst them alone. They lived by hunting and whiskey making; and when these failed by depredations.

> Their *legal* marriages however, were celebrated in one or other of the churches of the neighbouring villages; and on all such occasions, they marched in grand procession, adorned with ribbons, and having a fiddler at the head of them.'

Phillips explained that the community had largely broken up at the time he was writing, but the families now earned a living through 'cloth making or fancy weaving'. He also described an earlier visit he had made to the community, when he was invited into one of their huts, which were 'built of stone and mud, and at a distance have more the appearance of hovels than of human habitation'.

Sykes, in his *History of Huddersfield*, quoted from Phillips's article and remarked that these Burnplatters 'were the bogey-men of the children of those parts, and I remember that my grandmother, who resided in her early married life at Holme, not far from the seat of the Burnplatters, could find no more awful threat than "to send me to the Burnplatters"'.

Although everyone seemed to agree that the Burnplatters had all dispersed by the 1860s, there was no shortage of 'academic' interest in their origins. An idea persisted that they were 'foreigners' who had settled in the mid-eighteenth century. For example, a local historian called Walter E. Haigh suggested in 1928 that the 'small colony of foreigners', who had lived in the area from around 1750 to 1860 'in a few poor huts at Burnt Platt', were originally stragglers from the Highland Army of Prince Charles Edward Stuart ('Bonnie Prince Charlie') as it retreated from Derby. Haigh explained that the group, known as 'Duędiz' (supposedly based on the name 'Duęd' used by George II in signing proclamations against Bonnie Prince Charlie's rebels) were notorious in the area as pedlars, petty thieves and composers of crude songs; they dispersed over the years and the last of the Burnplatters' huts was pulled down in the 1860s. However, the theory does not stand up to scrutiny; subsequent research failed to uncover evidence of foreign names in local records such as parish registers, militia lists, or the 1841 census.

For Sykes, the Burnplatters were a kind of romanticised 'gypsy' and fertile ground for storytelling. It is unlikely that he genuinely thought that they were involved in the Bradbury murders. But as so often, readers latched onto anything connected to Bill's o'Jack's. Although the rest of *Miriam* was quickly forgotten, later writers have taken Sykes's storytelling device seriously and have suggested that William Bradbury was indeed trying to say 'Burnplatts'.

In reality, there is no evidence to connect the Burnplatters with the murders; on the contrary there are many issues with such a theory. Even putting aside the problem that their involvement was first suggested eighty years later, they lived over six miles from Greenfield and were unlikely to have encountered the Bradburys. And there is a distinctly legendary air about the Burnplatters. There is only one concrete account of anyone having met them: a recollection of a visit from 'a few years' before, written at a time when the community had already dispersed. Even the writer of *Miriam* remembered the Burnplatters as being a mythological 'bogeyman' used to scare children.

Those who have attempted to make them legitimate suspects have perhaps conflated the plot of *Miriam* with the account in which Thomas Bradbury overturned the hut of some Irish 'navvies', or the reports of Bradbury terrorising poachers and 'broom collectors' on Saddleworth Moor. And given the distortion of the actual evidence required to stretch William Bradbury's accusation of 'Pats' into 'Platts', a further tortuous interpretation that he was trying to say 'Burnplatts' enters the realms of the absurd. Overall, this is nothing but an imaginative idea invented by Sykes which associated a legendary murder with an equally legendary group of people. He was almost certainly not offering a serious explanation, and it should not be treated as such.

Whatever its artistic merits or the validity of its 'solution', *Miriam* influenced Alfred Denville, an actor who ran a repertory theatre company and who later became a member of Parliament for Newcastle upon Tyne Central. In 1919, he combined the theories in *Saddleworth Sketches* with the premise of *Miriam* to write a play, *Bill's o'Jack's*, which was first performed in 1919 in Oldham and in 1922 at the Theatre Royal in Ashton-under-Lyne. The characters include several Burnplatters (onc of whom is Miriam), the Red Bredburys, Abel Holmes (the main character in *Miriam*), 'Owd Kedlock' from *Saddleworth Sketches*, and – because the story opens (presumably inspired by the 'confession') with a man dying in Australia – 'an Aboriginal from Western Australia'. One newspaper enthused that Denville 'has constructed a play full of thrills out of the notorious mystery ... The author-actor claims to have given a common-sense solution of the mystery'. Denville had two culprits: the Red Bredburys, who were responsible for the injuries to William, and a Burnplatter called Patsy Mullins (played at some of the performances by Denville himself), who killed Thomas.

Other plays have also been written about the murders. In April 1911, a performance was given by a travelling theatre company at Uppermill playground, although no details survive. In 1960 *The Bill's O' Jack's Mystery* by Wylbert Kemp, a hairdresser from Huddersfield, was performed at the Oldham Coliseum; it was later repeated at Holmfirth Civic Hall in 1961 with a different cast. The original performance received a very good review in *The Stage*, which marvelled that Kemp 'should present [the story] so acceptably in terms of contemporary theatre'. In this play, the murderer was an illegitimate son of Thomas Bradbury living among the Irish workers in the area; Thomas was portrayed as a particular villain and, inevitably, gypsies made an appearance. The narrative jumped around, starting with the aftermath of the murder, returning to the time before it, and concluding with the events of 2 April 1832. The author noted at the time of the 1961 production that he had used strong language in the script, which he felt was necessary to capture the period. And the programme produced for the Holmfirth performance included a photograph of the cast mournfully gathered, in costume, around the Bradbury gravestone. The most recent play based on the murders, *The Moorcock* by Henry Livings, was performed between 23 January and 19 February 1982 at the Oldham Coliseum. In contrast to earlier plays,

The Moorcock was a musical and starred John Hallam, a nationally known actor who had appeared on television, as 'Bill Bradbury'.

A different kind of artistic depiction of the murders was created in 1936. A silent film by the Oldham Cine Society – a company that made several similar productions in the Saddleworth area – included some scenes shot in the shortly-to-be-demolished inn itself. Unfortunately, the film does not appear to survive.

Other works of fiction have also been produced about Bill's o'Jack's. In 1928, an author from London, William Groves, wrote something called 'The Bill's o'Jack's Mystery' which appeared in the September 1928 issue of *Week End Novels*. And two full-length novels about the murders have been written since *Miriam*. *The Murders at Bill's O'Jack's*, written by James Davenport and published in 1985, goes down a familiar romanticised route involving gypsies. A very different approach was adopted in 2023 by Sophie Parkes in *Out of Human Sight*. Her novel is a reimagining of what happened to Amelia Winterbottom in the years after she stumbled upon her dying relatives.

Despite the romance, gossip and speculation added to the legend after the publications of *Saddleworth Sketches* and *Miriam*, there were some serious attempts to examine the murders as history. Sometimes authors provided their own solutions to the mystery but more often simply provided an overview. For example, *Thomson's Weekly News* printed an article in 1915 as part of its 'Famous Lancashire Mysteries' series. The by-line, 'Specially Contributed by Noted Investigator', kept the author anonymous but he claimed that, while he had not been born at the time of the murders, he came across the story 'when for purposes of paralleling the incident with a similar happening, I was called upon to investigate "Bill's o'Jack's" murder'. He claimed that in so doing he 'was lucky enough to be brought into contact with a number of people who were professionally employed in trying to clear up the mystery'. Quite who these people were supposed to be – they certainly did not exist – is not clear. But the article drew from several sources and was fairly comprehensive, although it established nothing new. The author argued, as was the growing trend, that Thomas Bradbury was unpopular, had a vicious temper and was cruel. The 'investigator' mentioned the 'Irish gypsies' who collected brush from the moor and reconstructed what might have happened, blaming the three Irishmen seen heading towards Holmfirth; Thomas returned home to see them attacking his father in the corner and fought back with his fists before being overcome.

Unusually, the author absolved the Red Bredburys of blame, but muddied the waters by suggesting that one of the Irishmen had a sister who was in love with Thomas Bradbury. Even more unusually, he never used *Saddleworth Sketches* – William Bradbury's granddaughter was named Amelia rather than Mary. But the involvement of 'gypsies' and a troubled romance are indications that he might have read *Miriam*.

Another new theory emerged around ten years later. In 1926, an architect and local councillor called Alfred James Howcroft published *Tales of a Pennine People* in which he retold stories from the area around Saddleworth. In a chapter entitled 'A Moorland Mystery' he gave a straightforward retelling of the murder from 1832. The only 'new' details (which are plausible even if they don't help much) came in a description of Thomas as 'a tall muscular man of sandy complexion, devoted to sporting and the preservation of game. He had also been a fully qualified poacher in his day'. The account in this book was based largely on the contemporary articles from the *Manchester Guardian* but the author had read *Saddleworth Sketches*.

Howcroft first covered some very old ground. He cast doubt on Abraham Dawson's claim to have heard 'rough company'; he was sceptical sound would be heard through 'twenty-one-inch walls and grey slates and travel seventy yards to the road'. He concluded that Reuben Platt 'probably, mostly spoke the truth', but followed *Saddleworth Sketches* in suggesting 'his determination to drag in the Irishmen and their headgear' was strange. Howcroft also used *Saddleworth Sketches* as his source to discuss the Red Bredburys, although he dismissed the idea that they said that Thomas 'would not appear against them'.

But he also offered new interpretations. One had never been mentioned before in print but Howcroft wrote as if the theory was widely known: 'It was soberly believed by others that the two men [William and Thomas] had annihilated each other, as warranted by their temperaments'. But he – wisely – did not believe that. Instead, he offered an idea of his own: that there was a connection with Esther Porritt. He wrote: 'It was an extraordinary inquest, or rather, two inquests, first on two bodies, then on a third – three bodies in a row, all done to death – father, son and grandson'. Although Howcroft named neither the third body, nor the 'beautiful young woman' against whom a verdict of murder was returned, he was clearly referring to Esther Porritt and her dead child (who was in fact a girl). Once more, he must have used the *Manchester Guardian*, the only newspaper to make such a connection between Porritt and Thomas Bradbury.

This was followed by a long passage of slightly purple prose which gradually turned into a fictionalised account of what might have happened, based on his theory. He described a man travelling over the moors from Chapel-en-le-Frith carrying a pistol. Amid rather tedious descriptive passages, the man is never named but remembers saying goodbye to his daughter, Hester*, as she left home for the first time. But now, his daughter is a criminal and when he looks down at Bill's o'Jack's, all he sees is 'a little boy brought into his home without the wholesome joy and gladness known to honourable living'. The man arrives at the Moorcock – as Howcroft called the inn throughout – where William gets him a drink before going to bed. When Thomas arrives, he recognises the stranger and the two men fight, interrupted at one point as William tries to intervene before being struck. Having killed both men, the stranger flees, wracked with guilt and despair. Although never stated outright, the man was obviously supposed to be the father of Esther Porritt.

* The *Manchester Guardian* article on the inquest from 1832 called her Hester Porritt. Her actual name was Esther.

This account of Howcroft was the first time that Esther Porritt had been brought into the picture since 1832. Esther Porritt's father, Jonathan Porritt, lived in Chinley all his life and died in 1836, meaning he was alive at the time of the murders. And walking to Greenfield from Chinley over the moors was certainly possible, although it is roughly twenty miles. But there is no evidence to support Howcroft's theory.

The centenary of the murders produced a flurry of writing, at least some of which was intended to be accurate history. A publication called *Old Stand* featured two articles around this time. The first, published in March 1931, summarised A. J. Howcroft's theory; a second, published in February 1932 simply went over the well-established facts and followed *Saddleworth Sketches* almost exactly in suspecting Reuben Platt and the Red Bredburys.

Soon after, George Halstead Whittaker wrote one of the best summaries of the case, published in 1932 as *Bill's O'Jack's: A Moorland Mystery: Facts and Surmises*. As well as containing lengthy extracts from various newspapers and publications, including the play by Alfred Denville and the ubiquitous *Saddleworth Sketches*, the author made a coherent attempt to draw conclusions from the wide array of evidence. He also observed that, at the time he wrote, people remained as intrigued by the mystery 'as surely as though the event had been of recent date'.

Whittaker went over the facts as they were known. He ruled out, on the grounds of the 'very severe injuries to each man' that the two had fought between themselves. He theorised that Thomas was attacked and his father came to help, which is a reversal of most theories held at the time but which drew its inspiration from *Tales of a Pennine People*. Another idea was that the three men seen by Reuben Platt – he repeated the incorrect claim from *Saddleworth Sketches* that no-one but Platt had seen them – went into the inn, refused to pay and injured William in the resulting quarrel before waiting for Thomas, 'against whom they had some grudge'.

But most of his reasoning followed *Saddleworth Sketches*. Like Jonathan Hirst, he noted that Thomas Smith had not been called to the inquest; he discussed the five men recorded in that book who interrupted the game of pitch and toss; and he cast suspicion on Reuben Platt and wondered if he doubled back to 'plunder' the house. However, like Hirst he could not supply or provide a convincing motive and conceded that Platt alone was unlikely to overpower Thomas Bradbury (although this overlooked the possible advantage of both surprise and a pistol). These were not the only debts Whittaker owed to *Saddleworth Sketches*. He also included the text of the *Manchester Courier* articles as printed in that book – including the name Mary Winterbottom – and followed Hirst's line on the Red Bredburys: that one of them confessed in Australia and that 'Red Tom' died in agony near Holmfirth constantly talking about the murders. This dependence illustrated the influence that *Saddleworth Sketches* continued to have. What had been local rumour when Hirst was writing in 1871 had become accepted as fact.

Whittaker next discussed the possible connection – based on the plot of *Miriam* — with the 'Burnplatters'. But Whittaker sensibly noted that this connection was not made by anyone at the time, nor was it mentioned in *Saddleworth Sketches*. He also added some thoughts of his own about whether William said 'Pats' or 'Platts': 'It should be made clear that "Pats" a hundred years ago had a meaning more like "navvies" and did not necessarily mean Irishmen. "Pats" were navvies who lived in huts at Greenfield during the construction of the road hereabouts, which completed the turnpike from Manchester to Holmfirth.' However, the *Wheeler's Manchester Chronicle* recorded in 1832 that James Whitehead had indeed assumed 'Pats' to mean Irishmen and passed this information on to Hegginbottom.

Finally, Whittaker discussed how many attackers there were. He concluded that one person was unlikely to overcome both men and get away undetected, although it would have explained the 'savage butchery of the deed' if it was a single attacker who hated the Bradburys. Two could possibly have done it, especially if it was the Red Bredburys who wanted to stop Thomas giving evidence. Three 'is a likely number of assailants' and would point at the three Irishmen and a motive of robbery. Whittaker concluded by relating the solutions given in the stories presented in *Tales of a Pennine People*, *Miriam* and the play *Bill's o'Jack's.* Incidentally, although he quoted from *Tales of a Pennine People*, he did not identify the killer as the father of Esther Porritt nor give the motive implied by Howcroft. He was therefore likely to be unfamiliar with the supposed connection between Thomas Bradbury and Esther Porritt, especially as he included every other theory that had appeared in print. Therefore, despite his impressive array of sources, he did not have access to the *Manchester Guardian* articles.

Not long after Whittaker's book was published, an article by R. Hawkin, published in the *Yorkshire Weekly Post Illustrated* in 1935 – which, as usual, summarised the *Saddleworth Sketches* – concluded, perhaps unsurprisingly, that Reuben Platt was the most likely murderer, with theft as the motive. However, Hawkin observed that if robbery might explain the attack on William, it would not have provided a reason to kill Thomas except to prevent his identification of the attackers; if revenge against Thomas was the motive, there was no need to kill William.

After the centenary had passed, the outpouring of new material slowed. The next serious attempt to examine the case was a chapter in *Saddleworth Murder and Mystery* by Vera Winterbottom, published in 1960. The author, using a slightly different approach, began by setting the historical context that had been forgotten in most retellings: that there was social unrest at the time; that trade was depressed and the cost of living increasing after the wars of the late eighteenth and early nineteenth centuries; that a drought in 1826 had caused unemployment; that 'machine-wrecking riots' were spreading as mechanised mills threatened the traditional industry of handloom weaving; that the Great Reform Bill passed in 1832. She mentioned enclosure, believing it to be a factor in the murders because people still viewed the land as belonging to them as it had before enclosure. Winterbottom also set the scene at Greenfield – that it had no railway until 1848 and no police force until 1858 and the only means of rapid travel were the canals or the turnpike road, the coach fares of which were too expensive for most locals.

Winterbottom then related the facts about the murders. Her main source, inevitably, was *Saddleworth Sketches*. She named William's granddaughter as 'Mary Winterbottom' and therefore cannot have had access to other versions of the newspaper reports. Her explanations also took their inspiration from *Saddleworth Sketches* – the Red Bredburys were likely involved and Jamie Bradbury's daughter played a role – but she disagreed that Reuben Platt was a realistic suspect. But her account then devolved into myth and legend. She discussed the 'many lawless characters in the district': the 'navigators' working on the new roads and canals who had moved into Delph and Diggle, making the towns like 'Western outposts of Gold Rush days' through their wildness; 'wandering tribes of gypsies, and the "Burnplatters" or "Platts"', whom she linked with the story of Thomas Bradbury demanding money for access to collect broom. While still reliant on *Saddleworth Sketches*, she summarised the strength of case against each major suspect or group. The Red Bredburys were the most likely attackers. Reuben Platt had no motive except theft and was unlikely to overcome both men on his own. Alternative possibilities are examined and dismissed, including that the father and son wounded each other. Winterbottom ended by outlining the outstanding questions in the case and concluded that the murderer or murderers would never be known.

In 1967, an article appeared in the *Edgar Wallace Mystery Magazine* written by Geoffrey Whiteley called 'The Murders at the Moorcock'. The ten-page article gave a thorough background to the story; the author appears to have used Vera Winterbottom's book as his only source, and therefore followed the facts as given by *Saddleworth Sketches*. Whiteley agreed that Reuben Platt was unlikely to have been involved – particularly as he had no need to incriminate himself by saying that he saw Thomas Bradbury the night before – but argued that none of the theories really fitted the facts. He therefore followed the idea first suggested by Alfred Denville, that two different parties were responsible: William was attacked by thieves while Thomas was killed by the Red Bredburys.

None of the writing between 1832 and 1967 succeeded in being (or perhaps was ever intended to be) a serious study of the murders. Each author, particularly after the publication of *Saddleworth Sketches*, was too reliant on a single source. But finally, this changed in the 1970s and 1980s through the work of the Saddleworth Historical Society and the efforts of two men. In this period, three articles were printed in the *Saddleworth Historical Society Bulletin*, two written by Neil Barrow in the Summer 1978 and Autumn 1978 editions, and a further one by Barrow and Terry Wyke in 1987. The first two outlined newly rediscovered evidence, about the Australian 'confession' and information regarding the character of the Bradburys. The 1987 article went over the entire history of the case, its coverage and some possibilities for further investigation, including the role of Esther Porritt and the Burnplatters. This was by far the most rigorous examination of the evidence and circumstances of the case that had ever been attempted.

Even today, fascination with the unsolved murder has not faded. Bill's o'Jack's is occasionally mentioned on websites which investigate old mysteries. There have been threads on Reddit, YouTube videos, and Bill's o'Jack's has even occasionally reached the mainstream news, for example being mentioned in a *Mirror* article about 'pub murders' and a story on the BBC News website about unsolved English murders. The Bradburys have found their way into recent books of historical tales, although few of these reach the level of detail of earlier writing and usually follow one of the standard interpretations, with the inevitable appearances of the Red Bredburys, Reuben Platt or the Burnplatters. Probably the best recent writing on the subject is on a blog by wessyman137 which covers the tale admirably and succinctly and displays recent photographs of the many places involved, including the site on which Bill's o'Jack's stood.

But in all these thousands and thousands of words, no-one has yet come up with the definitive theory that explains what happened that night (or morning) in April 1832.

Conclusions

As the story continued to be told and the legend grew over the years, the world did not stand still. When Bill's o'Jack's closed for the last time in 1937, Britain – and Saddleworth – had changed enormously since the time of the murders. Work in the north of England was still concentrated in factories, but little else would have been recognisable to William and Thomas Bradbury. The long and fiercely resisted struggle that had begun with the reform movement and the scandal of Peterloo had been largely won; now all adults over the age of 21 had the vote. The battle over enclosure was largely forgotten; the lands around Saddleworth had been in private hands for a long time. Three reservoirs were by then situated in the valley where Bill's o'Jack's had done business.

Photography – still an experimental process in 1832 and not commercially viable for several years after – had captured Bill's o'Jack's for posterity; it had been filmed by the Oldham Cine Society. Technology had been invented that would have seemed like magic to the Bradburys. By the time that Bill's o'Jack's finally ceased business, it was possible to watch television, to travel by car and even by aeroplane. There had been a devastating world war in which far more people died than would have been dreamed of during the wars of the early nineteenth century. But people still talked about Bill o'Jack's and Tom o'Bill's. The story was embellished and added to and reanalysed, but it survived. And all that time, visitors came to St Chads and gazed at the famous memorial.

Since then, perhaps the mystery has faded, and the legend has become fixed; there have been no new expansions since the addition of 'Burnplatters'. The murders are still a local legend, although much diminished. The intense discussion that coincided with the centenary has ended. But today it is possible to get closer to the deaths of the Bradburys than at any point since 1832. The story has migrated online to websites fascinated with unsolved mysteries. Newspapers from that time can be accessed from the internet; even the letter from the Saddleworth magistrates to the Home Office can be read without leaving home, via a download from the National Archives. The remarkable Saddleworth Historical Society have made a huge amount of material available, along with careful analysis and discussion, through their journal.

Even so, the story still has a physical presence in the area, not just in the excellent Saddleworth Museum. Several buildings survive that would have been recognised by the Bradburys: Daniel Whitehead's shop closed a long time ago but the house in which it operated still stands; so too does the William the Fourth public house, which continues to do business under the same name; and the house at Sidebank where Ann Bradbury and Thomas's children lived is still there. Local rumour suggests that some of the stone from Bill's o'Jack's was recycled in the construction of new houses. Apart from the presence of the reservoirs and a few newer plantations, a visitor to the Greenfield hills today would see much of what the Bradburys saw.

However, there is one inescapable fact. More than 190 years after William and Thomas Bradbury were murdered, it is certain that whoever is responsible will never be discovered. In stories like this, it is natural for the reader to want an answer, but that is not possible here. It is tempting to opt for a neat solution: that one of those long-standing suspects was responsible, such as the Red Bredburys or Reuben Platt; or a man like Charles Mullen or John Mitchell or the hawker who 'confessed' in Australia. But it is equally, or perhaps more likely, that the killer was someone whose name was never associated with the story, someone who anonymously lived out their lives away from scrutiny.

Such a crime today would probably be easily solved through scientific analysis or DNA samples. Back in 1832, none of this was possible; even fingerprint evidence was many decades away from being used in criminal investigation. Even putting aside the lack of an investigating authority, it would have been almost impossible to find the culprit based on what was found at the scene. Other famous murders had been solved, but largely owing to factors – such as the location of the body or the discovery of evidence that incriminated an individual – that did not apply to Bill's o'Jack's. When the killer failed to be found in the immediate aftermath, they could only realistically have been caught and convicted if an accomplice had turned King's Evidence; such an accomplice provided the evidence that convicted John Thurtell in the Radlett Murder. This was how many murderers were caught and explained the incentive of a possible pardon that was often offered by the Home Office. Otherwise, there was simply nothing to work with; and when no such witness came forward in the Bill's o'Jack's case, there was little prospect of a conviction. In a way, it was the perfect crime for 1832.

As for the question of why the Bradburys were killed, that too is unanswerable. But there was no shortage of motivations, ranging from theft to revenge. Perhaps it was a poaching dispute, as suspected when the Red Bredburys attracted suspicion in 1832; maybe there was some untraceable link to enclosure or political disputes. Possibly even some connection with the dispute between William Bradbury and his landlord. Or an association with the Yeomanry Cavalry. Or something related to Thomas Bradbury's personal life, particularly if he fathered at least one child with Esther Porritt.

But in the end, it is necessary to accept that the truth will never be known.

However, the story lives on. When I went to Saddleworth Museum in early 2019, a woman was visiting because she had discovered she was related to the Bradburys. And the path to the grave in St Chad's churchyard is remarkably clear in what remains a wildly overgrown cemetery. On one rainy day I visited, the surrounding grass was trodden down as if I were not the only person to call.

The memorial is still easy to read, even if the stone is showing signs of age. Since photographs were taken for Vera Winterbottom's book in 1960 and to publicise Wylbert Kemp's play in 1961, the grave has suffered considerable damage. Of the metal rail surrounding the slab, intact in 1961, only a small section survives. A stone panel on the left-hand side has also disappeared. Maybe souvenir hunters have forcibly struck.

Below the poem, brief memorials are inscribed to William Bradbury junior and his wife, and to Thomas Bradbury's wife, all of whom were buried alongside the murder victims. There is enough space for the addition of more names – which might have been the original intention – but the grave has been undisturbed since Ann Bradbury's death in 1864.

The poem is a continuing reminder of how violently the two men died. And this violence has been the key to the longevity of the story of the Bill's o'Jack's murders. Thomas Bradbury cannot have suspected, as he set off down the hill on 2 April 1832, that his walk with Reuben Platt would still be the subject of discussion nearly two hundred years later. Nor that he and his father were about to achieve a macabre kind of immortality. Whatever it was that happened over the next twelve hours, we can still but only guess.

Acknowledgements

I would like to thank all the staff at Saddleworth Museum in Uppermill, but particularly Peter Fox, for their invaluable help throughout my inquiries and for the images within this book. I would also like to thank Tim Campbell-Green who was a huge help when this project got underway in 2019.

Mike Buckley of the Saddleworth Historical Society was kind enough to spend time explaining some of the local background to the case and providing some of the maps within this book. He also patiently answered my follow-up questions via email. And the resources placed online by the Saddleworth Historical Society have been immensely useful.

The staff at the Boston Spa Reading Room of the British Library were always helpful and friendly, particularly with the mysteries of microfilm readers. So too, over a very long period, were the staff at Oldham Local Studies and Archives where most of the information about Edwin Butterworth originated. And the staff at West Yorkshire History Centre in Wakefield offered every assistance in locating information about enclosure and deciphering the relevant records.

Dr Catriona Kennedy at the University of York was able to suggest some good background material about the Irish in England. Philip Spooner of West Street Antiques kindly responded to my request for information about the pistol found at Bill's o'Jack's. Sophie Parkes similarly answered my questions by email.

And I would like to thank Sarah-Beth Watkins at Pen and Sword for her assistance in putting all this together.

Bibliography

Archival

'Register of enrolment B44', Saddleworth Enclosure Award, 1834, QD5/3/B44; Quarter Sessions of the West Riding of Yorkshire (Q); West Yorkshire Archive Service, Wakefield.

Folio 125–129, Letter from the magistrates of Pontefract, Yorkshire, concerning the murder of William Bradbury and his son, Thomas, occupiers of the Beer House in Saddleworth, Yorkshire. A sworn statement given by Ammon Platt is enclosed and a handbill offering a reward of £100 to be paid on conviction of any of the murderers. The government is asked to offer a further reward. Letter annotated 'Gazetted in Thursday's Gazette April 10 – with offer of £100 and pardon'. 5 April, HO 64/3/46; Home Office: Criminal (Rewards and Pardons) Correspondence and Secret Service Reports; The National Archives of the UK (TNA).

Butterworth Papers

Edwin Butterworth, 'Reports of Occurrences or Local News', notebook, 12 March – 19 April 1832, BUT/F/7; The Butterworth Papers (1787–1859) of Edwin Butterworth (1812–1848) and James Butterworth (1771–1837) of Oldham, Lancashire; Oldham Studies and Archives, Oldham.

- 'Inhuman Murder' (initial account)
- 'Murders in Saddleworth' (inquest)

- 'Child Murder' (Esther Porritt)
- 'Saddleworth – Wednesday' (arrest at Rotherham)
- 'Saddleworth Murder' (reward available)
- 'Murders in Saddleworth' (revenge motive/broom cutters/Red Bredburys/collection for widow)

Edwin Butterworth, 'Oldham Reports', notebook, 20 April – 30 June 1832, BUT/F/8; The Butterworth Papers (1787–1859) of Edwin Butterworth (1812–1848) and James Butterworth (1771–1837) of Oldham, Lancashire; Oldham Studies and Archives, Oldham.

- 'Murders in Saddleworth' (Release of Red Bredburys).

Edwin Butterworth, Register of Oldham News No. 3, notebook, 12 March – 19 April 1832, BUT/F/4; The Butterworth Papers (1787–1859) of Edwin Butterworth (1812–1848) and James Butterworth (1771–1837) of Oldham, Lancashire; Oldham Studies and Archives, Oldham.

- 'Murders at Saddleworth' (abridged inquest).

Edwin Butterworth, 'Newspaper Account Book: All newspapers', account book, 1831–32, BUT/I/B/1/2; The Butterworth Papers (1787–1859) of Edwin Butterworth (1812–1848) and James Butterworth (1771–1837) of Oldham, Lancashire; Oldham Studies and Archives, Oldham.

'The Annals of Saddleworth', historical notes re: Saddleworth, with notes of 19th cent local meetings; stamped with H Brierley, Hill View Terrace, Delph 1892-1894; HEW/MF/6 (No. 40); Oldham Studies and Archives, Oldham.

Newspaper Reports

Initial reports:

'Horrid Murder near Oldham', *Liverpool Mercury*, 6 April 1832, p. 8.

'Horrid Murders in Saddleworth', *Manchester Times*, 7 April 1832, p. 3.
'Horrid Murder', *Manchester Courier*, 7 April 1832, p. 3.
'Barbarous Murders and Robbery', *Leeds Mercury*, 7 April 1832, p. 3.
'Horrible Murder in Saddleworth', *Manchester Guardian*, 7 April 1832, p. 3.
'Murders at Dobcross', *Wheeler's Manchester Chronicle*, 7 April 1832, pp. 2–3

Inquest reports:

'The Saddleworth Murders', *Liverpool Mercury*, 13 April 1832, p. 8.
'The Saddleworth Murders', *Manchester Times*, 14 April 1832, p. 4.
'The Murders in Saddleworth', *Manchester Courier*, 14 April 1832, p. 3.
'Saddleworth Murders', *Leeds Mercury*, 14 April 1832, p. 2.
'The Late Murders in Greenfield', *Manchester Guardian*, 14 April 1832, p. 3.
'The Late Murders at Greenfield', *Wheeler's Manchester Chronicle*, 14 April 1832, p. 2.

Books and Journals

Altick, Richard D. *Victorian Studies in Scarlet*. London: Dent, 1972.
Barrow, Neil. 'Bill's o'Jack's' in *Saddleworth Historical Society Bulletin* Vol. 8, no. 2 (1978).
Barrow, Neil. 'Bill's o'Jack's: Further Evidence' in *Saddleworth Historical Society Bulletin* Vol. 8, no. 3 (1978).
Barrow, Neil and Wyke, Terry. '"Savagely Murdered in an Unusually Horrid Manner." Bill o'Jack's Revisited' in *Saddleworth Historical Society Bulletin* Vol. 17, no. 1-2 (1987).
Bentley, David J. *English Criminal Justice in the Nineteenth Century*. London: Hambledon Press, 1998.
Bradbury, Joseph. *Saddleworth Sketches*. Oldham: Hirst and Rennie, 1871.
Buckley, Mike, Harrison, David, Petford, Alan. *Mapping Saddleworth: Volume I, Printed Maps of the Parish 1771–1894*. Uppermill: Saddleworth Historical Society, 2007.

Buckley, Mike, Harrison, David, Petford, Alan. *Mapping Saddleworth: Volume II, Manuscript Maps of the Parish 1625-1822*. Uppermill: Saddleworth Historical Society, 2010.

Corfield, Penelope J. *The Georgians: The Deeds and Misdeeds of 18th-Century Britain*. New Haven: Yale University Press, 2022.

Emsley, Clive. *Crime and Society in England 1750–1900*. Harlow: Longman 2010.

Fisher, Pamela Jane. 'The Politics of Sudden Death: The Office and Role of the Coroner in England and Wales, 1726–1888'. Unpublished PhD thesis, University of Leicester (2007).

Flanders, Judith. *The Invention of Murder: How the Victorians Revelled in Death and Detection and Created Modern Crime*. London: HarperPress, 2011.

Hilton, Boyd. *A Mad Bad and Dangerous People?: England 1783–1846*. Oxford: Oxford University Press, 2006

Howcroft, Alfred James. *Tales of a Pennine People*. Oldham: H.C. Lee, Whitehead, 1923.

Magee, Rob *Saddleworth Pubs and Their Licensees c.1674–1998*. Manchester: Neil Richardson, 1998.

Sykes, D. F. E. *Miriam: A Tale of Pole Moor and the Greenfield Hills*. Original edition Huddersfield (unknown publisher), 1912; online edition, produced by John Parkinson: Project Gutenburg, 2017.

Thornton, Joseph. *New Saddleworth Sketches*. Manchester: The Holt Publishing Service, 1967.

Whittaker, George Halstead. *Bill's O'Jack's. A Moorland Mystery. Facts and Surmises. Collated by G. H. Whittaker*. Stalybridge: G. Whittaker & Sons, 1932.

Wyke, Terry. 'Locating the "Far Famed Bill's o'Jack's"' in *Saddleworth Historical Society Bulletin* Vol. 50, no. 2 (2020).

Notes

Introduction

For the history of St Chad, see 'St Chad Saddleworth – Parish Church', The Church of England in Saddleworth: https://www.cofeinsaddleworth.org.uk/st-chad-saddleworth-parish-church.

Some of the many books to discuss the Bradbury grave include: Kenneth Lindley, *Graves and Graveyards* (London: Routledge and Kegan Paul, 1972), p. 34; Nigel Rees, *Epitaphs: A Dictionary of Grave Epigrams and Memorial Eloquence* (London: Bloomsbury, 1993), p. 34 (this also cites two studies from 1899 and 1980); William Atkins, *The Moor: a Journey Into the English Wilderness* (London: Faber and Faber, 2015), pp. 128–29.

The Morning After

For the history of the Bill's o'Jack's public house, and its earlier name, see Magee, p. 37. The description from 1828 comes from *Pigot and Co's National Commercial Directory for 1828–9* (London and Manchester: J Pigot & Co, 1828), pp. 1057–58.The three quotations about the area are from *Wheeler's Manchester* Chronicle, 7 April ('beauty and grandeur'); *Manchester Guardian*, 7 April ('the traveller finds himself'); and Butterworth 'Murders in Saddleworth' (inquest, BUT/F/7) ('the wildest, most barren…').

The description of the events of the morning of 3 April is largely drawn from the reports on the inquest. Any particular details about sourcing are given in the text. Of the specific details, the door being closed comes from *Wheeler's Manchester Chronicle*, 14 April; the description of the room comes from Thomas Smith's letter in *Liverpool Mercury* 6 April and *Manchester Courier* 7 April. Bradbury's reply that his son had been present was reported in Butterworth 'Murders in Saddleworth' (inquest, BUT/F/7); Whitehead's description of their being an 'Irishman' lying injured comes from *Manchester Guardian*, 14 April. The details about James Whitehead come from the 1841 census, accessed via Ancestry.com.

A Tumultuous Time

For the general background to the Georgian period, the growth of industry, and the population explosion, see Hilton, pp. 1–12, 15 and Corfield, p. 90. For a discussion of the fear and optimism, see Corfield pp. 43–66. For the growing public disorder associated with political grievances, see Corfield pp. 185–91. For the Reform Act, see Hilton, pp. 420–37.

For the growth of the wool industry in Saddleworth, see Bernard Barnes, 'Early Woollen Mills in a Pennine Parish: Saddleworth and the Upper Tame Valley' in *Saddleworth Historical Society Bulletin 13*, No. 2 (1983), pp. 24–38. For the improvement of transport in the region, see Wilfred Theakstone, 'Saddleworth' in *Manchester Geographies*, ed. Wilfred Theakstone (Manchester: Manchester Geographical Society, 2017), pp. 97–99. For the increase in Saddleworth's population and the effects of the collapse in the textile trade during the wars with France, see G. Woodhead, 'The "Peterloo Massacre" and the Saddleworth Connection' in *Saddleworth Historical Society Bulletin 32*, No. 1 (2002), pp. 3–10. The population figures come from the 1841 Census of Great Britain: *Abstracts of the Answers and Returns made pursuant to Acts 3 & 4 Vict. C. 99, and 4 Vict. C. 7, intituled respectively 'An Act for taking an Account of the Population of Great Britain', and 'An Act to amend the Acts of the last Session for taking an Account of the Population'.*

Enumeration Abstract, 1841. Part I England and Wales and Islands in the British Seas. (1843 xxii (496) 1), Great Britain Historical GIS Project (2017) 'Great Britain Historical GIS'. University of Portsmouth.

For the grievances in Saddleworth, see A. J. Brooke, 'The Working Class of Saddleworth in the Industrial Revolution 1795–1842 (Part one)' in *Saddleworth Historical Society Bulletin 10*, No. 2 (1980), pp. 24–39; A. J. Brooke, 'The Working Class of Saddleworth in the Industrial Revolution 1795–1842 (Part two)' in *Saddleworth Historical Society Bulletin 10*, No. 3 (1980), pp. 45–49. For poverty and the food riots in the area, see Alan Booth, 'Food Riots in the North-West of England 1790–1801' in *Past & Present*, No. 77 (1977), pp. 84–107 (http://www.jstor.org/stable/650388); 'Distress and Food Riots in Saddleworth 1795–1812' in *Saddleworth Historical Society Bulletin 43*, No. 3 (1984), pp. 38–41.

The study of Peterloo is a huge area, and there was no place to go into it in detail here. There have been numerous books and articles about it, and there are several excellent websites. But the Saddleworth connection, including its reputation as a political hotbed, is explored in Mike Buckley, 'The Saddleworth Casualties of Peterloo' in *Saddleworth Historical Society Bulletin* 49, No. 3 (2019), pp. 73–85; and G. Woodhead, 'The "Peterloo Massacre" and the Saddleworth Connection' in *Saddleworth Historical Society Bulletin 32*, No. 1 (2002), pp. 3–10.

Bill o'Jack's and Tom o'Bill's

For the literacy figures derived from marriage certificates, see *Second Annual Report of the Registrar-General of Births, Deaths, and Marriages, in England* (London: HMSO, 1840), pp. 8–9. For a broader discussion of literacy in this period, see David Vincent, 'The Modern History of Literacy' in John L. Rury and Eileen Tamura (eds.) *The Oxford Handbook of the History of Education* (Oxford: University Press, 2019), pp. 507–522. For a discussion of trends, see W. B. Stephens, 'Literacy in England, Scotland, and Wales, 1500–1900' in *History of Education Quarterly* 30, no. 4 (1990), pp. 545–71. (https://doi.org/10.2307/368946.)

The Bradbury Bible can be viewed at Saddleworth Museum.

The announcement of Mary Bradbury's death appeared in the *Manchester Courier*, 17 March 1827, p. 3.

The bankruptcy of the clothier, William Bradbury, was mentioned in *The London Gazette*, No. 16, 176, 27 August 1808, p. 1,178; see also, for example, 'Bankrupts', *General Evening Post*, 7 July 1808, p. 1.

For the turnpike road, see 'Greenfield and Shepley Lane Head Turnpike Road', Huddersfield Exposed: https://huddersfield.exposed/wiki/Greenfield_and_Shepley_Lane_Head_Turnpike_Road. See also the map from 1822 in *Mapping Saddleworth II*, pp. 202–03.

For the history of Bill's o'Jack's, see Magee, p. 37. Magee, incidentally, suggested that William Bradbury was a 'crack shot' and 'a bit of a poacher' in his youth; but he gave no sources and this has not been repeated anywhere else. The Shooter's Arms is named in Edward Baines, *History, Directory & Gazetteer of The County of York. Vol I: West Riding* (Leeds: Edward Baines, 1822), p. 268. By 1828, it was listed as Bill's o'Jack's in *Pigot and Co.'s National Commercial Directory for 1828–9* (London and Manchester: J Pigot & Co, 1828), pp. 1057–58.

The quotation from James Butterworth, and the information about the origins of Bill's o'Jack's are taken from Terry Wyke (2020), pp. 36–37. See also the background information in *Wheeler's Manchester Chronicle*, 7 April, which also includes the detail about the beer brewing by the Bradburys and describes the scenario in which the father and son were evicted from their home around 1830. For the Georgian relationship with beer and alcohol, see Hilton, pp. 576–77. Information regarding the Beer Act also comes from: Peter Fox, 'Saddleworth's Beer Houses' in *Saddleworth Historical Society Bulletin 41*, No. 4 (2011), pp. 98–106; Nicholas Mason, '"The Sovereign People Are in a Beastly State": The Beer Act of 1830 and Victorian Discourse on Working-Class Drunkenness' in *Victorian Literature and Culture* 29, No. 1 (2001), pp. 109–27 (http://www.jstor.org/stable/25058542).

For an overview of enclosure, particularly in this period, see Hilton, pp. 8–9; 'Enclosing the Land', UK Parliament, 19 November 2014:

https://www.parliament.uk/about/living-heritage/transformingsociety/towncountry/landscape/overview/enclosingland/. For an overview of the effects on Saddleworth, see Wilfred Theakstone, 'Saddleworth' in *Manchester Geographies*, ed. Wilfred Theakstone (Manchester: Manchester Geographical Society, 2017), pp. 97–100. But most of the detail regarding the long process of enclosure in early nineteenth century Saddleworth was kindly provided by Mick Buckley, although any mistakes are mine. See also *Mapping Saddleworth I*, p. 14.

For Ralph Fletcher, the Enclosure Commissioner, see *Saddleworth Historical Society Bulletin* 10, No. 4 (1980), pp. 69, 76. For the process of finding his replacement, see for example 'Saddleworth Inclosure', *Leeds Intelligencer*, 8 March 1832, p. 4. For the signatures of attendees at the meeting, see 'Register of enrolment B44', QD5/3/B44.

For Thomas Bradbury's employment, see *Wheeler's Manchester Chronicle*, 7 April. For his possible involvement in Peterloo, see TS11/1056 Statement of Captain Tench dated 13 January 1820, via Peterloo 1819: https://peterloo1819.co.uk/app/uploads/2019/06/TS11-1056-Tench.pdf.

For Thomas's reputation: details from George Shaw's diary come from Barrow, 'Bill's o'Jack's', p. 20. Newspaper accounts of the poisoning of the dogs can be seen, for example, in 'Atrocious Villainy', *Manchester Courier*, 29 August 1829, p. 3; 'Unexampled Villainy', *Sheffield Independent*, 29 August 1829, p. 2. For the story of Matthew Marsh, see 'The Annals of Saddleworth' (details above) and Barrow, 'Bill's o'Jack's: Further Evidence', pp. 37–39.

For Joseph Brierley of Delph (the likely author of 'The Annals of Saddleworth'), see 'Delph Mechanics and Literary Institute 1855–1954' in *Saddleworth Historical Society Bulletin* 2, No. 1 (1972), p.4; 'The Flint Implements Controversy' in *Saddleworth Historical Society Bulletin* 11, No. 2 (1981), p. 27. For the alternative suggestion that Henry Brierley was the author, see *Saddleworth Historical Society Bulletin* 1, No. 4 (1971), p. 3; nothing is known of Henry Brierley.

There is another possible family link to poaching. A man called William Bradbury was involved in poaching in March 1798. We know this because a meeting was held at Dobcross, looking into the possibility of refunding fines for breach of the Game Laws at which it was decided that William Bradbury should not receive anything back. Unfortunately, no further details are available and so there is no indication (as usual) whether this is our William Bradbury. But a family tradition of poaching would not be implausible. See Alfred Howcroft, *History of the Chapelry and Church of Saddleworth and the Township of Quick* (Oldham: Hirst and Rennie, 1915), p. 118. For the discussion of poaching on Saddleworth Moor a few years later, see 'Saddleworth', *Leeds Mercury*, 18 August 1838, p. 5. For details of poaching in general, see John E. Archer, 'Poaching Gangs and Violence: The Urban-Rural Divide in Nineteenth-Century Lancashire' in *The British Journal of Criminology* 39, no. 1 (1999): pp. 25–38 (http://www.jstor.org/stable/23638042). For a description of the two men at the time of their death, see *Wheeler's Manchester Chronicle,* 7 April.

'Men of obscure birth and imperfect education'

For Edwin Butterworth, see Michael Winstanley, 'News from Oldham: Edwin Butterworth and the Manchester Press, 1829–1848' in *Manchester Region History Review* 4 no. 1 (1990), pp. 3–10. For the alterations and text from his notebooks, see BUT/F/7. For his accounts of stories sold, see BUT/I/B/1/2 (full reference given above).

For literacy rates and the impact on reading/newspapers, see Corfield, p. 115, 1 and Hilton pp. 15 and 20. For newspaper circulation, see Moira Goff, 'Early History of the English Newspaper', *17th and 18th Century Burney Newspapers Collection* (Detroit: Gale, 2007). For newspapers in general, including unstamped newspapers, see Jean Chalaby, *The Invention of Journalism* (Basingstoke: Palgrave Macmillan, 1998), pp. 7–31. For the purposes of newspapers (and the origin of the word 'journalist'), see Matthew Rubery, *The Novelty of Newspapers: Victorian Fiction After the Invention of the News* (Oxford: University Press, 2009), pp. 3–10. For journalists in this period, and their social background, see Andrew Marr, *My Trade: A Short History of British Journalism* (London: Pan Macmillan, 2009), pp. 10–12. This also includes the quotes from Sir Walter Scott and the *London Review*.

For the murder of Timothy Marr, the murder of William Weare, the Red Barn Murder and Burke and Hare Murders, see Flanders, pp. 1–75. See also Altick, pp. 17–40. For details about Hannah Brown, see Altick, pp. 37–40. For De Quincey's 'On Murder…', see for example Altick, pp. 23–24, 305.

For statistics on murder, see Bentley, pp. 17–18; Emsley, p. 283. For the murder of Thomas Patrick, see James Moore, *Murder at the Inn: a History of Crime in Britain's Pubs and Hotels* (Stroud : The History Press, 2015), p. 25; Andrew Begent, '"And may the Lord have mercy on your soul … Amen": Executions at Springfield Prison, Chelmsford 1827–1914', *History Notebook*, No. 32, Essex Police Museum: https://www.essex.police.uk/SysSiteAssets/media/downloads/essex/about-us/museum/research/history-notebooks/32.pdf.

For newspapers in Saddleworth and the habit of 'recycling', see Corfield, pp. 179–80; Howard Lambert, 'Saddleworth Notices and Reports from the Leeds Intelligencer: Part 1, 1755–1780' in *Saddleworth Historical Society Bulletin 47*, No. 1 (2017), pp. 19–20. For the other Saddleworth cases, see 'Murder', *The Sun* (London), 13 April 1829, p. 4; 'Poisoning a Whole Family', *Morning Herald*, 7 November 1831, p. 4; 'Administering Poison', *Yorkshire Gazette*, 31 March 1832, p. 3.

For Thomas Smith and his letter, see *Liverpool Mercury* 6 April, *Manchester Courier* 7 April. The address printed on the *Manchester Courier* version was 'No. 16, Maskill-street, Chorlton Row, and warehouse, No. 17, Back George-street'. Although there was no Thomas Smith listed at either address on the 1841 census, *Pigot's Directory for Manchester* in 1829 included a man called Thomas Smith at 16 Maskell Street. Prior to this, a man of the same name, who worked as a book-keeper (meaning an accountant) was listed at number 18 Maskell Street in *Pigot & Dean's New Directory of Manchester and Salford* for 1821; see *Pigot & Dean's New Directory of Manchester and Salford, 1821–22* (Manchester: R. & W. Dean and J. Pigot, 1821), p. 149 and *Pigot and Son's General Directory of Manchester, Salford, &c. for 1829* (Manchester: J Pigot & Co, 1828), Appendix, p. 27.

For the reprints of the articles, see 'Horrid Murder near Oldham', *Lancaster Gazette*, 7 April 1832, p. 3; 'Horrid Murder near Oldham', *Lancaster Herald*, 7 April 1832, p. 5; 'Frightful Murders in Saddleworth', *Leeds Intelligencer*, 12 April 1832, p. 4; 'Frightful Murders in Saddleworth', *Leeds Patriot and Yorkshire Advertiser*, 14 April 1832, p. 2. One of the few newspapers to reprint the article from *Wheeler's Manchester Chronicle* was 'The Murders at Dobcross', *Baldwin's London Weekly Journal*, 14 April 1832, p. 4.

The main original articles are those listed in the general references above.

The independent – and largely inaccurate – versions of the story appeared in: 'Horrid Murders Near Saddleworth', *York Herald*, 7 April 1832, p. 3; 'Atrocious Murder', *Macclesfield Courier and Herald*, 7 April 1832, p. 2; 'Most Atrocious Murder', *Staffordshire Advertiser*, 7 April 1832, p. 4; 'Manchester, April 4', *The Globe* (London), 7 April 1832, p. 4; 'Manchester, Wednesday', *Morning Herald* (London), 7 April 1832, p. 3; 'Horrid Murder near Oldham', *Lancaster Herald*, 7 April 1832, p. 5; 'Murder of a Father and his Son', *Sheffield Independent*, 7 April 1832, p. 3.

For the letter from the Saddleworth magistrates, see Home Office: Criminal (Rewards and Pardons) Correspondence and Secret Service Reports HO 64/3/46; Folio 125–126. For the reward poster, see Home Office: Criminal (Rewards and Pardons) Correspondence and Secret Service Reports HO 64/3/46; Folio 129. For the sworn statement of Ammon Platt, see Home Office: Criminal (Rewards and Pardons) Correspondence and Secret Service Reports HO 64/3/46; Folio 127–128.

The Night Before

For the Platts of Primrose, see *Saddleworth Historical Society Bulletin* 3, No. 2 (1973), pp. 37–39. See the *Manchester Times* inquest report on 14 April 1832 for the description of Reuben Platt as a carter. This, and all other newspaper references to Platt (including his evidence at the inquest), are from the newspapers listed in the general references above. Any particular details about sourcing are given in the text.

Ammon Platt told the magistrates that he 'inquired into the circumstances connected with the murder and was informed that on the evening of the second day of April … the said Thomas Bradbury in company with Reuben Platt was on his way to Road End…' As written, it seems more likely that a third party, and not Reuben Platt, was the source of the story. However, it is not impossible that Reuben spoke to Ammon Platt.

On Irish clothing, see for example Rachel Sayers, 'The History of Irish Dress 1750–1850', What Grandma Wore, 27 January 2020: https://whatgrandmawore.wordpress.com/2020/01/27/guest-blog-post-from-rachel-sayers-the-history-of-irish-dress-1750-1850/. But as that blog article says, there has been little academic study of Irish clothing trends in this period.

The description of the men comes from the first reward poster: see Home Office – Criminal (Rewards and Pardons) Correspondence and Secret Service Reports HO 64/3/46, Folio 129. Reuben Platt's quote on what the three men were wearing is taken from the *Liverpool Mercury* (13 April), which in turn comes from Butterworth 'Murders in Saddleworth' (inquest, BUT/F/7). For the linking of fustian and working class identity, see Katrina Navickas, '"That Sash Will Hang You": Political Clothing and Adornment in England, 1780—1840', *Journal of British Studies* 49, No. 3 (2010): pp. 540–65, http://www.jstor.org/stable/23265378; and Paul A. Pickering, 'Class without Words: Symbolic Communication in the Chartist Movement', *Past & Present*, No. 112 (1986): pp. 144–62, http://www.jstor.org/stable/651001.

The Hunt for Suspects

Charles Mullen revealed at the inquest that his family were in Cumberland. There are two census records of a man called Charles Mullen living in that area. The 1841 census lists him as a labourer living with his wife Elizabeth, a 9-year-old called Charles (born in Cumberland) and a 2-year-old called John (born in Ireland) at Maryport. This suggests that Charles junior was born sometime between June 1831 and June 1832 (June was the date of the 1841 census) but there are no records to indicate precisely when. However, he said at the inquest that he had left behind his wife and family, indicating the presence of at least one child. On the 1851 census, Elizabeth is living alone but still married and listed as the 'wife of an agricultural labourer'; there is also a 5-year-old boy called Dennis, born in Maryport. There is no trace of Charles nor John; nor is there a record of their death or any other explanation. Finally, Charles Mullen senior re-appeared on the 1861 census, living with Elizabeth and Dennis in Maryport and still working as a labourer. He died in Maryport in 1868; Elizabeth seems to have lived until 1890. All details from Ancestry.com; the two deaths come from Find a Grave via Ancestry.

The account of where Mullen had been working and how he lost his job, and his own version of what happened comes from *Wheeler's Manchester Chronicle* (7 April) and from details revealed at the inquest. The latter account is jumbled which might reflect Mullen's attempt to hide his drunkenness or the nature of the questioning by which it emerged. The *Wheeler's Manchester Chronicle* article (7 April) provides the most detailed account of his arrest and detention, as well as his appearance before a magistrate. The *Manchester Guardian* (7 April) also gave a briefer account of his arrest. The two newspapers identified different men as being responsible for Mullen's capture: the *Chronicle* said that Benjamin Wheeler had questioned him but the *Guardian* identified him as 'a gentleman named Bradbury'. Similarly, the former newspaper said that John Wrigley arrested Mullen; the latter said it was the man Bradbury.

Details about the King's Head were kindly provided by Mike Buckley.

For the number of Irish-born people living in England, the West Riding of Yorkshire and Lancashire in 1841, see 1841 Census of Great Britain, *Abstracts of the Answers and Returns made pursuant to Acts 3 & 4 Vict. C. 99, and 4 Vict. C. 7, intituled respectively "An Act for taking an Account of the Population of Great Britain", and "An Act to amend the Acts of the last Session for taking an Account of the Population".*

Enumeration Abstract, 1841. Part I England and Wales and Islands in the British Seas. (1843 xxii (496) 1), Great Britain Historical GIS Project (2017) 'Great Britain Historical GIS', University of Portsmouth. The figures for Manchester and Saddleworth come from the database records of FindmyPast.

A detailed discussion of attitudes towards the Irish in early nineteenth-century England is beyond the scope of this book and there is an enormous amount of scholarship on the issue. A good overview can be seen in Graham Davis, 'The Irish in Nineteenth Century Britain' in *Saothar* 16 (1991): pp. 130–135. *JSTOR*, www.jstor.org/stable/23197151 and M. A. G. Ó Tuathaigh, 'The Irish in Nineteenth-Century Britain: Problems of Integration' in *Transactions of the Royal Historical Society* 31 (1981): pp. 149–173, www.jstor.org/stable/3679050.

For the formation of the West Riding police force, see Martin Stallion and David S. Wall, *The British Police: Forces and Chief Officers 1829–2012* (Hook: Police History Society, 2011), pp. 198–99. For the role of magistrates in this period, see for example Matthew White, 'Crime and Punishment in Georgian Britain', British Library, 14 October 2009, https://www.bl.uk/georgian-britain/articles/crime-and-punishment-in-georgian-britain. For constables, see Peter Stone, 'Crime and policing in Georgian London', The History of London, https://www.thehistoryoflondon.co.uk/crime-and-policing-in-georgian-london/.

For an overview of the court system from magistrates to assizes, and the prosecution process in general, see Bentley, p. 7; Emsley, pp. 13–14, 188–202. The process in cases of murder is described in Clive Emsley, Tim Hitchcock and Robert Shoemaker, 'Crime and Justice – Trial Procedures', Old Bailey Proceedings Online, https://www.oldbaileyonline.org/static/Trial-procedures.jsp; and John Langbein, *The Origins of Adversary Criminal Trial* (Oxford: University Press, 2003), pp. 40–47, 120–23, 284–87.

On the practice of offering rewards, and the dangers of doing so (such as in the Macdaniel Affair), see Bentley, p. 7. For statistics on murder, see Bentley, pp. 17–18, Emsley, p. 283.

The progress of the rather desperate and haphazard search for suspects can be seen in the usual newspaper articles from 7 April, 14 April and from Butterworth's notes (see above). The quote from Butterworth about visitors comes from his largely unpublished notes on the inquest.

The timeline of the involvement of Saddleworth magistrates in 1832 can be worked out from Home Office: Criminal (Rewards and Pardons) Correspondence and Secret Service Reports HO 64/3/46; Folio 125–129. Further details can be seen in *Wheeler's Manchester Chronicle* for 7 April 1832 (see above). The reward notice was published in *London Gazette*, No. 18,925, 10 April 1832, p. 801. For the practice of offering pardons in return for information, see Bentley, p. 7.

The Inquest

For Michael Stocks senior, see Malcolm Bull, 'Stocks', Malcolm Bull's Calderdale Companion, 1 July 2023, http://www.calderdalecompanion.co.uk/mms97.html. For his attempted removal as a magistrate, see 'Michael Stocks Esq', *Leeds Patriot and Yorkshire Advertiser*, 9 April 1831, p. 1; and 'Case of Michael Stocks Esq', *Leeds Intelligencer*, 28 July 1831, p. 3. For his attempt to become the first member of Parliament for Halifax, see 'Halifax Election', *Leeds Mercury*, 15 December 1832, pp. 7–8.

For Michael Stocks junior, see 'Election of Coroner', *Yorkshire Gazette*, 23 December 1826, p. 4 (his election); 'Vacancy in the Office of Coroner in the Halifax District', *Leeds Intelligencer*, 4 November 1837, p. 7; Malcolm Bull, 'Michael Stocks', Malcolm Bull's Calderdale Companion, 24 May 2021, www.calderdalecompanion.co.uk/x2056.html (although some of this entry confuses Stocks with his father).

For an overview of the election of coroners, see Fisher pp. 25–27. For their role, see Fisher, pp. 91, 119–20. The delay in the inquest owing to Stocks' presence in Pontefract is noted in *Wheeler's Manchester Chronicle* 7 April 1832.

Description of the house comes from the *Manchester Guardian* 7 April 1832 (which also features the crude plan), *Wheeler's Manchester Chronicle* 7 April 1832 and Thomas Smith's letter from *Liverpool Mercury* 6 April and *Manchester Courier* 7 April. The more accurate plans can be found in Howcroft, p. 99 (1832) and Howcroft, p. 109 (1926). Other description comes from the 7 April 1832 newspaper reports (and Butterworth) but further details come from the inquest reports from 14 April and Ammon Platt's statement in Home Office: Criminal (Rewards and Pardons) Correspondence and Secret Service Reports HO 64/3/46; Folio 127–128. The photograph is in the Saddleworth Museum collection; a similar but slightly different photograph was printed in 'It Happened Yesterday', *Leeds Mercury*, 9 April 1936, p. 12.

Regarding Stocks' request to keep details out of newspapers (as solely reported by the *Manchester Guardian* on 14 April 1832), the battle of courts to ensure fair coverage by the press, and the issue of newspaper contempt of court, see Bentley pp. 43–45.

For coverage of the inquest in the newspapers, see the main reports as published on 14 April 1832 (see above).

Regarding 'Amelia Winterbottom', and the children of Nancy Winterbottom née Bradbury and her husband Benjamin see *Anglican Parish Registers*, Manchester, England: Manchester Libraries, Information and Archives. Other family details come from various census and baptism records accessed via Ancestry.com. It could be argued that 'Amelia' was the daughter of Nancy's sister Mary, who married Benjamin Winterbottom's brother, John. But they never had a child called Amelia either.

On the shift towards expert testimony in criminal trials, see Stephan Landsman, 'One Hundred Years of Rectitude: Medical Witnesses at the Old Bailey, 1717–1817' in *Law and History Review* 16, No. 3 (1998): pp. 445–94, https://doi.org/10.2307/744241. On the changes to the role of coroner, and the move towards a greater professionalism, see Fisher, pp. 91–108. On medical evidence at inquests, see Fisher, pp 184–93.

For Samuel Hegginbottom, see *Pigot and Co.'s National and Commercial Directory for 1828–29*, (London and Manchester: J Pigot

& Co, 1828), p. 1059. Other details come from census returns and marriage records accessed via Ancestry.com, and from his gravestone. Hegginbottom's evidence comes from the main newspaper sources, particularly those reporting the inquest on 14 April (see above). The quotes are mainly taken from Butterworth but the essence of what he said is the same in each report. The details about the pistol (the description of which is from the *Manchester Guardian* from 7 April 1832), and its association with the Yeomanry Cavalry were kindly provided by Philip Spooner of West Street Antiques in Dorking. For Durs Egg, see 'D. Egg (Biographical details)', British Museum, https://www.britishmuseum.org/research/search_the_collection_database/term_details.aspx?bioId=231715.

On firearm possession, see 'Gun Control: The Right to Bear Arms', Stephen Cooper, *History Today*, 2 October 2015, https://www.historytoday.com/gun-control-right-bear-arms; also see Vagrancy Act 1824, 5 George IV c. 83, Section IV.

For the later court case against Mullen, see 'County Sessions', *Cumberland Pacquet, and Ware's Whitehaven Advertiser*, 9 January 1838, p. 4; also England & Wales, Criminal Registers, 1791–1892 on Ancestry.com.

For the information about visitors to the house as late as 21 April, the diary of George Shaw is quoted in Barrow, 'Bill's o'Jack's', p. 20.

The claim of Joseph Matthews appears in *Manchester Guardian* 14 April. The other details come from the 1841 census, accessed via Ancestry.com.

Details of Thomas Bradbury's children come from various census returns and baptism records accessed via Ancestry.com. Butterworth's report on the money being used for a funeral comes from Butterworth 'Murders in Saddleworth' (Motive, BUT/F/7). The report on the sale of furniture was in 'The Late Murders at Greenfield', *Wheeler's Manchester Chronicle*, 21 April 1832, p. 2; and 'The Saddleworth Murders', *Manchester Guardian*, 21 April 1832, p. 3 (which stated that Thomas had five children). The advertising of the auction was printed in *Manchester Guardian*, 21 April 1832, p. 1. See also Barrow and Wyke, p. 2.

On funeral costs in Saddleworth, and for the Delph Independent Sunday School funerary society and the Saddleworth Friendly Family Burial Society of Uppermill, see 'Records of the Saddleworth Friendly Family Burial Society' in *Saddleworth Historical Society Bulletin* 21, No. 3 (1991), pp. 8–9. For a discussion of costs in general, see for example Teerapa Pirohakul (2015) *The funeral in England in the long Eighteenth Century,* PhD thesis, London School of Economics and Political Science; Walvin, James. 'Dust to Dust: Celebrations of Death in Victorian England' in *Historical Reflections / Réflexions Historiques* 9, No. 3 (1982): pp. 353–71: http://www.jstor.org/stable/41298792.

On the money made from the Thurtell case, see Flanders, pp. 34–35.

For the spread of the Bill's o'Jack's story, see 'Barbarous Murders and Robbery', *The Times*, 9 April 1832, p. 4; 'Saddleworth Murders', *The Times*, 5 May, p. 3; 'Barbarous Murders and Robbery', *Morning Chronicle*, 9 April 1832, p. 3; 'Barbarous Murders and Robbery', *Brighton Guardian*, 11 April 1832, p. 1; 'Frightful Murders in Saddleworth', *Morning Chronicle*, 16 April 1832, p. 3; *Leeds Intelligencer*, 12 April 1832, p. 4; 'The Late Murders in Greenfield', *Morning Chronicle*, 17 April 1832, p. 4; 'The Murders Near Saddleworth', *Albion and Star*, 24 April 1832, p. 4. Articles appeared in the *True Sun* on 9 April 1832, p. 3; 16 April 1832, p. 3; 21 April 1832, p. 1; and 16 May 1832, p. 3.

A simple – if unscientific – comparison can be made between the interest in the Bill's o'Jack's case to other murders. The sensational 'Red Barn Murder' generated enormous interest. Searching the British Newspaper Archive for 'Red Barn' generates 236 results in April and May 1828 (when Maria Marten's body was found) and 323 for August (when William Corder was tried and executed). The killing of Thomas Patrick, the landlord of the Yorkshire Grey in Colchester, has 211 entries for December 1827, the date of the murder (using a search for the phrase 'murder' and 'Colchester'). A search for 'Bradbury' and 'murder' gives a result of 135 articles in April 1832. But the Colchester case had far less lasting impact than the Bill's o'Jack's murders, and most of the articles concern the trial and execution of the murderer, James Winter. In contrast, there was no trial to fuel the interest in the Bill's o'Jack's murders.

The Red Bredburys and Other Unlikely Candidates

The 'hutch'd of a lump' quote comes from the *Manchester Guardian*, 14 April.

For the arrest of other suspects, see: 'The Saddleworth Murders', *Leeds Intelligencer*, 12 April 1832, p. 3 (Manchester arrests); 'The Saddleworth Murders', *Liverpool Mercury*, 13 April 1832, p. 8; Butterworth 'Saddleworth – Wednesday' (Rotherham arrest); 'The Murders in Saddleworth', *Manchester Courier*, 21 April 1832, p. 2 (discharge of Rotherham suspects); Butterworth 'Murders in Saddleworth' (inquest, BUT/F/7) and 'Saddleworth – Wednesday' (Hooley Hill suspects); 'The Late Murders at Greenfield', *Wheeler's Manchester Chronicle*, 14 April 1832, p. 2 (false rumours of Liverpool arrest); 'The Saddleworth Murders', *Huddersfield and Halifax Express*, 21 April 1832, p. 3 (cigar-maker); 'Murders in Saddleworth' (BUT/F/8) and 'Saddleworth Murders', *Manchester Courier* 28 April 1832, p. 2 (arrest and release of men in Liverpool).

For the 'Red Tom Bredburys' see: Butterworth 'Murders in Saddleworth' (Motive, BUT/F/7); 'The Murders in Saddleworth', *Manchester Courier*, 21 April 1832, p. 2; 'The Saddleworth Murders', *Manchester Guardian*, 21 April 1832, p. 3; 'The Saddleworth Murders', *Huddersfield and Halifax Express*, 21 April 1832, p. 3; 'The Late Murders at Greenfield', *Wheeler's Manchester Chronicle*, 21 April 1832, p. 2. For their release, see 'Murders in Saddleworth' (BUT/F/8); 'Saddleworth Murders', *Manchester Courier* 28 April 1832, p. 2; 'The Saddleworth Murders', *Huddersfield and Halifax Express*, 28 April 1832, p. 3.

For records of the Pontefract Session, see for example 'Pontefract Spring Sessions', *Leeds Mercury*, 7 April 1832, p. 3. The official records can also be seen on Ancestry.com.

For the death of James Bradbury and the continued rumours against the Red Bredburys, see 'Death of James Bradbury of Whitewalls', *Huddersfield Chronicle*, 11 October 1851, p. 8.

For records of other possible members of the family, see for example 'West Yorkshire, Non-Conformist Records, 1646-1985', tax records and census returns on Ancestry.com.

Hannah Bradbury (probably née Platt but not apparently any connection to Reuben's family) was born at Saddleworth (according to the 1851 census) in 1786 (although a Hannah Platt was baptised at St Chad's in 1781) and probably married Job in 1803. She was widowed by the time of the 1841 census, when she lived with six children aged 12 and over. But the woman on the 1841 census was almost certainly the wife of Job Bradbury as one of her children was also called Job. And she is possibly the 'Widow Bradbury' listed as holding land at Austonley on tax records from 1829. Another son of hers, John (born around 1820), is likely the John Bradbury (1820–1875) of Bradshaw, who was buried at the Independent Chapel in Holmfirth.

For the suggestion that the Red Bredburys were cousins of Thomas Bradbury, see 'The Annals of Saddleworth' (details above); this also names Jamie Bradbury as one of the suspects.

Job Bradbury/Bredbury is listed on several tax returns: in 1810 and 1817, a man called Job Bredbury was listed in tax records; in 1822, he was listed as Job Bradbury. And Thomas Bradbury is listed on tax records for 1802, 1803 and 1805; there were actually two men of that name living in Austonley. One of these was listed as Thomas Bredbury in 1809.

For James Bradbury at the Quarter Sessions of 1819, see *Yorkshire, England, Quarter Session Records, 1637–1914* [database on-line]. Provo, UT, USA: Ancestry.com Operations, Inc., 2016. For the date of James Bradbury's death, see 'Deaths', *Huddersfield Chronicle*, 4 October 1851, p. 5. A James Bradbury of the same age, born in Quick, Saddleworth, was imprisoned in York Castle when the 1851 census was taken. He was a 'clothier and farmer' but was incarcerated as a debtor. Possibly the same James Bradbury was living at Fairbanks as a farmer in 1841 with his wife and several children. However, several details, including the place he lived, do not match with the death notice in the *Chronicle*, so this may be a different man. Another man called James Bradbury, born around 1796, lived at nearby Digley Mill at the time of the 1841 census.

For the switch back to the Irishmen as suspects, see 'The Saddleworth Murders', *Huddersfield and Halifax Express*, 28 April 1832, p. 3. And for the lingering suspicion that those three Irishmen were those responsible, see 'Final Examination of the Irish Highwaymen', *Manchester Courier*, 9 April 1836, p. 3.

For the play, see for example 'The Saddleworth Murders Dramatized', *Leeds Mercury*, 5 May 1832, p. 3.

For the 'confession' of Nathaniel Stannyer, see for example 'Murder at Saddleworth', *Macclesfield Courier and Herald*, 23 March 1833, p. 2. For the 'confession' of John Mitchell, see 'The Greenfield Murder', *Bradford Observer*, 24 April 1845, p. 5. And for the Australian 'confession', see 'Confession of the Murder at Bill's o'Jack's', *Huddersfield Chronicle*, 5 March 1853, p. 3. Analysis of the latter confession comes from Barrow and Wyke, pp. 17–20.

Finding a Motive

The descriptions of the alleged theft come from the main newspaper sources (see above) on 7 April and from Butterworth 'Inhuman Murder'. For the rarity of murder associated with burglary, see Emsley, pp. 42–44.

The descriptions of Thomas Bradbury come from the later articles (details of specific articles are given in the text and are listed above). Butterworth's discussion of the motive comes from Butterworth 'Murders in Saddleworth' (Motive, BUT/F/7).

The account of Matthew Marsh (including quotes) comes from 'The Annals of Saddleworth' (details above) and Barrow, 'Bill's o'Jack's: Further Evidence', pp. 37–39.

For the admissibility of 'dying declarations', see Bentley, pp. 214–15. On William Bradbury speaking, see the usual newspaper articles from 7 April, 14 April and from Butterworth's notes (see above). For the use of 'Pats' to refer to the Irish, see for example Jonathon Green, 'Pats', Green's Dictionary of Slang, 2023, https://greensdictofslang.com/entry/jnlcq3a. For the later information, see Thornton, pp. 90–91.

The dating of the information in 'The Annals of Saddleworth' is very problematic. Much of the detail such as when the turnpike road was built, the idea that the Red Bredburys appeared at Pontefract, and even the use of the name 'The Moorcock' all indicate that the information comes from the 1890s, when the document was written. But some of the details could well have originated with Matthew Marsh and be based on much earlier writing – perhaps from close to the 1830s. The strongest suggestion along these lines is the very precise date on which Thomas Bradbury supposedly attacked the hut of the Irish workers and some of the details about the land not being enclosed at the time. And the similarity – although neither copies the other, nor do they clearly have a source in common – between what appeared in the 'Annals' and the report by Butterworth on the 'broom collectors' might support the idea that the information came from Marsh and was written around the time of the murders.

The accounts of the Porritt inquest come from Butterworth 'Child Murder'; 'Child Murder', *Wheeler's Manchester Chronicle*, 14 April 1832, p. 2; 'Child Murder', *Liverpool Mercury*, 13 April 1832, p. 8; 'Child Murder', *Manchester Times* 14 April 1832, p. 4; 'Charge of Infanticide', *Huddersfield and Halifax Express*, 14 April 1832, p. 3; and – the only newspaper to mention the connection with Thomas Bradbury – 'Painful Disclosure', *Manchester Guardian* 14 April 1832, p. 3. The details from the hearing at York Assizes, which heard the fullest account of what happened, come from 'Yorkshire Assizes', *York Herald*, 8 September 1832, p. 4. The official record of her imprisonment can be found in the *Criminal Registers, 1791–1892*, accessed via Ancestry.com. On infanticide in this period, and the reluctance of grand juries to find mothers guilty of murder, see Emsley, p. 48.

For the baptismal record of Esther Porritt, see the records of Chinley Chapel, listed as an independent chapel under *England & Wales, Non-Conformist and Non-Parochial Registers, 1567–1936* on Ancestry.

com. For the birth of James, son of Esther Bradbury, see the baptismal records of Ashton-under-Lyne parish (listed in the Bishop's Transcripts), accessed via Ancestry.com.

For the later association of her with the case, see Howcroft, pp. 92–109 and Barrow and Wyke, pp. 16–17.

The quote on rumours comes from Butterworth 'Murders in Saddleworth' (inquest, BUT/F/7).

Saddleworth Sketches

For Joseph Bradbury, see 'Death of Dr Bradbury', *Isle of Man Times*, 4 May 1895, p. 5. Further details can be seen in his advertisement in *Heywood Advertiser*, 26 June 1874, p. 2 and in various census returns (accessed via Ancestry.com).

The initial two articles in the *Oldham Chronicle*, which were combined to make the opening chapter in *Saddleworth Sketches* are: 'F. D. M.', 'Saddleworth Sketches No. I: Bill's o'Jack's and Greenfield' *Oldham Chronicle*, 19 November 1870, p. 7; and 'F. D. M.', 'Saddleworth Sketches No. II: Bill's o'Jack's and Greenfield', *Oldham Chronicle*, 26 November 1870, p. 7 (the latter has the subheading 'The Inquest'). There is no explanation of who 'F. D. M.' is, but *Saddleworth Sketches* (and all subsequent writing) made clear that they were the work of Joseph Bradbury, and he later claimed credit independently of anything published by the *Oldham Chronicle*.

For dialect literature, see Graham Shorrocks, 'Working-Class Literature in Working-Class Language: The North of England' in *English Literature and the Other Languages*, eds. Marius Buning and Ton Hoenselaars, (Amsterdam: Rodopi, 1999), pp. 89–95; Larry McCauley, '"Eawr Folk": Language, Class, and English Identity in Victorian Dialect Poetry' in *Victorian Poetry* 39, No. 2 (2001): pp. 287–301. http://www.jstor.org/stable/40002680.

For discussion of who wrote the extra section of *Saddleworth Sketches*, and the suggestion that it was Jonathan Hirst, see Wyke, p. 35. Details about Hirst can be found in 'The Late Mr Jonathan Hirst',

Huddersfield Examiner, 23 September 1876, p. 5 and in various census returns.

The sketch entitled 'Bill's o'Jack's and Greenfield' is found in Bradbury, pp. 1–43. The editing of Bradbury's original text is described in the anonymous 'Publishers' Preface'. For Bradbury's original account (including the altered reprint of the *Manchester Courier*), see pp. 11–17; for the additional writing, see pp. 17–34. After this, Bradbury's original narrative resumes.

For 'Owd Kedlock' (James Horsfall) see 'Death of a Saddleworth Celebrity', *North Cheshire Herald and Hyde and Glossop News*, 24 March 1877, p. 3. Further details can be seen in census returns, and Horsfall's burial records, accessed via Ancestry.com. And 'Owd Kedlock' featured in a second sketch by Bradbury; see Bradbury, pp. 166–73.

The review of *First Davenport of Bramhill* comes from *The Saturday Review*, 5 January 1895, p. 23. The extract comes from: Joseph Bradbury, *First Davenport of Bramhall*, (London: Digby & Long, 1894), p. 1.

For the other views of the Red Bredburys written after *Saddleworth Sketches* but with an alternative interpretation of who they were, see 'The Annals of Saddleworth' (details above) and (for the quote about 'Jamie Bradshaw') Thornton, p. 90. For the details regarding Joseph Bradbury, the supposed son of James Bradbury, see the 1841 census (accessed via Ancestry.com) and the record of Lane Independent Chapel, Holmfirth (also on Ancestry.com).

'Morbid Pilgrimage'

All family information comes from various census returns, from the parish records of Saddleworth church, and from death records, all accessed via Ancestry.com.

On Edwin Butterworth, see Alan G. Crosby, 'Butterworth, Edwin (1812–1848), topographer and journalist' in *Oxford Dictionary of National Biography*, 23 September 2004: https://www.oxforddnb.

com/view/10.1093/ref:odnb/9780198614128.001.0001/odnb-9780198614128-e-4229; and Michael Winstanley, 'News from Oldham: Edwin Butterworth and the Manchester Press, 1829–1848', *Manchester Region History Review* 4 No. 1 (1990), pp. 3–10.

For the change of name to 'The Moorcock', and for Augustus Bradbury at the Clarence, see Magee, p. 39.

The alterations to Bill's o'Jack's can be seen in by comparing Howcroft, p. 99 (1832) and p. 109 (1926), although the date of the alterations is unclear. For the 1855 visit to Bill's o'Jack's, see Geraldine Jewsbury, 'The Great Saddleworth Exhibition' in *Household Words*, 1 October 1853, p. 110. For Joseph Bradbury's visit to the Clarence, see Bradbury, pp. 3–4. For the later history of Bill's o'Jack's, see Wyke, pp. 37–39. The directory entries for Bill's o'Jack's can be accessed via a file held by Saddleworth Museum.

The visit of the journalist in 1899, and the quote about 'fireside story' comes from Harwood Brierley, 'A Yorkshire Itinerary', *Leeds Mercury*, 7 October 1899, p. 26. This also mentions a booklet on sale; a similar leaflet is mentioned in 'A Holiday Visit to Bill's o'Jack's', *Stockport County Express*, 5 September 1912, p. 2. Some of the various souvenirs on sale (and the 'relics' from the murder or those belonging to William Bradbury) are on display at Saddleworth Museum. See also Barrow and Wyke, pp. 2–4. The story of the journalist who declined to see bloodstains is from 'Notes of a Trip to Bill's o'Jack's', *Ashton Reporter*, 1 September 1855, p. 4. For visits of groups (including the 3000 from Oldham in 1894) to Bill's o'Jack's, and takings at Easter meeting expenses for the year, see Wyke p. 41–42. Joseph Bradbury's quote on the 'lovely inn' comes from Bradbury, p. 11. The 1899 quote on a 'famous place for ham and eggs' is from 'A Visit to Bill's o'Jack's', *Halifax Courier*, 27 April 1889, p. 2.

Much of the information on the Saddleworth Wakes (and the association with Bill's o'Jack's) comes from newspaper cuttings held at the Saddleworth Museum; see also Bradbury, p. 76. A larger overview of Wakes is given in Susan Barton, *Working-Class Organisations and*

Popular Tourism, 1840–1970, (Manchester: University Press, 2005), pp. 74–76.

An example of the popularity of Bill's o'Jack's as a venue for an outing (and the quote about 'no other outing') can be found in Harwood Brierley, 'A Yorkshire Itinerary', *Leeds Mercury*, 7 October 1899, p. 26.

For the later landlords of Bill's o'Jack's, see Magee, p. 39; Bradbury's dismissive remark about the dancing shed is from Bradbury, p. 11. For the clashes between English and Irish workers, see 'Attempted Murder at Bill's o'Jack's', *Stalybridge Reporter*, 2 November 1878, p. 8. The history of the establishment up until its demolition can be found in newspaper cuttings held by Saddleworth Museum; Macgee, pp. 39–40; Wyke (2020), pp. 40–42. And the quote from the time of its closure about it being a '"Mecca" of morbid pilgrimage' comes from 'Bill's o'Jack's', *Bradford Observer*, 16 February 1937, p. 8.

The continuing fascination with the murders (including the supposed 'relics' held in other local public houses) and the poetry produced is described in Barrow and Wyke, pp. 4–6. Examples of comparison between later crimes and the 1932 murders can be found in the newspaper cuttings held by Saddleworth Museum. The story of the excise officer is from 'The Greenfield Mystery: Bill's o'Jack's Romance', *Halifax Evening Courier*, 15 April 1912, p. 2. The other 'relics' and the postcard are described in Whittaker, p. 18. The date for the postcard of around 1915 comes from Saddleworth Museum. The centenary article (and the information about William Bradbury's great grandchildren) comes from 'Northerner', 'This World of Ours', *Yorkshire Post*, 2 April 1932, p. 8.

'Such interest did their tragic end excite'

See Altick, pp. 17–40 for a discussion of how reading about murders in the pre-Victorian period became a form of entertainment. For Eugene Aram, see for example Flanders, pp. 99–108.

The Greenfield Tragedy, or the Unknown Assassins was mentioned in several newspapers, for example 'The Saddleworth Murders Dramatized',

Leeds Mercury, 5 May 1832, p. 3. The longest account is 'The Theatre', *Wheeler's Manchester Chronicle*, 5 May 1832, p. 3. Details of the plot come from Frederick Burwick, *British Drama of the Industrial Revolution* (Cambridge: University Press, 2015), pp. 218–19. For the performance at the Saddleworth Wakes, see Barrow and Wyke, p. 6. Samples of the poetry can be found in Barrow and Wyke, p. 5. For the song about the murders, see 'The Greenfield Murder', *Bradford Observer*, 24 April 1845, p. 5.

James Platt is identified as the author of the tombstone epitaph in Bradbury, p. 83. Details of his life come from Whittaker, pp. 28–29, and his obituary, 'Death of James Platt', *Huddersfield Chronicle*, 2 April 1864, p. 7. The latter does not mention the tombstone. The omitted final verse of the poem, and the quote about the 'approbation' comes from 'An Inhabitant of Holmfirth', 'Sketches, Tales, and Legends of the Valley of Saddleworth', *Huddersfield Chronicle*, 24 July 1852, p. 8.

The book giving religious instruction: Anonymous, *Bill O'Jack's: A Conversation Between Dick the Carder and John the Slubber, on Sunday Afternoon, about William Bradbury and Thomas his Son* (London: Wertheim, Macintosh & Hunt, 1860).

The 1852 retelling is from 'An Inhabitant of Holmfirth', 'Sketches, Tales, and Legends of the Valley of Saddleworth', *Huddersfield Chronicle*, 24 July 1852, p. 8. The 1887 account, with its concluding poem, comes from Thomas Gibbons, 'No. III: The Greenfield Tragedy', *Manchester Courier*, 13 August 1887, p. 9.

For Joseph Burgess's serialised retelling, see Wyke, pp. 35–36. Its success was trumpeted in 'Enormous Success of Our New Serial', *Cotton Factory Times*, 14 March 1902, p. 1.

The quote from *Miriam* is p. 12 in the Project Gutenberg edition. The idea that William Bradbury said 'Platts, Platts' is from pp. 360–61. Sykes's earlier writing about Burnplatters can be found in D. F. E. Sykes, *The History of Huddersfield and the Valleys of the Colne, the Holme and the Dearne* (Huddersfield: The Worker Press, 1906), p. 233. His source material (and the inspiration for the mythical status of Burnplatters), and the original 1847 article comes from George S. Phillips, 'Walks Round Huddersfield: No. V: Burn Platts; and St John's Chapel in the

Wilderness', *Bradford and Wakefield Observer*, 18 November 1847, p. 7. The idea of the Burnplatters being 'foreign' was described in Walter E. Haigh, *A New Glossary of the Dialect of the Huddersfield District* (London: Humphrey Milford, 1928), pp. 23, 157. A more modern interpretation (including the idea that the name arose from their practice of burning the moors) and a partial refutation of the 'foreign' theory can be found in George Redmonds, *Slaithwaite: Place and Place-names* (Huddersfield: GR Books, 1988), p. 10.

Details of Arthur Denville's play come from Whittaker, pp. 19–23. The mysterious 1911 performance is briefly described in Barrow and Wyke, p. 5. For Wylbert Kemp's *The Bill's o'Jack's Mystery*, see 'True Murder Makes Good Theatre' in *Stage*, 29 September 1960, p. 19; see also the souvenir programme produced by Holmfirth Amateur Dramatic Society for the 1961 performance, available to view online: '*The Bill's o'Jack's Mystery* (1961) – Holmfirth Amateur Dramatic Society', Huddersfield Exposed, https://huddersfield.exposed/wiki/The_Bill%27s_o%27_Jack%27s_Mystery_(1961)_-_Holmfirth_Amateur_Dramatic_Society. For *The Moorcock* by Henry Livings, see Barrow and Wyke, p. 5; and Alan Hulme, 'Murder on the Moors', *Manchester Evening News*, 22 January 1982, p. 9. For the lost 1936 film, see Barrow and Wyke, p. 7; Wyke, p. 44.

The story by William Groves is listed in Whittaker, p. 4. The 1985 novel is James Davenport, *The Murders at Bill's O'Jack's: A Fictional Account of the Murders at the Moorcock Inn, Saddleworth, in 1832* (Manchester: Neil Richardson, 1985). And for Sophie Parkes's 2023 book, see 'Books', Sophie Parkes: Writer, https://www.sophieparkes.co.uk/books; Sophie Parkes, *Out of Human Sight* (Manchester and Sheffield: Northodox, 2023).

The 1915 article is from Anonymous, 'Famous Lancashire Mysteries. No. 5 – The Unsolved Tragedy of Bill's o'Jack's', *Thomson's Weekly News*, 15 May 1915. This was accessed via a clipping in Oldham Local Studies and Archives, so there was no page number available. The version of the story as told by A. J. Howcroft can be seen in Howcroft, pp. 92–109. For information on Howcroft, see for example, 'Alfred James Howcroft', Architects of Greater Manchester 1800–1940, https://

manchestervictorianarchitects.org.uk/architects/alfred-james-howcroft. Howcroft based his account of Abraham Dawson on the articles in the *Manchester Guardian* in 1832 but made some odd changes; in his version, Dawson heard sounds around 9 pm and mentioned this 'rough company' to 'Mr Patterson, constable of Manchester' (the original source gave a time of half-past nine and said that he told Joseph Matthews). Later in his account, he also got the lettering on the pistol wrong despite having access to the *Manchester Guardian* description.

The two articles from *Old Stand* are held in clippings files at the Oldham Local Studies and Archives. The page numbers of the articles were not preserved. They are held in *Oldham News* Volume 8: pp. 113, 121.

The summary by G. H. Whittaker comes from Whittaker, pp. 5–18.

The 1935 article is from R. Hawkin, 'Shocking Murder at Bill's o'Jack's', *Yorkshire Weekly Post Illustrated*, 28 September 1935, p. 13. The account by Vera Winterbottom can be found in Vera Winterbottom, *Saddleworth Murder and Mystery* (Oldham, 1960), pp. 1–11. Geoffrey Whiteley's article can be found in Geoffrey Whiteley, 'The Murders at the Moorcock', *Edgar Wallance Mystery Magazine* Vol. 4, No. 30 (January 1967), pp. 82–91.

For some of the more recent features and writing, some examples include: 'Bill's o'Jack's – Murder in Saddleworth, England', Reddit, 2015, https://www.reddit.com/r/UnresolvedMysteries/comments/2ej701/bills_o_jacks_murder_in_saddleworth_england/; Boudicca Fox-Leonard, 'The UK's most notorious pub murders – when terror strikes the heart of our communities', Mirror, 21 February 2015, https://www.mirror.co.uk/news/uk-news/uks-most-notorious-pub-murders-5203884; David Lumb, 'English murder mysteries that have baffled detectives', BBC, 13 January 2015, https://www.bbc.co.uk/news/uk-england-29604413; 'Daft Monkey', 'The Bill's o'Jack's Murders Saddleworth (unsolved), YouTube, 28 February 2021, https://www.youtube.com/watch?v=i7LzVKRavqk. By far the best version is Wessyman137, 'Bill's o'Jack's', Wessyman blog hosted by Wordpress, 20 July 2014, https://wessyman137.wordpress.com/2014/07/20/bills-o-jacks/.

Index